A CONCISE HISTORY *of* CHRISTIAN DOCTRINE

A
CONCISE
HISTORY
of
CHRISTIAN
DOCTRINE

Justo L. González

ABINGDON PRESS / *Nashville*

A CONCISE HISTORY OF CHRISTIAN DOCTRINE

Library of Congress Cataloging-in-Publication Data

González, Justo L.
   A concise history of Christian doctrine / Justo L. González.
     p. cm.
   Includes bibliographical references.
   ISBN 0-687-34414-X (binding: pbk. 6x9 : alk. paper)
   1. Theology, Doctrinal—Popular works.   I. Title.

BT77.G66 2005
230'.09—dc22
                                    2005023306

05 06 07 08 09 10 11 12 13 14—10 9 8 7 6 5 4 3 2 1
MANUFACTURED IN THE UNITED STATES OF AMERICA

To David C. White,
who first introduced me to the
history of Christian thought

CONTENTS

PREFACE

I have lost track of how many times I have told and retold the history of Christianity and its doctrines. I have told it in books; I have told it in university and seminary classrooms; I have told it in Sunday school classes; I have even told and retold it to myself! Yet every time I tell it, there is something new about it. Some of this newness has to do with more recent research that I have done. Some of it has to do with a different audience, a different angle, or a different emphasis. But above all the story is always new and exciting to me because I claim it as my story. In reading about believers long gone and what they said and did, I often come to a better understanding of who I am, what I believe, and what I do.

In the particular case of this book, I have been renewed by revisiting the relationship between worship and belief, and also by the very task of summarizing the history and trying to bring the big picture into focus. In this task of summarizing, I feel very much as if I were speaking of one friend to another. The time is limited; the descriptions must be brief; it is simply not possible to tell all I would like to tell about my friend. In a way, this is a frustrating task, for one is keenly aware that much that is important has been left unsaid. But in another way it is profoundly rewarding, for in deciding what it is that I most need to say about my friend I am also forced to think about what it is that makes our friendship important—and the end result is that the friendship itself is enriched! So, while I hope and I have made every effort to make the pages that follow enlightening and rewarding to the reader, the truth is that I have already had my reward!

Now a word of gratitude. Thanks to Abingdon Press and to Robert Ratcliff for suggesting that I write this book. Thanks to Catherine, who is not only my wife, but also a friend, a colleague historian of theology, and a most perceptive and useful critic. And thanks to the legion who have lived the story, and to the many who have told it before me, for without their labors, mine would come to naught!

Justo L. González

INTRODUCTION

Do not believe every spirit, but test the spirits to see whether they are from God.
1 John 4:1

Are doctrines good? Are they even necessary? What is a "doctrine," anyway? How did we get them? These are legitimate questions that Christians have every right to ask. They are good questions, for it would seem that doctrines do nothing but divide us. Besides, we have all known wise and saintly Christians who do not seem to know much about Christian doctrine, but are true exemplars of Christian living. Hasn't the church just complicated matters with all kinds of doctrine about the authority of Scripture, about creation, about God and the Trinity, and so on? Is there any value in all that? How did these doctrines come about? Obviously, much could be said about each of these issues. One could write—I have written—volumes about some of them. But that might just be one more case of the same problem—our apparent penchant to complicate what is in itself so simple. If there is a suspicion that doctrines are, at least in part, a means to hide ignorance and to claim authority on the basis of supposedly higher knowledge, that suspicion cannot be allayed by weighty tomes that claim to clarify matters while in fact obscuring them. If we are asked about the woods, to talk about each particular tree is not very helpful and may well hide our uncertainty about the woods.

For these reasons, I shall try to keep this book as simple as possible, without oversimplifying matters. This is important to me, not only because the questions themselves require straightforward answers, but also because in writing this book I am putting myself to the test. Do I really believe that doctrines are all that important? If so, I should be able to explain their importance in words that the

1

average believer can understand. In fact, I fear that if I cannot explain the significance of doctrines in relatively intelligible terms, this may be an indication that I too am baffled by them, and that all my research and writing on the minutiae of doctrines and their development is actually an attempt to hide my confusion from myself!

So I begin to write this book, not just as a study guide for others, but also as part of my own pilgrimage. I set out on this pilgrimage with only one certainty, that of faith. I am a believer, and as such I set out—and I invite my readers to set out—without really knowing where this journey will end, much as Abraham set out from the land of his ancestors. And, like Abraham, I know that wherever God leads us in this pilgrimage will be a good place.

What Is a Doctrine?

Obviously, this word, like most words, can have several meanings. It can be someone's opinion on a particular subject, as when we speak of "Plato's doctrine of the soul." It can be a principle that guides the actions of a person or of an entire nation, as when we speak of the "Monroe doctrine," establishing a policy to keep the European powers out of the Western Hemisphere. It can have negative connotations, particularly in derivatives such as "indoctrination" and "doctrinaire." In spite of all these meanings and connotations, "doctrine" simply means "teaching" or "instruction"; and, like any teaching or instruction, doctrines can be good or bad, freeing or enslaving, inviting or forbidding.

In the particular context of this book, however, a "doctrine" is much more than someone's opinion, and certainly much more than the act of communicating such an opinion. A doctrine is the official teaching of a body—in this case, the church—that gives it shape, coherence, and distinction. All social bodies have doctrines, either explicitly or implicitly, for without such doctrines they would become an amorphous mass without identity or purpose.

What complicates matters in the case of the church is that the very word "church" has different levels of meaning. "Church" is the Lutheran Church of the Redeemer down the street; it is also a denomination, such as The United Methodist Church or the Roman Catholic Church; and it is the body of believers through the ages and throughout the world. At each of these levels, churches have doctrines, even though we might not think so. The Church of the Redeemer has its own views of reality, most of them shared with other Lutherans, but some of them the result of its own history and its context. The Roman Catholic Church holds to the doctrines of the Assumption of Mary and the infallibility of the pope, while The United Methodist Church does not. And there are some tenets that are held by the church everywhere—at least by the vast majority of it.

It is mostly in this latter sense that I shall be considering doctrines in this book. My purpose is to focus our attention on those doctrines that are generally held by Christians everywhere, rather than on the points that divide them. Certainly, on occasion we will deal with differences among Christians; yet our concern will be mostly with that which distinguishes Christians as such from the rest of the world, with those doctrines that give Christianity its shape, regardless of denominational differences. Furthermore, quite often doctrinal disagreements—either among theologians or among denominations—should be seen, not as mutually exclusive positions, but rather as ways to remind the entire church of something that otherwise it might be apt to forget.

How does a particular view on some issue become a doctrine of the church? Some doctrines—in fact, very few of those that are accepted by the church at large—were declared to be such by an official body of the church. Most of those few official declarations took place in the fourth and fifth centuries, when a number of church councils discussed and eventually proclaimed what have become some of the most universally held doctrines of the church. To those we shall return in due time.

However, most doctrines have become official teaching of the church by simple and often even undeclared consensus. As we shall see, even the matter of which books are to be included in the New Testament, and which not, was settled by means of a slowly developing consensus. It was not until the sixteenth century that an authoritative body—in this case the Roman Catholic Council of Trent—made a list and declared that these are the books that form the New Testament. In fact, we will see in the next chapter that this declaration did not make much difference, since well over a thousand years earlier, by a slowly developing consensus, the church had already come to agree on the books that form the New Testament, and therefore on this particular point the Council of Trent was saying nothing new. (Regarding the Old Testament, the story is a bit more complicated, as we shall see in chapter 2.)

Thus, although some of the basic tenets of Christianity have been proclaimed as doctrine of the church by an official act of an authoritative body, in most cases a particular tenet becomes a doctrine of the church when the church at large acknowledges it as a necessary consequence or expression of the gospel by which it lives.

Many of the distinctive doctrines of particular denominations have been proclaimed as official doctrines by authoritative bodies in those denominations. This is the case, for instance, of the Assumption of Mary and the infallibility of the pope in the Roman Catholic Church. In the Reformed tradition, the statements of the Canons of Dort and of the Westminster Confession have doctrinal authority; and the same is true of the Confession of Augsburg among Lutherans.

It is also important to note that the main source of doctrine is not theological speculation, but the life of worship. Scholars have usually referred to this principle as *lex orandi est lex credendi*—the rule of prayer becomes the rule of belief. Modern rationalism would have us think that ideas evolve mostly from purely logical and *objective* thought, when in fact ideas often spring from, and are always shaped by, life. We tend to think that doctrines emerge primarily out of theological debate; but in fact most of them are expressions of what the church has long experienced and declared in its worship. The church had long been worshiping Christ as God when the first debates emerged as to what this meant. The church had long been reading the gospels in worship before anyone declared that they are the Word of God. The church had long been baptizing and sharing in communion before any doctrines were developed as to the meaning of baptism or the presence of Christ in communion.

Theological debate does often have a role in the development of doctrine. The most common process is one in which someone proposes a particular way of understanding some aspect of the Christian faith, and others respond by declaring that what is being proposed is not true to the life of the church—particularly as it is expressed in worship. In the ensuing debate, as issues are clarified, the church at large—either by implicit consensus or by official action—decides that a particular view actually contradicts or ignores an essential aspect of the faith as the church has long experienced it in life and in worship. The most common outcome of such debates is that one party is declared to be wrong—often given the title of "heretical"— and the views of the rest are declared to be the official position—the doctrine—of the church.

Think about it as parallel to the case of a local church in which the pulpit has always been placed at the center of the chancel. Probably the pulpit was put there for a number of reasons. Some of those reasons may have been merely practical. For instance, when there were no systems of amplification, it was easier to hear a sermon if the pulpit was at the center, and not off to one side. Some may have been aesthetic: a pulpit in the center makes the chancel look more balanced. Some may have been merely a matter of tradition: those who designed this church were used to churches where the pulpit was at the center, and they simply copied what they had seen elsewhere. Some may have been theological: a pulpit at the center affirms that the center of worship is the preaching of the Word of God. Now some members of the church—or the pastor—suggest moving the pulpit to one side. Again, their reasons may be varied, some practical, some a matter of aesthetics, and some theological. As justification for their proposal, people in this group argue that the center of worship should not be the pulpit, but the communion table. In the ensuing debate, aesthetic, practical, and theological arguments become entwined and practically indistinguishable—furthermore, personal animosities, friendships, and other invisible agendas also play a role. Eventually one side wins, or a compromise is reached that satisfies most of the membership of the church. Some of those whose views have been rejected decide to abide by the will of the majority, and comply with the decision. Some others, however, will not accept the decision. They continue trying to move the furniture, insisting that the others are wrong. Eventually, they will probably leave the church—if they are not expelled first.

Somewhat similar, but dealing with much more serious matters, is the process that usually leads to the decision that a certain view is the actual doctrine of the church. Someone offers a position, or a solution to a theological problem, or a new form of worship, and the proposal results in debate, experimentation, attempts at compromise, alternative solutions, and so on. When eventually a consensus

5

is reached, this usually reflects what the church has long believed and expressed in its worship and in its life. But as a result of the debate, a new consensus has also arisen, that certain positions or views actually deny or threaten a central aspect of the Christian faith. At that point, and in order to avoid repeating the debate constantly, the conclusion that has been reached becomes a doctrine of the church.

It is easy to disparage doctrine and to think that all those who in centuries past tried to define Christian doctrine were overzealous inquisitors or hunters of heretics—which some in fact were—or simply people who were far too certain about things that are in fact inscrutable. We live at a time when the principle of "live and let live, think and let think" is so prevalent that we fear that any doctrinal statement is an undue invasion into other people's rights to their own opinions. It is true that there are still Christians who insist on compliance with every detail of doctrine, and with absolute agreement with what they declare to be true belief. You probably have good reason not to wish to be like them. Right now, some denominations are being torn asunder because some insist on a particular way of reading the Bible, and they declare that there is no place in the church for those who think otherwise. However, this should not lead us to the other extreme, as if doctrines were absolutely irrelevant. Imagine that someone came to church Sunday, put a rock in the chancel, and invited all to worship the rock, dancing around it and praying to it. No matter how open-minded you are, you would probably object to such a suggestion, arguing that it goes against your convictions and against Christian monotheism. Some things are clearly out of bounds. No matter whether you call them doctrines or not, the fact is that there are certain things and beliefs that are important to you as a Christian, as well as to the church as a whole.

Perhaps the best way to explain the proper function of doctrines is to think of them as the foul lines on a baseball field. There is no rule that forces the shortstop to stand to one side of second base, and the second baseman to the other. There is no rule that says that the ball must be hit to a particular area of the field. As long as they stay within the foul lines, players have a great deal of freedom. The foul lines, however, do set limits to that freedom. There are certain areas that are simply out of bounds. You may hit a ball as hard as you wish; but if it is foul it is not a home run. To try to legislate where each player must stand, and where the ball must be hit, would destroy the game; but to try to play without any sense of limits, without any foul lines, would also destroy the game.

When properly employed and understood, good Christian doctrine performs a similar role. It does not inhibit people's freedom to hold a variety of opinions, to explain matters in a variety of ways, to emphasize different elements of the Christian faith. But it does tell us what the limits are beyond which you are no longer within the bounds of what the church at large considers to be its faith. When it is a doctrine of a particular denomination, it may serve to emphasize or to protect something that may be of value for the entire church, but which is also that denomination's heritage.

Or, think of doctrines in terms of fences atop a mesa, at the edge of a series of cliffs. The fences do not tell you where to stand, or where to go within the entire area of the mesa. They simply warn you that if you go beyond a certain point you are no longer safe. Perhaps others have already fallen from atop the mesa, and that is why the fence has been built. As we study the development of Christian doctrine in the pages that follow, you will see what are some of the cliffs or pitfalls against which such doctrines seek to guard us, and will thus gain greater appreciation for them, not so much as limits to your freedom of opinion, but rather as warnings or signs of dangers that others have discovered.

The Development of Doctrine

Do doctrines evolve? They most certainly do. Otherwise, the very title of this book would be an oxymoron, for things that do not change cannot have a history. Doctrines change first and foremost because they are human. Doctrines are not divine; they are not even *from* God. They are *about* God and God's will. This does not make them irrelevant or unimportant. They are ways in which the church through the ages has sought to clarify what it has heard from God, regarding both God's nature and God's will for creation. We may often wish doctrines had come directly down from heaven, as infallible and unalterable descriptions of God. Indeed, one of the most common errors in the life of the church—and a very costly one—has been to confuse doctrine with God, as if God could be contained in a verbal formula. This is understandable. One of the most common expressions of human sin is our wish to control God. We wish we had God in a bottle, to carry around in our pocket. Or, even more, we wish God were like a genie trapped in a magic lamp, ready to do our bidding at our request, and always under our command and control. That is the essence of idolatry. The difference between God and an idol is not that one is visible and the other is not; the difference is that God is a sovereign whose subjects we are, and an idol is an object subjected to our will.

This is crucial, for to confuse doctrines about God with God is to fall into idolatry. The very common tendency to turn doctrines into infallible statements whereby we describe and circumscribe God is the same tendency that has led others to take a piece of wood, place it on an altar, and say, "You are my god." The person who worships a block of wood recognizes that life is not under human control, but is not ready to relinquish control to an uncontrollable God. The prophet Isaiah makes this point quite strongly by commenting on those who "hire a goldsmith, who makes it into a god; then they fall down and worship! They lift it to their shoulders, they carry it, they set it in its place, and it stands there; it cannot move from its place" (Isa 46:6-7). Likewise, when we insist that doctrines are absolutely fixed, infallible, exact descriptions of God, we are acknowledging that we must rely on someone beyond ourselves; and yet at the same time we are refusing to relinquish control to a God we cannot control—again, the genie in the bottle. And, just as Isaiah says about an idol of gold, we then act as if those idolized doctrines rested on our shoulders, and we become militant "defenders of the faith"—as if God's truth needed to be defended!

Another reason we dislike the notion that doctrines might evolve is that too often we have confused doctrine with faith, and because we have been told that it is by believing in a particular way that one is saved we may conclude that one is saved—in other words by holding to a particular doctrine. It is said that when Servetus was burned at the stake in Geneva, William Farrel, one of the leaders of the Reformation in the city, heard him cry at the very last moment, "Christ, Son of the eternal God, have mercy on me," and that Farrel commented that it was a pity that Servetus had not cried, "Christ, eternal Son of God, have mercy on me," because in that case he could have been saved, when in fact he had gone to hell. In one sense Farrel had a point. After much debate, the church had come to a certain consensus about Christ—a consensus reflected in Farrel's phrase, and not in Servetus's—and that consensus is valuable and important. Yet, do we really believe in a God whose love is such as to be swayed by a doctrinal formula? Is it not possible that Servetus, mistaken as he was, still loved God as much as did Farrel? Is God's love limited to those who think correctly about the divine? Although doctrines have much to do with faith, and are an expression of faith, salvation is not by doctrine—not by the doctrine of the Trinity, nor by the inerrancy of Scripture, nor by any other doctrine. Let doctrines develop, and change, and grow. The love of God remains the same!

Doctrines evolve in various ways and for different reasons. One of these ways—perhaps the most common—is by responding to a new challenge. Just as nobody says much about the furnishings in a local church until someone suggests moving the pulpit, there are aspects of Christian belief that are unexpressed, and even unthought, until someone suggests something that challenges what until then has been implicit. In the pages that follow we will see many such instances. Most of the early councils that issued declarations regarding the godhead, or about the nature of Christ, were responding to the challenge of dissenting opinions. Some of those opinions were incorporated into the final decisions, and others were excluded and declared heretical; but in all cases the result was that matters that until then had gone generally unexpressed, once challenged and clarified, became official doctrine of the church.

Another way in which doctrines evolve has to do with the constant flow of Christianity into new cultures, and with change in those cultures themselves. Christianity was born in Palestine, in the midst of Judaism; and therefore the first Christians, all Jews like Jesus himself, interpreted their faith in terms of their Jewish background. Very soon, however, this Jewish sect began expanding among other Jews outside of Palestine—the Jews of the Diaspora, mostly Hellenistic Jews. This became the bridge through which Christianity began making inroads into the Hellenistic world and culture, first among those Hellenists who looked favorably on Judaism—those whom the Jews called "God-fearers"—and eventually among pagan Gentiles. The Roman Empire into which Christianity made such headway was culturally divided between a Latin-speaking West and a Greek-speaking East—and this slowly resulted in different views regarding Christianity. Christianity itself had barely become the dominant religion in the Roman Empire, when the Western portion of that Empire was invaded by a variety of people of Germanic origin, with very different ideas about the nature of reality, the ordering of society, and so on. So the process continued, to the point that Christianity is now represented in practically every culture and nation in the world. In each of those cultures, both past and present, Christianity has developed its own roots, has been nourished by the soil of that culture, and thus has developed its own particular ethos. Even though some have thought that doctrine should remain untouched and unchanged by these varying contexts, the fact is that from the very beginning it has been impossible—even if it were advisable, which it may not be—to separate gospel from culture, as if there were an expression of the gospel unmarked by its cultural context that one can then transfer unchanged from culture to culture.

Clear proof of this is the issue of language and translation. Languages are not equivalent symbol systems, so that one word in one language has its exact equivalent in another. This is true even in the apparently most concrete and apparently simple words. *Table* in English may be a noun referring to a piece of furniture. In that case, the Spanish word would be *mesa*. Then, it could be a multiplication chart; in which case it would be a *tabla* in Spanish. Or it could be a verb, something an assembly does when deciding not to discuss a matter, which in Spanish would be expressed as *prorrogar* or *aplazar*. This means that translators must constantly make choices on the basis of what they understand a text to mean. Those choices determine what the new readers understand. Did you know that the word "atonement" was invented by translators trying to convey a biblical notion for which they found no equivalent in English? Yet now that word has its own established meaning, and Christians in other parts of the world coming before an English text with the word "atonement" must find their own ways to translate it. Or take the matter of the very doctrine of God. Every culture and language into which Christianity has penetrated has had a notion of divinity. Some had several different words, expressing various aspects of the divine. When Christians then have to choose among such terms, this results in a challenge similar to those discussed above, by people "trying to move the furniture." In China, for instance, Roman Catholic missionaries in the seventeenth century found two possible ways to translate the name of God, each with its own particular connotations. The Jesuits opted for one translation, and the Dominicans for another. Eventually, the matter reached Rome, which had to make a decision. The process itself had an effect on the way people spoke about God, not only in China, but also in Rome.

Sometimes the change is produced not by crossing cultural borders, but by the evolution of cultures in which Christianity is already established. In the thirteenth century, there was a great change in the culture of Western Europe, as the monetary economy, long forgotten in favor of a barter economy, was restored; as a new merchant class developed; as cities and universities grew; and as new philosophical ideas were imported from Muslim Spain and from Sicily. In that changing society, many of the traditional statements of doctrine were challenged. The result was a series of new understandings of matters as diverse as creation, revelation, and the practice of voluntary poverty. In the nineteenth and twentieth centuries, Darwin's theory of the evolution of the species led to debates on the doctrine of creation that would have been inconceivable before. The development of modern technology, and its undeniable power to affect nature in unprecedented ways, has led to serious discussion among Christians on the subject of ecology and how it relates to Christian doctrines such as creation and eschatology—the doctrine of the last things. Today, many are claiming that modernity is coming to an end, and we are moving into postmodernity. If so, we should expect traditional doctrinal statements to be challenged—as is indeed the case. We do not know what the outcome will be; but we may be rather certain that as culture and society evolve, so will doctrinal statements evolve.

Sometimes this development is so slow as to be imperceptible. For instance, in the course of our study we will see that during the Middle Ages the preoccupation with being right before God led to the development of a complex penitential system, to the point that people came to believe that salvation is something we attain by our own good works, and not something freely given out of God's love. The Reformation of the sixteenth century was to a large extent an effort to undo this and other developments, which the Reformers said were undue changes in Christian doctrine and practice, and their opponents held were simply the continuation of what the church had always taught and done.

11

Furthermore, these unnoticed changes are constantly taking place around us and are not only a matter of times past. The closer they are to us, and the more ingrained they are in our culture and our ways of understanding life and society, the more difficult they are for us to notice. A case in point is the manner in which during the last two or three centuries Western Protestantism has come to reflect the values of the society in which it exists. Take for instance the matter of wealth and poverty. I have already referred to the issue of voluntary poverty. In times past—and still in some traditions—when churches were named after people, these were most often people who had distinguished themselves by their voluntary poverty and their service to the needy—people such as St. Augustine, St. Francis, St. Claire, or St. Ignatius. Today, in some of our denominations, when churches are named after people, quite often these people have distinguished themselves by their accumulation of wealth and by their contributions to the church. This reflects a change in the attitude of many Christians toward wealth—a change that so closely reflects the values of our society that we scarcely note it.

In short, like it or not, doctrines do change. They will continue changing as long as they are living realities, expressions of a living faith. If they cease changing, they are no longer living and have become dead relics of a faith that is probably also dead or in the process of dying.

The Continuity of Doctrine

Having said all of this, it is important to underscore the other side of the coin: the continuity of doctrine. In the pages that follow you will note that, just as doctrines evolve, there is also a certain continuity in their evolution. Doctrines are not capricious statements or suggestions that someone makes "out of the blue," or so to speak by trying to make Christianity relevant to the latest fad. Precisely because most of the basic doctrines of Christianity have been established by a slowly developing consensus, they prove to be quite resistant to faddist changes, no matter how successful such changes might momentarily seem. In the nineteenth century, for instance, there were numerous attempts among Protestant liberals to redefine the uniqueness of Jesus in terms that were more acceptable to modern times, but that also radically changed what the church had traditionally understood that uniqueness to be. For a time, some of these attempts were so successful that their proponents claimed that traditional Christology was a matter of the past. Yet, as time passed, those proposals have faded into the background, certainly making significant contributions to the understanding of traditional Christology, but not replacing it.

Probably the best way to think about the continuity of doctrines as they develop is to think about ourselves and our own continuity. Over the almost seventy years of my life, I have changed quite a bit—and so have my friends. As a boy, I enjoyed horseback riding and canoeing. Today, I prefer a good book or a comfortable cruise. As a boy, I was skinny, always trying to gain weight. Today, I have to watch my weight, and I would very much like to get rid of a few extra pounds. Day in and day out, I have changed. Some of those changes have been dramatic to the point that I can almost date them—changes in career, in perspectives, in values. Others have been constant and imperceptible. Today, I look at myself in a mirror, and at a photograph from my childhood, and I can scarcely believe that the two are the same person. And yet, I am still myself. There is a certain continuity. The mischievous, stone-throwing lad that I was, I still am—even though I no longer throw stones at my friends, and my mischievousness takes a different direction.

In the same manner, although doctrines do evolve, when that evolution is proper, they retain their identity. The fact that they evolve is not sufficient reason to conclude that their earlier form was false, or that their newer form is a distortion. I do not think that I am a distortion of who I used to be, or that I used to be less than I am now—even though in the past there was less of me! I have simply grown, matured, aged, been shaped by changing circumstances. Likewise, a doctrine may grow, be clarified, reflect changing circumstances, and still retain its identity.

Much of this continuity is provided by the continuity in the life of the church. The church has undergone many changes and has taken many shapes in the course of its almost twenty centuries of existence. It has been a persecuted church and—in less glorious times—a persecuting church. It has been a small minority, and a dominant majority; a small enclave in the midst of an alien culture, and a force shaping culture; a pilgrim people, and a place for those who "have arrived." Throughout all these changes and configurations, we can still see continuity in the life of the church. The faith we now hold and we so cherish has come to us through the toils of martyrs who died for their faith, of unknown monks who copied manuscripts, of mothers who taught their children, of missionaries and preachers who staked their lives on it. It is within this unbroken line of believers, great and small, wise and foolish, weak and strong, believing, worshiping, serving, dreaming, doubting, struggling—in short, within the church—that we stand, and that doctrines have emerged and evolved.

Thus, just as the church is ours, even though we may have difficulties with much that goes on in the life of the church, doctrines are also ours, even though we may have difficulties with some of them. And, just as we have the responsibility of making the church ours to the point that we are able both to serve and to criticize it as necessary, so are we called to study its doctrines to the point that we are able both to affirm and to seek to reform them as necessary.

The Chapters That Follow

In any study such as this, it is possible to organize the material in two different ways. The first is chronological. Were we to follow an essentially chronological scheme, it would be necessary to divide the history of Christianity into a series of periods. Then we would discuss the various Christian doctrines in a particular period (for instance, before the time of Constantine), from that move to the next period, and so on. The second main option would be to organize our material thematically. Such an approach would be based on a more or less traditional ordering of theological subjects, so that there would be a chapter on revelation, one on God, one on creation, and so on, and in each of these chapters one would follow the development of that particular heading of theology from the very earliest times to our day. Each of these two approaches has its advantages and its drawbacks, and the truth is that it is impossible to follow one of them strictly without ever lapsing into the other.

The approach I have chosen to follow here is a combination of the two outlined above. It is based on the fact that various headings of theology have become a main subject of discussion at different times.

Thus, while one can find discussions regarding the Trinity both before and after the fourth century, it was in the fourth century that this particular doctrine came to the foreground and was debated in such a way that the decisions of that time have determined much of the later discussion on the subject. Likewise, while Christology has always been a main concern of the church, it was in the fifth century that this was the center of attention, and that some decisions were made that became the mark of orthodoxy. On this basis, the book is organized thematically in the sense that each chapter deals with a particular set of doctrinal issues—Scripture, God, creation, humankind, Christology, and so on—and that each chapter sketches the development of that particular set of issues throughout the history of the church. Yet it is also organized chronologically in the sense that the ordering of the various chapters follows roughly the same chronological order in which the particular issues discussed therein came to the foreground. For this reason, for instance, the chapter about the doctrine of God and the Trinity—focusing mostly on the fourth century—appears before the chapter on the doctrine of Christ—which was the main subject of debate during the fifth century.

Perhaps a more pictorial image would be useful to explain this. Imagine each of the chapters that follow as a highway along which traffic flows. Over most of the length of the highway, it flows at a steady pace. If you are driving along, you hardly think about traffic. Yet there are certain points in every highway in which traffic becomes congested. The reasons for this may be many, and most often there is more than one reason—traffic merging from another road, a particularly busy intersection, a steep incline, and so on. Thinking of each theme as a highway where traffic flows along the centuries, the place where traffic becomes congested is the particular time when that theme became dominant in theological discussion, or when the debate led to decisions that have marked the history of Christian theology from that point on. In some highways, traffic will become congested earlier than in others—the church debated the doctrine of the Trinity long before it debated whether salvation is by faith or by works. Generally, in the pages that follow those highways where traffic became congested earlier—those themes that were hotly debated earlier—will appear first, followed by other chapters dealing with subjects that were debated later. Yet each chapter seeks to outline the development throughout the entire history of Christianity of the theme or themes under discussion. Thus, the chapter on Christology, while focusing on the debates of the fifth century, follows those debates through the ages. Since each chapter summarizes the entire story, each concludes with some observations as to the relevance for today of the issues debated back then.

The above outline would be simple, were it not that some highways become congested at more than one point. Thus, the place of tradition in Christian thought and life was an important subject of discussion in the second century, and also in the sixteenth; and the role and participation of humankind in the entire process of redemption has been discussed rather vigorously at various times. In such cases, I have made decisions that, although somewhat arbitrary, are based on my perception of the best way to present the argument clearly and succinctly. I trust that the reader will forgive me if at some points I have failed to make things sufficiently clear by following this scheme.

A Final Word

Now, a final word of introduction and invitation. This book is written as a believer addressing believers. Although sometimes we tend to act as if theology were purely an intellectual matter, for believers it is much more than that. It is part of our attempt to practice and to show the love of God with all our minds. Even if its content is correct, theology fails when it is not a hymn of praise to God, an acknowledgment of our own sin, a joyful recognition of God's power and God's grace. Writing theology, an author has the uneasy yet joyful feeling that the One about whom one is writing is looking over one's shoulder; that one is addressing not only the reader, but also the unseen Author of every line of life and history. One also has the hope and the consolation that the reader likewise will not read alone, but will read in the presence and for the service of the same One about whom one writes, and that therefore these lines one writes will invite others to the same praise and joy with which they are written. So be it!

For Further Reading

On the nature and function of doctrine:

Lindbeck, George A. *The Nature of Doctrine: Religion and Theology in a Postliberal Age.* Philadelphia: Westminster Press, 1984.

Hart, Trevor. *Faith Thinking: The Dynamics of Christian Theology.* Downers Grove, Ill.: InterVarsity Press, 1995.

On the history of the self-understanding of theology:

Congar, Yves M. J. *A History of Theology.* Garden City, N.Y.: Doubleday, 1968.

On the actual history of doctrines, in much more detail than the present book:

González, Justo L. *A History of Christian Thought,* in three volumes; revised edition. Nashville: Abingdon Press, 1987.

1.

ISRAEL, THE CHURCH, AND THE BIBLE

Their delight is in the law of the LORD,
and on his law they meditate day and night.
Psalm 1:2

The Jewish Roots of Christianity

As we read the New Testament, it is clear that one of the issues the church first had to face was its relationship to Israel and to the promises made to Abraham and his descendants forever. According to the witness of the Gospels, during Jesus' lifetime there were those who associated him with Elijah, John the Baptist, or others among the prophets (Matt 16:14; Mark 6:15; 8:28; Luke 9:18-19). Jesus himself repeatedly referred to the sacred Scriptures of Israel. The same was true of his earliest followers, as well as all the writers of the New Testament.

Even Paul, the "Apostle to the Gentiles," usually began his preaching in the cities he visited by speaking at the synagogue, constantly quoted the Hebrew Bible—although in a Greek translation—and according to Acts declared himself to be preaching "the hope of Israel" (Acts 28:20).

Yet it was some of the religious leaders of Israel who, according to the Gospels, believed Jesus to be a danger to the nation and its religion, and therefore turned him over to the Roman authorities to be crucified. When, after the events of Holy Week and Pentecost, his disciples began their preaching, they had to contend with the opposition of many in the Jewish Sanhedrin, which ordered them to cease their activities, and punished them when they did not obey.

As Christianity spread into the Gentile world, many of its first converts were either Jews or those whom the Jews knew as "God-fearers," that is, people who believed in the God of Israel and who followed most of the moral teachings of the Hebrew Scriptures, but who were not ready to accept circumcision, nor to follow all the ritual and dietary laws of Israel. Traditionally, when such God-fearers decided to join Judaism, they were accepted into Israel's fold through a series of steps that included a baptismal rite and were known as "proselytes." Now the preaching of Christianity provided such God-fearers with a new option. They could join the church through a process that also culminated in a baptism, and within this community they could worship the God of Israel without having to submit to the ritual strictures that had stood in their way to becoming Jews. Many actual Jews accepted the preaching of Christians, and Jesus as the Messiah—to the point that for quite some time a large proportion of Christians were of Jewish origin. For some, this new form of Judaism that seemed to make it easier to be part of the surrounding society without fear of being defiled by ritually unclean Gentiles seemed less demanding, and therefore more appealing, than a stricter form of Judaism. In this, they were continuing a trend that had developed in some Jewish quarters, for even before the advent of Christianity there were many Jews who were seeking ways to bridge the gap that separated them from Hellenistic culture and society. For many such Jews, and not only for God-fearers, Christianity seemed to provide an attractive alternative.

Thus was set up a spirit of competition and often suspicion between Christians and Jews—a competition that centered mostly on the question of whose interpretation of ancient Scripture was correct. Christians claimed the Hebrew Bible as their own, accusing Judaism of misinterpreting its own scriptures. They insisted that there were prophecies in the Hebrew Bible that pointed to Jesus. Soon they began circulating lists of "testimonies"—passages from the prophets and other sacred Jewish writings that, according to Christian polemicists, foretold the coming of Jesus and many of the events of his life. In the heat of competition and controversy, Christians increasingly blamed Jews in general—and not just the religious leadership of Jerusalem—for the death of Jesus. Blaming Jews for the death of Jesus served their anti-Jewish polemics, and it was also more convenient and less dangerous than constantly reminding themselves and others that Jesus had been executed as a subversive criminal by the powerful Roman Empire.

In the midst of polemic and competition, Judaism also stiffened its opposition to Christianity, particularly after the destruction of Jerusalem in the year 70 left it devoid of a temple and territorial identity. Judaism, until then the national religion of a people with a land and an ancient center of worship, now found itself having to define itself by means other than a temple and a land and competing for a place in the maelstrom of religions of the Greco-Roman world. In that competition, its most serious rival was Christianity, precisely because Christianity had Jewish roots and now claimed for itself much of the religious inheritance of Israel. A center of the ensuing revival of Jewish scholarship and polemics was in Jamnia (now Yavneh, in Israel). In the year 90, the rabbis in Jamnia listed the official books (the "canon") of the Hebrew Scriptures. Scholars still debate to what degree this was simply a reaffirmation of what most Jews had long held, and to what degree it was a reaction to Christianity and its propaganda. At any rate, the canon of Jamnia excluded many of the more recent books that for a number of reasons were often quoted by Christians.

It is difficult for us today to understand the full measure of the debate and controversy involved in this process. For many centuries—even though there have always been differences in the midst of each of the two—Christianity and Judaism have been fairly well defined. For much of that time, Christians have had the upper hand politically and socially and have often used their power to suppress Judaism and to harass its followers. But such was not the case in the early centuries of the Christian era. Both Christianity and Judaism were in the process of taking shape—Christianity because it was new, and Judaism because it was learning to live under new circumstances. Thus, neither Judaism nor Christianity was exactly what it is today—and which of the two would eventually win out was still much in doubt.

The Hebrew Bible

The first Christians, like Jesus himself, were Jews. They did not think they were part of a new religion. They were convinced that the "gospel," the good news, was that in Jesus and his resurrection the ancient promises made to Israel were being fulfilled—in other words, that "the hope of Israel" was now coming to fruition. As Acts tells the story, at first they did not even conceive that this was a message of hope for all humankind, and it was only after some astonishing experiences that they decided that their good news was also for the Gentiles. Even then, all you have to do is read the epistles of Paul to realize that the good news for Gentiles is that they, too, are invited to become children of Abraham by faith—or, as Karl Barth put it in the twentieth century, that they could become "honorary Jews."

As Jews, no matter whether by physical descent or by adoption through faith, Christians had a Bible—the Hebrew Bible, to which we shall return later in this chapter. This was the Bible they read in their meetings, as they gathered to worship God and to try to discern God's will for them and the meaning of the events to which they had become witnesses—the life, death, and resurrection of Jesus of Nazareth. In the book of Acts we have several examples of Paul and others speaking at a synagogue, and there using the Hebrew Scriptures to tell their fellow Jews that Jesus is the fulfillment of the promises made to Abraham, and to invite them to believe in Jesus. Thus, the first Christian Bible was the Jewish Bible. This they used in teaching. This they used in controversy. And this they used in worship. Apparently no one even dreamed of adding other books to the Hebrew Scriptures.

However, as the first generation of witnesses began disappearing, Christians felt the need for some instrument of instruction that preserved the teaching of those early witnesses. It was not enough to read in church the books of the prophets, or the Law of Moses; it was also necessary to read materials that dealt more directly with Jesus himself and with the duties and beliefs of Christians. In a way, Paul's letters were intended to meet this need. He could not be present in all the churches he founded, so he wrote to them. His letters—with the exception of his personal note to Philemon—were intended to be read aloud to the gathered congregation. They were letters of instruction, entreaty, challenge, inspiration, and sometimes fundraising, addressed to particular churches with particular needs. He even dared write a long letter to the Christians in the city of Rome, most of whom he had never met. He apparently did this to prepare the way for a planned visit to Rome; but the power and insight of this letter were such that people continued reading it in church long after Paul's death. In fact, the effect that Paul's letters had led churches to make copies and share them with one another, and then to read them in their services, using them as materials for instruction parallel to the ancient books of the Hebrew Bible. Toward the end of the first century, while exiled in Patmos, John "the theologian" wrote a book to the churches in the Roman province of Asia—the book of Revelation—that soon began circulating among other churches in the region and eventually was recopied and read throughout the church.

Paul and John of Patmos wrote for specific occasions, and therefore did not write about the entire life and teaching of Jesus. They were still alive when people began feeling the need for teaching documents to be read in church—documents presenting the entire life of Jesus, as well as his teachings, or what we now call the Gospels. Most scholars agree that the first of these was the Gospel of Mark, followed shortly thereafter by the Gospels of Matthew and Luke, and eventually by the Gospel of John.

As they began reading these books in church, Christians did not debate whether they were "the Word of God," nor whether they were inspired. At first they did not even seem to have considered the matter of their relative authority vis-à-vis the books of the Hebrew Bible. They simply found them valuable for their worship—particularly for that part of the worship service that consisted mostly in Scripture reading and exposition—and began using them in that context. Some time before the middle of the second century a Christian writer, Justin Martyr, tells us that Christians gathered "on the day that is commonly called of the Sun" and read, "as time allows, the memoirs of the apostles or the writings of the prophets."[1] Thus, apparently without much debate, in the context of worship, the "memoirs of the apostles"—perhaps the Gospels, or perhaps the Gospels as well as some of the epistles—were being equated in authority with the prophets.

The Challenge of Marcion

At about the same time as Justin was writing those words, however, a controversy was beginning to brew regarding the authority

23

and value of the Hebrew Scriptures—a controversy that was related to the attempt on the part of some Christians to reject everything Jewish.

There were those whose opposition to Judaism went to such an extreme that they were ready to disown any connection between their faith and the religion of Israel. There was, for instance, an obscure sect called the Ophites—that is, followers of the snake. According to them, the real hero in the garden of Eden was the serpent, who sought to liberate humans from the tyrannical power of the God of the Jews. Others, the Cainites, held similar opinions, making Cain their hero. To what extent they made use of Christian doctrine is not clear. In any case, the most famous and most influential among Christians who sought to do away with the religion of Israel was Marcion.

Marcion was born in the town of Sinope, on the Black Sea, the son of the Christian bishop of the city. Although little is known of his early life, by the middle of the second century he was in Rome, where his teaching caused quite a stir. Eventually his followers withdrew from the rest of the church, giving birth to a Marcionite church with its own bishops and its own structure. The existence of this rival body was the reason Marcion became so influential, and why some of the intellectual leaders of the church, including some who wrote polemical treatises against Judaism, also wrote treatises against Marcion.

Marcion claimed there was a sharp contrast and even opposition between the God of the Hebrew Bible and the Father of Jesus. These were not even two different concepts of God; they were two different gods. According to Marcion, the Yahweh of Hebrew Scriptures is an inferior god, one who—either out of ignorance or out of mischief—created this world and now rules it. This is a vengeful and even vindictive god, one who insists on justice and punishment for disobedience, and whose willfulness is manifested in his having arbitrarily chosen the Jews as his own privileged people. In contrast, the Father of Jesus Christ—and the God of Christian faith—is high above the petty god of Israel, and high above any concern for matter and this physical world. This high God, rather than demanding every last ounce of what is owed to him, forgives the sinner. This is not the Yahweh of law and justice, but the Father of love and grace, who has sent Jesus into this world of Yahweh's in order to save what was lost—that is, our spirits that Yahweh had imprisoned in this material world of his.

According to Marcion, this message of grace was soon forgotten by most Christians, and it was only Paul, the apostle of grace, who had retained the message of the high God of love and forgiveness. Yet even Paul's writings had been taken over by people who did not understand this message, or the contrast between Yahweh and the Father, and who had corrupted Paul's epistles by introducing in them all sorts of references to the Hebrew Bible and to the God of Abraham and Jacob.

This meant that Marcion, unlike the rest of the church, rejected the ancient scriptures of the Jews—not because they were false in the sense of being untrue, but because they were the true revelation of an inferior god. It was for this reason that he felt compelled to propose a new Christian Bible, one that would not include any of the books of the Jews, nor any positive reference to such books. This was the first canon of the New Testament. It included ten epistles of Paul and the Gospel of Luke, who, because he had been Paul's companion, was a true interpreter of the Christian message. What, then, of the many references to the Hebrew Scriptures in the Gospel of Luke and in the epistles of Paul? Marcion claimed that these had been interpolated into the original text by "Judaizers." The writings of both Luke and Paul, therefore, had to be purged of every reference to the Hebrew Bible or to the God of the Jews.

The rest of the church was appalled at such teachings. Although there certainly were conflicts and competition between Jews and Christians, the latter had always recognized their Jewish roots, and their argument with Judaism had to do with whether or not Jesus was the Messiah, and not with whether the God of Abraham was the true and highest God, or whether this God had created all things. The passages from the Hebrew Bible that Christians had previously used to prove to Jews that Jesus was indeed the Messiah were now put to a different use, which was to prove that the books in which such prophetic utterances were found were indeed the Word of the same God who had spoken in Jesus. Thus, for instance, although Christians had long claimed that Isaiah 53 had predicted that the Messiah would suffer, and in their polemics against Jews this was used to prove that Jesus was the Messiah, now in the attempt to refute Marcion, the same claim was used to prove that God did speak through Isaiah.

The Canon of the New Testament

However, it did not suffice to refute Marcion and to claim that God spoke in the Hebrew Bible. It was also necessary to determine which Christian books could and should be used in the churches to teach its members, much as the Hebrew Bible was used in the synagogue to instruct its faithful. As we have seen, by Marcion's time it had become customary to read and expound in church, not only the Hebrew Bible, but also the writings of the apostles. Now, partly as a response to Marcion's strange canon, and partly out of the unavoidable need to determine which books should be granted that authority, and which should not, the church began developing lists of authoritative Christian books.

This was a long process. The church had no centralized government, nor anyone who could make decisions for the whole. There was no great church council or legislative body to decide which books should form part of the new list of sacred books. In the absence of such means, agreement developed slowly, through consultation and mutual influence among churches. Some churches used some books and not others. The Fourth Gospel was slower than the other three in gaining full acceptance. From a very early date, most lists included the four Gospels, Acts, and the letters of Paul, as well as most of the books that now appear toward the end of the New Testament. It took a long time for all to agree on including the Second and Third Epistles of John, Second Peter, James, and Jude. By the middle of the third century, the canon of the New Testament was generally agreed upon. It certainly included the four Gospels, Acts, the epistles of Paul, and several other books. But some lists included books that eventually the church rejected, not as bad or as mistaken, but simply as not bearing apostolic authority. (An example is the *Shepherd* of Hermas, a book of visions and instructions written in Rome in the middle of the second century.) Eventually the present-day canon of the New Testament became a matter of general consensus. Yet it is not until 367 that we find the first list that agrees exactly with what we have now, including all our present books, and no others. By the end of that century, after much hesitation on matters of detail, the canon of the New Testament was generally fixed, and it is this canon that we follow to this day. Significantly, at that time the church did have the means to resolve matters of controversy—the great "ecumenical councils," of which more will be said later—and yet there was no attempt to resolve the question of the exact list of books in the New Testament by such means. The often heard assertion, that the Council of Nicea established the canon of the New Testament, has no basis in fact. The differences among various lists—by then quite minor—were not considered a subject of acrimonious debate to be adjudicated by a council or any other official means, and were left to be solved by the slow process of developing a consensus.

At this point it is important to say something about the commonly held notion of the "forbidden books" of the New Testament. Commonly, usually in the context of discussions about the occult wisdom of the ancients, or in works of fiction such as *The Da Vinci Code*, one hears that there were a number of gospels competing with the present four for admission into the New Testament and that they were forbidden for one reason or another—because they claimed that Jesus was married, because they spoke of the feminine side of God, or because they included ancient wisdom that the church rejected or suppressed. This is simply not true. The "gospels" and other similar writings that are not included in the New Testament fall generally into one of two categories. Most of them are pious legends embellishing the story of the four canonical Gospels or of Acts, written long after the basic list of New Testament books had been formed. Thus, there are stories about Jesus playing with his friends, about the actions of the Virgin Mary, about the travels of Peter and John, and so on. Some of these stories and books are attributed to various apostles, to Mary, or to other figures in the New Testament. These were never suppressed or forbidden. Many of the stories they tell became popular legends that sometimes made their way into church decorations and sermons. They simply never had the authority of the canonical four Gospels.

The other category includes books written in order to promote a particular point of view that the church rejected. Probably the earliest of these—which has not survived—was Marcion's version of the Gospel of Luke eliminating all references to the Hebrew Scriptures

27

or to the God of Israel. Another such book was the second-century Gospel of Truth, written by Valentinus in support of his teaching. Groups that employed such gospels rejected all other gospels and therefore it was never a question of whether their gospels were to be included in the New Testament. It was rather a question of whether they were to supplant the New Testament. Although there are several such books, most of them are clearly later than the four canonical Gospels, and scholars are in general agreement that they are mostly works of fiction, adding nothing to our knowledge of Jesus himself. The one possible exception is the Gospel of Thomas, a document discovered in Egypt in the twentieth century, consisting mostly of sayings of Jesus. Many of these sayings are included in the canonical Gospels; others are clearly apocryphal; and a few may be actual sayings of Jesus that are otherwise unknown. But even in the case of the Gospel of Thomas, there is no indication that there was ever an attempt or a desire to have this document included as a fifth gospel in the New Testament—nor that it was "forbidden," for apparently it was used only by a dwindling sect of Christians, and its disappearance was simply the result of the disappearance of the sect itself.

The Apocrypha of the Old Testament

Regarding what we now call the Old Testament, Christians rejected Marcion's views and insisted on using the Hebrew Scriptures as their own, on the grounds that the history of God's revelation to Israel was the history of God's preparation for the coming of Jesus, and that therefore, now that Jesus had come, those who followed him had the right to use them and the obligation to accept them as authoritative. The Hebrew Scriptures had been translated into Greek even before the advent of Christianity—a translation called the *Septuagint*. This was the Bible that most Christians used. In fact, the writers of the New Testament, except the author of Revelation, usually quote Scripture not from the Hebrew text, but from this Greek translation.

The problem is that, for complex reasons that scholars still debate, the *Septuagint* included a number of Jewish books that are not part of the Hebrew canon—1 and 2 Esdras, Tobit, Judith, the Wisdom of Solomon, Ecclesiasticus (not to be confused with Ecclesiastes),

Baruch, 1 and 2 Maccabees, and some additions to Esther, Daniel, and Jeremiah. Whether these books were ever part of a Hebrew canon is still a matter of debate. They certainly are not now and have not been, at least since the first century, when the rabbis in Jamnia proclaimed their canon of Scripture.

These books are generally known as the Apocrypha of the Old Testament, or as the deuterocanonical books—that is, the books of a second canon. Unfortunately, and causing some confusion, the term "apocrypha" does not mean the same thing with reference to the Old Testament as it means with reference to the New. The Apocrypha of the Old Testament are the deuterocanonical books just listed, that form part of the longer canon of the Old Testament, and not of the Jewish canon. In contrast, the Apocrypha of the New Testament includes all those books mentioned before, attributed to an apostle, to Mary, and even, in the case of one brief letter, to Jesus himself that have never been part of the canon. With reference to the Old Testament, books attributed to ancient writers, and never part of the canon—in other words, the counterpart of the Apocrypha of the New Testament—are called "Pseudepigrapha," and include such books as the Testaments of the Twelve Patriarchs, the book of Enoch, the Ascension of Isaiah, and many others.

Thus, although the deuterocanonical books are not part of the Hebrew canon, they have been considered part of Scripture by most Christians at least until the time of the Reformation. At that point Luther and other Reformers raised objections against them. Luther placed them at the end of his translation of Scripture, as an appendix, arguing that, although good for edification, these books did not have the full authority of Scripture. Eventually most Protestants followed suit, so that today most Protestant Bibles do not include the Apocrypha of the Old Testament—not even as an appendix. In contrast, Roman Catholic and Eastern Orthodox Bibles do include these books. Thus, although the canon of the New Testament is exactly the same for all Christian churches, this is not true of the Old Testament.

Jewish-Christian Relations

Unfortunately, the early controversies between Christians and Jews—in which each sought to establish an identity separate from the other—have continued to mar what should have been the close relationship between the two religions, long after the original circumstances have changed. For a very brief time, at the very beginning of the Christian movement, the balance of power was tilted toward the Jewish leadership in Jerusalem. The Gospels present a picture in which the Judean leadership of Jerusalem resents the Galilean intrusion represented by Jesus and his followers. In the early chapters of Acts, "the people," that is, the common Jewish population, tend to favor Christians until the inclusion of Hellenistic Jews among the leadership of the new sect leads to greater suspicion, and to the martyrdom of Stephen. Paul is depicted as a Jewish religious leader persecuting Christianity. Thus, there is much in the New Testament that reflects an early situation in which Christians had reason to fear the religious leadership of Jerusalem.

What we often forget in reading these books of the New Testament is that those writing them were also Jews, that the Messiah about whom they wrote was Jewish, and that so were all of his first disciples. Thus, when these authors speak of "the Jews" they are not referring, as we tend to think today, to all Jews, nor even to Judaism itself—whose fulfillment they believed they were—but to a certain group of religious leaders who saw the Galilean movement of Jesus as a threat both to their faith and to their power. In some cases, they are not even referring to Jews in general, but to Judeans—that is, to the people of Judea—and particularly to their leading elite in Jerusalem.

But then the situation began to change. Once out of its Palestinian cradle, Christianity and Judaism competed on what was to a large extent an even playing field. Judaism had the advantage of its antiquity and its recognition by Roman authorities. Christianity had the advantage of its greater capability to adapt to Hellenistic culture, and its greater appeal to Gentiles. Neither had the power to persecute or to punish the other—although there were some cases in which Christians felt that some overzealous Jews had found ways to bring the wrath of Rome to bear on them.

Soon, however, the playing field began to tilt in favor of Christianity. Early in the fourth century Emperor Constantine began showing favor toward Christianity, and by the end of the century practically the entire population of the empire had become Christian. The old religions subsisted mostly in remote places in the countryside and therefore received the name "paganism"—which literally means the religion of rustics and peasants. At the beginning of that century, Judaism was still competing with Christianity for the allegiance of those who found the old religions insufficient; but by the end of the century it had lost that battle and thus became mostly a hereditary religion, tolerated by the authorities, but still regarded as an old rival by the victorious church.

This did not mean, however, that the old arguments and rhetoric against Judaism were now abandoned by Christians. Old habits die hard. Long after Judaism had ceased being a real rival to Christianity, Christian preachers and teachers—and even more the Christian populace—continued their ancient polemics against Judaism. As that polemic became increasingly vitriolic, it was claimed that the Jews had crucified Christ; that in rejecting God's offer of Jesus, they had in turn been rejected by God; that they were an accursed people.

Christians continued claiming the Hebrew Scriptures for themselves and insisting that Jews did not really understand their own Scriptures. When Jerome (347–419) learned Hebrew in order to translate the Bible into Latin, he was severely criticized for imagining that he could learn something about the Bible from Jewish teachers. Given the new circumstances, Jewish scholars had little opportunity to respond to such charges. Art began depicting the contrast between the synagogue and the church—the first as an elderly, blindfolded woman, often with a broken spear, and the latter as a young, healthy woman, often with a sword of victory in her hand.

Throughout the Middle Ages, the mythology about the evils of Judaism and of Jews grew. Jews had crucified Jesus, and for that reason God had rejected them. Common gossip had it that Jews practiced black magic. They would steal the consecrated host of communion in order to use it in their evil incantations. In their nefarious worship, they even sacrificed Christian children. Because of these insidious prejudices, when the Crusaders left for the Holy Land in order to take it back from "the infidel," along the way many practiced massacring defenseless Jewish "infidels." A number of bishops and other church leaders condemned such atrocities; but the general preaching of the church, the legends depicted in church after church, and the piety and prejudices of the populace could not be undone or stopped by a few ecclesiastical declarations.

When the Black Death swept through Europe in the fourteenth century, Jews were often spared and, as a result, were accused of killing Christians by poisoning their wells. (Some scholars now suggest that, since the plague was spread by fleas on rats, what actually happened was that, for fear of being accused of witchcraft, Christians often refrained from keeping cats. Since Jews did keep cats, the rat population in their neighborhoods was lower, resulting in fewer cases of the plague.) Late in the fifteenth century, Jews in Spain were charged with ritual murder and desecration of the host. The Inquisition was brought to bear against them. Finally, in 1492, all Jews were expelled from the land.

The Reformation did little to change this situation. Luther declared that "the Jews are worse than the devils." Protestants often claimed that, in their insistence on salvation by works, Roman Catholics were Judaizers. Soon the countercharge appeared, that in their efforts to translate the Bible anew from the Hebrew, and not simply to use Jerome's Vulgate, Protestants were "judaizing." In short, "Jewish" became an epithet and an insult, rather than a term referring to a real people and to their faith.

Theologically, matters were made worse by a surreptitious new form of Marcionism that had begun creeping into the church during the Middle Ages, but became more noticeable in certain Protestant circles in the eighteenth and nineteenth centuries. According to this view, the Old Testament speaks of God as demanding, vindictive, and even cruel, while the New Testament presents God as a loving Father, forgiving and calling believers to forgive. No matter how often you may have heard this in Sunday school or even from the pulpit, it is simply not true. The God of the Old Testament is a just and merciful God; and so is the God of the New Testament. If the God of the Old Testament punishes, so does the God of the New. If the God of the Old Testament desires justice, so does the God of the New. And if the God of the New Testament loves and forgives, so does the God of the Old.

An even more subtle form of Marcionism stands behind the commonly heard assertion that "we must interpret the Old Testament in the light of the New." This is true. But it is also true that we must interpret the New Testament in the light of the Old. As Christians, we affirm that Jesus Christ is the culmination and the fulfillment of the promises made to Abraham and his descendants. This means that the promises are best understood through their fulfillment, and that the fulfillment is best understood through the promise.

Contemporary Relevance

Why is all of this important today?

It is important first of all because the consequences of an error in these matters can be nefarious. Christian prejudice against Jews and Judaism was greatly responsible for the Holocaust of the twentieth century. True, there were many Christians who rejected and opposed Nazi claims and policies, both in Germany and abroad. In Germany, many of these came together in the Confessing Church, which opposed the quiescent attitude of the official churches, and some of whose members paid for their faithfulness with their lives. Still, commonly held notions that the Jews crucified Christ, that for this reason they have been rejected by God, that they do not understand their own Scriptures, that their God is not the loving Father of Jesus Christ, stood behind much of the Nazi propaganda and behind much of the acquiescent attitude of many Christians, both in Germany and abroad.

Second, this is important because there are Christians today who, led by similar prejudices, but in a strange theological twist, follow and promote policies that, although apparently supportive of Judaism, are in fact anti-Semitic. Thus, there are Christians who claim that God does not listen to the prayers of Jews, and that all Jews are condemned to eternal damnation, and who, however, have become ardent supporters of the state of Israel and of all its policies. This they do, not out of respect or love for Jews, but, exactly the opposite, because they are convinced that when Israel is fully restored, the Lord will come and, among other things, will prove how wrong and unfaithful the Jews were. On this score, it may be helpful to reflect on Jesus' words to the effect that the end and its time are not for us to know or to determine.

Third, this is important because, as it affects our reading of Scripture, it also affects all of our life of faith. The New Testament was written during a brief span of less than a century. During that time, Christians were a very small, often persecuted, generally powerless minority. The Old Testament, in contrast, refers to a wide variety of situations in which the people of God may find themselves: in slavery, in exile, as rulers of a nation, having to organize social and political life, and so on. By ignoring the Old Testament, or by reading it only in the light of the New, Christians have often failed to see that when we are in positions of power we have responsibilities of which the Old Testament speaks most clearly. By ignoring the Old Testament, we have often reduced the gospel to a message of individual salvation and have lost sight of the vast cosmic dimensions of the full gospel of Jesus Christ. To this we shall return in the next and other chapters.

For Further Reading

On the formation of the New Testament:
Blackman, E. C. *Marcion and His Influence*. London: SPCK, 1948.
Bruce, F. F. *The Canon of Scripture*. Downers Grove, Ill.: InterVarsity, 1988.
Harrington, Daniel J., S. J. "Introduction to the Canon." In *The New Interpreter's Bible*, vol. 1, 7-21. Nashville: Abingdon Press, 1994.

On Jewish-Christian relations:
Carmichael, Joel. *The Satanizing of Jews: Origin and Development of Mystical Anti-Semitism*. New York: Fromm International, 1992.
Cohn-Sherbok, Dan. *The Crucified Jew: Twenty Centuries of Christian Anti-Semitism*. Grand Rapids: Eerdmans, 1992.
Perry, Marvin, and Schweitzer, Frederick M., eds. *Jewish-Christian Encounters over the Centuries: Symbiosis, Prejudice, Holocaust, Dialogue*. New York: Peter Lang, 1994.

Note

1. *I Apology*, 67.

2.

CREATION

*In the beginning when God created the
heavens and the earth ...
Genesis 1:1*

The Jewish Roots of Christianity

In claiming the Scriptures of Israel, and in declaring themselves honorary children of Abraham by faith, Christians also accepted much of the ancient faith of Israel. This included, among other things, the firm conviction that all that exists has been created by God.

Although the Bible opens with two parallel stories of creation (Gen 1–2), scholars are agreed that this is not the most ancient part of Scripture, and that Israel's conviction that Yahweh was its redeemer and liberator is prior to the doctrine of creation. In other words, Israel experienced and worshiped God first of all as a loving and saving God and, out of that experience and that worship, developed its doctrine of creation, making it clear that the God who redeems Israel is the only God, the God by whom all things are made.

A World Viewed as Evil

As the first Christians went out into the Hellenistic world living and seeking to communicate their faith, they encountered conditions and opinions that were similar to some that Israel had encountered among its neighbors much earlier, at the time when the stories of Genesis and other literature on creation were written. Just as Israel's faith was constantly threatened and challenged by its neighbors' polytheism, the Hellenistic world that Christianity now began to penetrate was populated by gods and other heavenly beings. There was a god—actually, there were several gods—of the sea, and gods for each direction of the wind, and gods fertilizing land and herds, and national gods, and regional gods, and family gods, and gods in the heavenly bodies, and gods of wine and of learning and of war. There were local gods worshiped in small, ancient shrines, and gods imported from distant lands worshiped in strange and mysterious rites.

These many gods served to explain the confusing and conflicting realities of nature and history. If seasons changed, it was because gods died and rose again. If the wind blew fiercely, this was the action of a certain god. If it stopped, that was the action of another god. If a nation conquered another, this proved that its gods were more powerful than the other nation's gods. If a nation declined, this was either because its gods were powerless before other gods, or because the gods had withdrawn their support. The world was the confusing and mysterious plaything of the gods, and all that humans could do was to pray to their gods and hope that these gods would both offer their blessing and be powerful enough to withstand the attacks of other, competing gods.

Such a chaotic world was also a hostile world. A world in which events are determined by the capricious and conflicting whims of a multiplicity of gods is a world in which no security and no meaning can be found. In consequence, the Hellenistic world was swept by a confusing and intermingling variety of religions and philosophical outlooks, all of them offering a way of escaping from what amounted to a hostile and undependable world.

In the field of philosophy, Platonism had developed into a mixture of philosophy and mystical religiosity whose followers sought meaning and hope by the contemplation of "eternal truth"—that is, truth beyond this confusing world of matter and change. On their part, Stoics coped with the apparent capriciousness of the world both by claiming that all of history is a repeating cycle, so that all that happens has happened before and is foreordained to happen again, and by declaring that the truly wise do not resist or become anxious over what they cannot change. Thus they promoted a spirit of victory over pain and anxiety by means of *apatheia*, lack of feeling.) Over against them, the Epicureans did affirm life in the world, teaching that after all, since the world and life are the unpredictable result of mysterious and whimsical forces, the best one can do is to cease trying to find meaning or direction in it and to live as best one can, enjoying life's goods and pleasures; yet even this apparent affirmation of the world was in fact a surrender to the meaningless capriciousness of the world.

In the field of religion, an ill-defined but powerful movement known as Gnosticism taught that the physical world is the result of an error or sin in the spiritual world, and for that reason is not good. Human spirits are like sparks of the spiritual world that have somehow become trapped in physical bodies, and whose goal is to escape from the realm of matter into the realm of spirit, where they belong. In some Gnostic systems, the earth stood at the center of a series of celestial spheres, each of them an obstacle on the path of the spirit's return to its own, and salvation could only be attained by knowing the secrets that would allow the soul passage through each of these spheres. Thus, not only earth, but also the heavens and all the heavenly bodies, were seen as enemies to be overcome.

Then there were mystery religions, some of them local in origin, and others imported from distant and supposedly mystical lands— Isis and Osiris from Egypt, the Great Mother from Syria, Mithras from Persia. Many of these originated in ancient fertility cults that had evolved through the centuries; but, while those ancient fertility cults focused on the production and reproduction of land, herds, and people, their new forms focused on life after death.

From Persia came strongly dualistic influences, teaching that all of reality is formed by two conflicting principles, light and darkness, and that the human predicament is that these two are mixed in the present world as well as in each one of us. According to these views, our spirits are part of the light that is trapped in the darkness, and salvation will come when the two principles are separated—not destroyed, since the two are eternal—so that we shall live in pure light, and all darkness will be kept out.

Such views were so widespread that even within Judaism and early Christianity there were some who held them. This evil world is about to pass. All matter is to be destroyed, leaving only spiritual realities. Then will God's purposes be fulfilled.

37

Official Roman religion took a different tack altogether. Rome was interested in convincing people that the present order was as it should be, that the world as Rome had organized it was worth living in, and that the gods affirmed and supported this world as well as its existing order. Therefore, although Rome most often allowed the peoples it conquered to continue worshiping their gods, policies were developed that fostered the assimilation of such divinities into Roman religion, as supporters of the existing order. This was done in part by equating gods, so that people would feel that their religion was also that of Rome. Thus, for instance, an ancient goddess worshiped in Ephesus was equated with the Greek Artemis, and then with the Roman Diana. As a result, Ephesians could worship a Roman goddess while still following their ancient tradition, and Romans would come to Ephesus to worship their own ancestral goddess. To all of this, Rome added emperor worship. Dead emperors were declared divine and subject to worship throughout the empire. Eventually, particularly in the eastern regions of the empire, the reigning emperor was also considered divine and worthy of worship. In brief, then, while much of the religious impetus of the time focused on escaping the world, official Roman religion focused on living in this world as Rome had shaped it.

The World Is Good

On their part, Christians did not originally approach the matter of the origin and value of the world as an intellectual puzzle to be solved, nor as a doctrine to be defended, nor even, surprising as it may seem, as an explanation for the origin and functioning of the world. Creation was important to them because in worship they praised God the Creator. Just as the ancient Hebrews had come to the realization that the God who was their redeemer was also the creator of all things, Christians had come to the realization that the God whom they worshiped in church, and whom they trusted for their salvation, was also the God who had made all things and called them good. In short, the Christian doctrine of creation, like most doctrines, did not emerge originally from intellectual puzzlement, but rather from the experience of worship. In several of the earliest Christian writings there are portions of hymns of praise to the

Creator and Redeemer God, and it is safe to surmise that these brief passages are quotations from hymns that Christians knew and repeated in their worship.

These convictions that the church celebrated in worship also implied a certain attitude regarding the world and life in it. Both in Judaism and in Christianity, the capricious, meaningless world of paganism, subject to the whim of a variety of competing gods, became a single world, made with a certain purpose, moving toward its intended end, which included God's purposes of salvation. Once again, the notion of creation was profoundly entwined with the experience and the hope of salvation—a salvation that, although still awaiting its final consummation in the end, was already foreshadowed by the joy of living in a world that, even though often hostile, was subject to the one God, and this the God of redemption.

Thus, the Christian doctrine of creation was important, not simply or even primarily as an explanation of the origin of the world, but as the foundation for life in the world and as an expression of the faith the church celebrated and shared in its acts of worship. The official doctrine of the church on these matters was developed in response to challenging and opposing views. Yet the challenge and the contrast were not among competing philosophical or scientific theories, but rather between the faith that the church expressed and celebrated in its worship and the views and practices of the surrounding culture.

In that situation, Christian leaders felt compelled to think and write about the doctrine of creation for two reasons: First, there was always the danger that the views of the surrounding culture on the nature and value of the world would penetrate the life of the church, and that this would undermine Christian obedience in the present world and undercut faith in the Redeemer and Creator God whom the church worshiped. Second, it was necessary to show to society at large that what the church celebrated in worship, and the manner in which the church looked at the physical world, was not entirely irrational—otherwise Jesus and faith in him would become objects of mockery and scorn. It was in response to this dual challenge that Christians developed the doctrine of creation—a doctrine, and this is worth repeating, that they shared with the faith of Israel.

The danger that views from outside would undermine the life of the church was quite real. By the second century people of Gnostic tendencies were embracing Christianity, or at least trying to bring some of the elements of Christianity into their Gnostic worldview. They still held to their basic notion of the origin of the world as the result of an error or a sin on the part of purely spiritual beings, and of the human predicament as the entrapment of souls, which are spiritual sparks broken off from the divine, in this world of matter. Into this framework they would then introduce some Christian teachings. They would speak, for instance, of Christ as Savior; but then they would turn Christ into a purely heavenly being, a messenger from abroad with no physical human reality. Or their concern for what they took to be salvation, and their neglect and underrating of physical reality, were such that they felt no compulsion to respond to the needs of widows, orphans, and those who are needy. Or they claimed that, since this creation is not the work of God, physical creatures are not to be used in the worship of God, and therefore they rejected the central act of Christian worship, which was a physical meal—the Eucharist. Indeed, early in the second century a Christian bishop of Antioch, on his way to martyrdom, wrote against Christian Gnostics who, precisely because they rejected the doctrine of creation by the Redeemer God, would "have no regard for widows and orphans . . . and also withdraw from the Eucharist."[1]

Marcion, whom we met in chapter 1, looked upon this physical world with such contempt and perhaps even horror that he felt that the supreme God, the Father of Jesus Christ, could not be blamed for it, and laid the responsibility for creation at the doorstep of the inferior and ignorant god of the Hebrews. By making redemption the act of the supreme God, and creation the act of a lesser one, Marcion rejected the connection between creation and redemption that had long been held by Jews as well as Christians.

Although the church repeatedly rejected such views, they proved quite attractive and resilient. People who did not consider themselves Gnostics or Marcionites would embrace Gnostic ideas, sometimes even unwittingly, since they were so commonly held in the surrounding culture. It is for this reason that the Apostles' Creed follows Genesis in declaring that God is "maker of heaven and earth." Likewise, the Nicene Creed depicts God as "maker of all things visible and invisible." Neither heaven nor earth, neither the visible nor the invisible, neither matter nor spirit, are excluded from this creative power of God.

The World as a Reasonable Creation of a Reasonable God

In addressing those outside the church, the task of Christian leaders was somewhat different, for here their purpose was to show these outsiders that Christianity was not the irrational faith that its critics claimed it was. In order to do this, some of the earliest Christian theologians—usually called the "second-century apologists"—looked for points of contact between what the church taught and the most respected opinions and traditions within the surrounding culture—a theme to which we shall return in chapter 3. This was important both because it removed obstacles in the Gentiles' path to faith, and because it contradicted many of the evil rumors that circulated about Christians—rumors that often led to persecution.

This task was made easier because there were already a number of thinkers and philosophers who had sought to explain the world in a more rational and coherent way than by simply referring to a multitude of gods. Some of these views Christians rejected, and some they accepted and modified. The views that many Christians found most appealing were those of Plato and his followers. The great attraction of Platonism for Christians was based on its monotheistic overtones. Plato and his teacher Socrates were part of a long succession of Greek thinkers who criticized the multiplicity of gods of traditional religion, and particularly their capriciousness and even immorality. As we shall see in chapter 4, such views, and their use in Christian theology, left a profound impression on the Christian doctrine of God. For the present, however, suffice it to say that the Socratic and Platonic tradition provided at least the possibility of the world being the result of a single principle or creative force.

This offered the opportunity to present the Christian doctrine of creation by a single God in terms that at least the intellectual elite in the Hellenistic world could understand and perhaps even respect. Therefore, as early as the second century, Christian thinkers were busily trying to construct bridges between what Platonists taught about the origin of the world and the Christian doctrine of creation.

The problem with the Platonic tradition was that it did not distinguish sufficiently between the First Principle and its creatures. This was particularly true of Neoplatonism, the form that Platonism took in the second century, at the time when Christians were first forced

41

to consider these matters. According to this view, all of reality is a series of emanations from the One—much as a series of concentric waves created by a rock falling on a pond. At the center of this system stands the One, pure, ineffable, perfect. While all of reality is good, for it comes from the One, as the successive spheres of emanation become more distant from the One they are less good—not really evil, but simply less good. This helped Augustine and others grapple with the problem of evil. According to this view there is ultimately only one reality, the One, for the various spheres emanating from the One are still part of it—they are part of a single whole, of a single reality, of a single and ultimate Being.

Although this may sound attractive, in the end it leads to pantheism—to the view that all things are part of God and that God is the sum total of all things. This understanding of the origin and nature of the world means that the soul is divine, that the body is divine, that mountains are divine, that an ant is divine, that the stars are divine.

Obviously, these are views that the Judeo-Christian tradition has rejected from its earliest times. When Genesis says that God made the sun and the moon and also the stars, it is actually counteracting the commonly held notion among the neighbors of Israel that the sun, the moon, and the heavenly bodies in general are in themselves divine. The people around Israel would worship the mountains, or they would build altars on the mountains, because they were closer to heaven, which they took to be divine. Over against them, the Hebrew prophets and other religious leaders affirmed that only God is divine, and only God is worthy of worship—all the rest has been created by God and is dependent on God. Thus, the psalmist asks whether he should look to the mountains for help, and he immediately answers: "My help comes from the LORD, who made heaven and earth" (Ps 121:2). In other words, the help and salvation of Israel comes from the same and only God who is also the creator of all things. Without such a doctrine of creation, separating God from creatures, idolatry would seem acceptable, for after all the piece of wood or the stone one worships is part of the Eternal.

In summary, the urge to make their teachings more readily understandable and even acceptable to their pagan neighbors and prospective converts made the Neoplatonic theory of the world as a series of emanations from the One attractive to Christian apologists. At the same time, however, this theological accommodation risked bringing into Christian doctrine views that ultimately were incompatible with it. It was between these two impulses, and in part as a result of the tension between them, that the Christian doctrine of creation took shape.

Another way of looking at this development is by comparing what Christians were affirming with the three main alternatives they rejected. The first such alternative is polytheism, which has already been discussed. Polytheism ultimately makes the world a hostile or at best a capricious place, where humans are the playthings of the whims of the gods. This was not really an alternative for Christians, whose monotheism, stemming from the Jewish roots of Christianity, was one of the basic tenets of their faith.

The second alternative was dualism. According to this alternative, there are two eternal principles, one good and one evil. This results in a tension between those parts of reality under the control of the good—usually, according to these views, spiritual reality—and those others under the control of evil—usually, material reality. This alternative would also contradict Christian monotheism. Furthermore, it would result in a radical discontinuity between creation and redemption, as in the case of Marcion.

The third alternative was a radical monism—the claim that all reality is one and that what to us seem to be different realities are in fact manifestations or parts of a single one. On the surface, this view was compatible with Christian monotheism. But by making all things divine it would ultimately lead to idolatry and would surrender the sovereignty of God over creation as one who stands over and above it and is not simply part of it.

The most common position among Christian theologians was to accept the support of the Neoplatonists for monotheism, while seeking to safeguard it from the extreme consequences of monism: pantheism and idolatry. This led Christians to stress the doctrine of creation as an act of God's will. God does not create out of necessity, simply because it is God's nature to create, as it is the nature of a dog to bark or as it is the nature of the Neoplatonic One to produce emanations. God creates out of a free and sovereign decision. Simply stated, in terms that would become an important subject of discussion in the fourth century (see chapter 4), creation is not the outcome of God's nature or of God's substance, but is the result of God's loving will. Furthermore, precisely because it is not the extension of the divine nature, creation, while reflecting God, is not itself divine. The world is clearly other than God.

Radical monotheism also led Christians to affirm creation "out of nothing"—in the traditional Latin phrase, *ex nihilo*. The most commonly held notion in the Hellenistic world was that there was an original, eternal, primeval matter—chaos or, as they would say, "unformed matter." Although at first some Christians suggested that this was the case, eventually monotheism prevailed, insisting that there can be only one eternal principle of all that exists and that to posit matter or chaos as coeternal with God is to deny the uniqueness and universal sovereignty of God. Thus Christians affirmed their monotheism, taking a position in which, although all things are created by God, they are not God.

The Question of Evil

This still left a very difficult problem: the problem of evil. Polytheists had no problem explaining evil, both moral and natural. Moral evils such as greed and war, as well as natural evils such as earthquakes, could be explained by blaming the gods' whim and conflicts. Dualism also offered a rational explanation for evil: there is an eternal principle that opposes the principle of good. All evil in the world is due to the intervention and the power of this evil principle.

Christian monotheism, in contrast with polytheism and with dualism, could not explain evil simply as the result of conflicts among gods or eternal powers, and therefore had a serious difficulty with the undeniable experience of the existence of evil. This may be seen in the life of St. Augustine (354–430), who eventually became one of the most influential theologians of all time, but who for a time could not accept his mother's Christian faith, because, among other reasons, he was puzzled by the problem of evil. He became a Manichean, a follower of one of the most influential dualistic religions of his time, precisely because Manicheism seemed able to account for the existence of evil. Eventually, it was Neoplatonism that offered him an explanation for evil: evil is not a reality, but rather is the absence of good. Although all reality is good, some parts of it are better than others because they stand closer to the One source of all. An example that Augustine himself offers is that an ape may seem ugly as compared to a human being; but as an ape, being what it is supposed to be, it is good and beautiful.

Throughout his life, even after he abandoned Neoplatonism and became a Christian, a bishop, and a theologian, Augustine held that evil is not a reality. It is not a substance. Nothing that exists is in itself evil. On this point, Christian doctrine has always agreed with him: God made the world—the entire world, including the sun and the moon, humans and beasts, mountains and insects—and declared it to be good. Nothing is evil in and of itself. Evil, rather than a reality, is a corruption of reality—or, as some would say, a nonbeing.

This still does not explain how the present world, with its hatreds and its crimes, with earthquakes and floods, can be the work of a good God. Augustine's explanation—and the traditional Christian view—is that God made all things good, that this good included free beings—humans and angels—and that it is in the exercise of their free will that angels and humans have produced not only moral evil and sin, but also the corruption of nature, thus resulting in all sorts of natural evils and disasters, as well as in the existence of demons, which are angels that have fallen. This is what is usually called the doctrine of the Fall.

The Fall means that, although the world and all that is in it were created good, evil has invaded God's good creation, so that the world and humankind as we now know them are a fallen world and a fallen humanity. In suggesting such a view, early Christians found support in the prevalent view of the time, that the golden age of the world was sometime in the past. Indeed, many writers, both pagan and Christian, believed that the world was growing old and that the problems and natural disasters they had to face were simply signs of the aging of the world. Within that context, it was not difficult to believe that there had been an original state in which creation was perfect, and then evil intervened. In this, many pagans agreed with Christians. The main difference was that, while this led pagans to despair regarding the future of the world, Christians proclaimed their hope for the redemption of the world and the restoration of creation—to which we shall return in another chapter.

A Hierarchical Creation?

The influence of Neoplatonism and other similar doctrines on Christianity, however, was felt in another way. Neoplatonism held that there was a hierarchy of being. Spiritual reality, since it belongs to a sphere that is closer to the One, is higher than material reality. This is not a view that is supported by Scripture, in which God makes everything and declares it good. Although in the Genesis stories the crown of creation is the human creature, this does not mean that there is a hierarchy of being, nor that intellectual or spiritual or invisible reality is better than physical or bodily reality. But now, through the influence of Augustine and others, Christians came to think of the whole of creation as a ladder of being, with matter on the lower rungs and spirit on the higher.

This had important consequences for the development of Christianity and Western civilization. If spiritual, invisible reality is better than the material, then our main concern must be about invisible souls and spirits, and not about bodies or any other part of the material world. Furthermore, if being is ordered in a hierarchy, ascending from the material and visible to the spiritual and invisible, then the only knowledge that is worthy of our attention—the only knowledge deserving of that name—is the knowledge of eternal, spiritual, and invisible realities. To look at material reality is a waste of time, not because the material is bad—which it is not—but simply because it is less good. Along these lines of thought, there is a passage in Augustine's *Confessions* in which he bemoans the time he once spent looking at a lizard and its antics, when he should have been contemplating the divine!

The result of such an attitude was the irony that for centuries Western Christian civilization, which claimed that God is the creator of all, and that all things are good and true because they come from God, paid little attention to physical reality. While Christian scholars, most of them monastics and all followers of Augustine, spent their entire lives meditating on spiritual realities, Muslim scholars, who also believed in creation and were also monotheistic, studied the world that God had created and, on the basis of those studies, developed what was then the most advanced civilization in the Mediterranean basin.

It was not until the thirteenth century, when Christian scholars from Western Europe traveled to Muslim Spain and to formerly Muslim Sicily in order to learn from the wisdom of that civilization, that the philosophy of Aristotle was reintroduced into Western Europe. This new philosophy affirmed the value of observing and studying physical reality—that part of creation that Christians had always declared to be the result of God's work and therefore good, but that they had come to consider as "less good" thanks to the influence of Neoplatonism. At that point, there were a few brave scholars who dared contradict the commonly held wisdom, and argue that Christianity was compatible with an alternative view of the world—a view in which the senses play an important role in knowledge and in which knowledge thus attained is good and valuable. This was mostly the work of St. Thomas Aquinas (ca. 1215–1274).

The opposition to Thomas and his proposals was strong and enduring. Both in Paris and in Oxford, several of his views were declared heretical. Eventually, however, his teachings prevailed, thus promoting a view of creation in which all of reality is worthy of study. It is not too far-fetched to suggest that Western technology would never have been possible without this revolution brought about by St. Thomas and his followers, and that therefore one of the foundations of Western civilization is the view of the world resulting from a properly understood and applied doctrine of creation.

From Thomas to Modernity

Time passed, and the observation of the universe that Thomas proposed led to unexpected consequences. Although it is true that modern science and technology developed out of Thomas's revolution in the theory of knowledge, it is also true that eventually the very progress of the new science would result in a view of the world that precluded the action of God.

After the Enlightenment, the modern age came to see the world as a vast machine in which nothing happens that cannot be explained by previous events—or that could not be explained, even if we knew all the facts. In other words, the modern world is a closed system allowing no intervention from outside, no event or development that does not have a purely "natural" explanation—by which is meant an explanation within the closed system itself. This was one of the greatest challenges of modernity to traditional Christian doctrine, and in particular to the doctrine of a God who creates the world and then leads it toward the fulfillment of the divine purposes.

The response of many Christians was to retreat to the claim that God did indeed create the world, but then simply let it function on its own principles, much like a mechanic who builds an engine and then lets it run. This position, which became particularly popular in England in the eighteenth century, was called Deism. The Deists believed in God, and they believed in creation; but they believed in both only as an explanation of the origin of the world. Eventually, the most generalized view of creation among the leading thinkers of the time was summarized by Reimarus (1694–1768) when he declared that the only miracle in which he believed was the miracle of creation.

While such views clearly followed from the spirit of modernity, and many Christians came to hold them, in fact, they amounted to a practical atheism. If God is reduced to an explanation for the origin of the world, and no more, one might as well be an atheist, for such a God is irrelevant once the world is set in motion.

It is also significant to point out that the retrenchment of the doctrine of creation into a theory for the origin of the world has two other theological consequences. One is that the continuity between creation and redemption—or, even more, the reading of creation from the point of view of redemption—was undercut. Redemption now became not the final purpose of creation, but a reality beyond creation, parallel to creation, yet having little to do with creation itself. The second consequence was that Christian thought now found itself desperately trying to defend this last bulwark of the doctrine of creation.

This is one of the main reasons Darwin's theory of evolution proved such a threat to some Christian theologians. All that was left of a relationship between God and the world had been reduced to the origin of the world; and now even this the theory of evolution called into question. There may well be other reasons Christians should question Darwinism. To this we shall return later in this chapter. But to reject Darwin's theory on the basis that it denies the doctrine of creation is to reduce that doctrine to a hypothesis about the origin of things.

During the second half of the twentieth century, and increasingly as that century came to a close and the next millennium now dawns, there are many indications that modernity has run its course. The closed, predetermined world of modernity is being seriously questioned. So is its claim to objective and universal knowledge. As a result, the coming decades will see much discussion of a number of Christian doctrines, many of them neglected during the apogee of modernity. One of these is the doctrine of creation.

Contemporary Relevance

As we face this renewed discussion on the doctrine of creation, it may be well to highlight some of the most important elements and consequences of that doctrine, so that as we look at emerging views we may be able to judge their adequacy as well as their shortcomings.

First, creation means that the entire universe and everything in it, being the result of the loving action of the redeemer God, is good. There certainly is evil in the world. But the physical world in and of itself is not evil. God is the maker of "all things visible and invisible."

Second, and deeply related to the first point, we must remember that, even from its very origins in the faith of Israel, the doctrine of creation was an expression and a consequence of the experience of God's care and redemption. In their struggle against Marcionism and other forms of dualism, Christians affirmed time and again that salvation is not salvation *from* creation, but rather salvation *into* the culmination or perfection of creation (see chapter 9). An adequate understanding of creation affirms the connection between the love that stands before our redemption and the love that stands behind our very existence—between creation and redemption.

This means that creation is not so much about the beginning of things as it is about their meaning. Creation is not about six days long ago, but about God's love for us and for all things in the beginning, in all our days, and forever. Thus, although much that Darwin said and suggested may be valuable, there are two unfortunate consequences of Darwinism that we must seek to undo. The first of these is the reduction of the doctrine of creation to a theory about origins. This is the greatest shortcoming of much of what today is called "creationism": it reduces creation to something that supposedly happened in six long-gone days, requiring nothing of us but that we believe in it. The second tragic and unacceptable result of Darwinism is the notion of the "survival of the fittest" as the proper order for the world and its progress. When this becomes the universal rule by which species evolve and by which history progresses, with no sense that there is something inherently wrong about it—of which the doctrine of the Fall reminds us—the consequences are nefarious. Here Christians must make a decision: we must decide whether we shall accept the notion that the guiding force of life and of history, and the guiding principle of our own lives, is the law of claw and fang, or is the love of God. Given the immediate and drastic consequences of each of these alternatives, this is a much more urgent matter than whether God created the world in six days or over unfathomable eons.

Third, in distinguishing between creation and emanation, this doctrine affirms that there is a difference between God and the world. While the world is God's creation, it is not God. God transcends the world. The world is a positive, valuable reality, since it comes from God; but when humans confuse the world or anything in it with the divine—when we worship it or when we grant it our ultimate allegiance—we put it to a twisted and even evil use, substituting it for God—as Paul would say, worshiping the creature instead of the Creator.

In the fourth place, this last statement reminds us that, although the world is the good creation of God, it is also a fallen world. No matter whether we understand the story of the fall as a literal event or not, we must acknowledge that the world is not what God intends it to be. The world is a fallen world, and we are fallen creatures. Thus, although all that exists is good, all that exists has also been tainted by sin and may be used for evil. This means that an adequate view of creation must affirm both its value and its corruption; both its creation by God and its corruption by sin. This is the difficult paradox that any understanding of creation must preserve.

The fifth point affirms one of the elements of that paradox: creation is good. Creation is not to be despised or abused or neglected.

As the product of God's hand, it deserves respect. All creatures are part of the same creation. In a way, we are related, not only to all of humanity, but to every being that exists or has ever existed in the universe. This affirmation has become increasingly urgent as we come to realize the degree to which human mismanagement is affecting and polluting the rest of creation—and humans themselves. Global warming, acid rain, mercury-laden fish, deforestation, desertification, and many other modern-day phenomena, are signs and consequences of defective views on creation.

Finally, the other element of the paradox reminds us of a sixth point that an adequate understanding of creation must take into account. The fact that everything in the world is a creature, and therefore not to be confused with God, and the added fact that every creature is somehow affected by sin and corruption, must subvert every human claim to absolute or final authority. All humans are corrupt. All nations are corrupt. All governments are corrupt. All churches are corrupt. There is no creature—neither nation nor church nor government nor flag nor cause nor established social order—that has an absolute and final claim on those who believe in the Christian doctrine of creation. This was one of the reasons the Roman Empire persecuted early Christianity: it could not tolerate a religion that relativized the authority of the empire and the emperor—a relativization symbolized in the Christians' refusal to worship the emperor.

Today, as the church for the first time in its history has become a truly universal community, represented in every nation and continent, these last two points become particularly urgent for Christians in the poorer or "underdeveloped" nations of the world—who are by far the majority of Christians. They experience the consequences of decades and most often centuries of "development" based on the ruthless exploitation of nature and its resources, often by Christians who did not show nature or the rest of humankind the respect that the doctrine of creation should foster. Many of these Christians in poorer nations also experience exploitation and oppression in the hands of oppressive national governments and international trade systems that demand an allegiance similar to what the Roman Empire demanded of early Christians.

The result of all of this is that thoughtful Christians throughout the world are calling us to a recovery of the Christian doctrine of creation—not to a recovery of a particular view of the manner in which the world originated, but to a recovery of the understanding of creation and therefore of the universe in the light of the love of God revealed to us in Jesus Christ.

For Further Reading

Bonhoeffer, Dietrich. *Creation and Temptation*. London: S.C.M. Press, 1966.

Brunner, Emil. *The Christian Doctrine of Creation and Redemption*. Philadelphia: Westminster Press, 1952.

Moltmann, Jürgen. *God in Creation: A New Theology of Creation and the Spirit of God*. Minneapolis: Fortress Press, 1993.

Plantinga, Cornelius. *Not the Way It's Supposed to Be*. Grand Rapids: Eerdmans, 1995.

Note

1. *Ep. to the Smyrneans*, 6.2-7.1.

3.

CULTURE

The true light, which enlightens everyone,
was coming into the world.
John 1:9

If, as Christians claim, all of reality is God's creation, the question immediately arises of the relationship between the Christian faith and all that goes on in the rest of creation. How is God active in times and places where no one has heard of Jesus Christ? To deny such activity would be tantamount to establishing a chasm between creation and redemption similar to that proposed by Marcion and quickly rejected by the church as a whole. Thus, logically, the very doctrine of creation would eventually have required Christians to discuss the origin and value of cultures that do not know the name of Jesus Christ.

However, what pressed Christians to consider these matters were not mere logical considerations. It was not as if some Christian scholars or church leaders simply sat down to consider quite leisurely the relationship between Christianity and the surrounding culture. The matter was much more urgent, at least for two reasons.

The first of these was the task itself of communicating the gospel to people of a different cultural background—in this case, Hellenism. The more cultured among these prospective Christians were aware and proud of the achievements of their civilization and their philosophers. Should they now be invited to reject all of this, to declare it purely evil, entirely wrong, valueless? Or was there something in the Christian view of the world, of creation, and of history that could serve to interpret, to evaluate, and to accept or transform some of the most valuable achievements of Greco-Roman civilization? Was the Christian message so radically new that nothing that had existed before—except perhaps within the faith of Israel—was of any value? To affirm such radical newness would both play into Marcionism and require pagan converts to deny all of their culture and traditions before they could call themselves Christian.

The second reason that made this question urgent was persecution in the hands of Roman authorities. The attitude of the empire toward Christians throughout the second century was generally expressed in an instruction from Emperor Trajan, at the beginning of that century, to the effect that authorities should not waste their time seeking out Christians, but that if any were brought before the magistrates they were to be given three chances to renounce their faith, and if they refused they would be condemned—usually to death.[1] For all practical purposes, this meant that actual persecution was generally in the hands of local magistrates, and even of the local populace. If, on the one hand, people had a negative attitude toward Christians and became convinced that they were an evil or subversive influence, it was a simple matter to point them out to the authorities, and bring the weight of the state to bear against them. If, on the other hand, there was general goodwill or at least acceptance from the populace and from the local leadership, actual persecution was less likely. Given such circumstances, it was important for Christians to present their faith in the best possible light. One way to do this was to relate it to the best of the Hellenistic cultural tradition.

Pressed by such demands, Christians felt an urgent need to speak of the relationship between their faith and the surrounding culture. To this end, the doctrine of creation was of great value, for it led Christians to think that the action of God—and therefore also, in one way or another, the truth of God—is not limited to the Christian message and to the Jewish tradition. Still, how were Christians to understand and to express this connection in ways that were both true to their convictions and understandable for those outside the church?

A Solution Is Found

The main way Christians found to respond to these demands was the doctrine of the Logos. The Greek word *logos* had a variety of meanings. It could mean "word," "reason," "discourse," "treatise," "speech," or a number of other related ideas. Long before the advent of Christianity, it had begun to play an important role in Greek philosophy, as a means to explain the rationality of the world. Why is it that my mind tells me that two and two are four, and when I then look at the world I discover that indeed, two apples and two more apples make four apples? Why is it that if I then look at stones I find that in this case too, two stones plus two stones make four stones? There must be an underlying rationality, a common denominator, to my mind as well as to every other mind and every reality in the world. If it were up to the confusing and conflicting multiplicity of the gods, there would be no order in the world, for the gods do not seem to agree on anything. And yet, the world shows a rational order. Thus, this order, this Logos of the world, stands even beyond the gods, as the permanent and unshakable power shaping all reality.

In some philosophical systems, this Logos was "hypostatized," as historians of philosophy would say. This simply means that the Logos had become a being, itself a reality, standing behind all other reality, behind all rationality, and therefore also behind all knowledge.

Already early in the first century, roughly during the time of Jesus, Jewish philosopher Philo of Alexandria had taken this philosophical theory of the Logos and tried to relate it to Judaism, explaining that the Logos was the creative principle through which God acted in the world.

As Christians now faced the culture around them, and sought ways to validate what was positive in it, they found all of this earlier work ready at hand. Furthermore, the Fourth Gospel began by declaring that Jesus was the incarnation of the eternal Logos or Word that had always been with God, and through whom all things were made. Quite possibly, the author of the Fourth Gospel, in writing such words, was not thinking so much of Hellenistic philosophy as of the stories of creation in Genesis, in which God creates by speaking, and perhaps also of the Wisdom of God as seen in Proverbs 8, which had already led some Jews to hypostasize Wisdom. However, some of the Christian apologists of the second century now took the Prologue of John, joined it with the Hellenistic philosophical tradition, and claimed that Jesus was the incarnation of the Logos that is the rationality behind all creation.

One line in the Prologue to the Fourth Gospel was particularly helpful to Christian apologists seeking to build bridges between their faith and the dominant culture of the times. This is where John says that this Logos is "the true light which enlightens everyone." This assertion could readily be joined to the Hellenistic notion of an underlying reason pervading all reality and therefore making all knowledge possible. Jesus is the incarnate Logos of God. All knowledge comes from the Logos. This means that the Logos or Word whom we have known in Jesus is the one who taught philosophers all they knew. In consequence, these apologists concluded, we need not reject the teachings of the philosophers, we need not condemn all the achievements of civilization. It all comes from the same Lord! We can claim it all for ourselves! As Justin, one of these apologists, would say, not only Abraham, but even Socrates and Plato, were in fact Christians, for whatever truth they knew or taught was Christian truth.[2]

However, not all Christians were thrilled by such notions. Some feared that this simply opened the way for all sorts of strange doctrines. Foremost among these was Tertullian, a Christian writer and apologist from Carthage, in North Africa, who felt that the heresies that were plaguing the church had their origin in philosophy. His words to that effect have become famous: "What indeed has Athens to do with Jerusalem? What concord is there between the Academy and the Church? What between heretics and Christians?"[3]

Yet the matter is not so simple. Tertullian, while rejecting Platonism as the origin of most heresies, was himself profoundly influenced by Stoicism. Thus, his treatise *On the Soul* is a combination of what the Bible says and Stoic doctrine on the subject. Probably, had he been told that he himself was much of a Stoic, he would have been offended, for in his mind he was simply expounding and defending what he took to be traditional Christian doctrine. Culture is not just what we see and read in books and philosophical theories. It is the environment in which we live, and the more immersed we are in it, the more difficult it is for us to realize the degree to which it affects our lives and shapes our views.

In general, Justin's view prevailed, although there were always elements of resistance continuing Tertullian's line of thought. Christianity was increasingly interpreted in terms of Hellenistic culture and Platonic and Neoplatonic philosophy. As we shall see repeatedly in other chapters of this book, this affected the way Christians understood the nature of God, how they envisioned the human creature, and a host of other issues.

Culture Is More Than Being Cultured

The case of Tertullian, however, should also serve to alert us that culture is always present and is a wider matter than what the "cultured" consider it to be. There is culture in the way food is cooked, how families are organized, and how the state is governed. There is culture in what is praised and what is denigrated. All human beings are affected by culture—and so is every Christian and every church. As Christians moved into the Hellenistic world, and even as they disagreed among themselves on their attitude toward such items in the culture as Greek philosophy, they all were affected by that culture. They worshiped in houses built according to the patterns and practices of the culture. They dressed as everyone else dressed, and they ate what everyone else ate. In some cases they organized churches following the pattern of the funerary societies that were then common. Eventually, their churches were grouped in jurisdictions copied from the provinces and dioceses of the Roman Empire. And yet, they insisted that they were different. This paradox was expressed eloquently by an anonymous second-century Christian:

> Christians are not distinguished from others as to their lands, their language or their uses. They do not live in cities that are only theirs, nor do they speak a strange tongue, nor is their style of life separate from others.... Rather, while living in Greek or barbarian cities, according to their lot, and joining others as to dress, food and way of life, they give signs of a particular behavior that is admirable, and that all find surprising. They live in their own lands; but as pilgrims. They partake in all as citizens, and yet suffer all as aliens. Every land is their motherland; and no land is their homeland. They marry and beget children as others do; but do not abandon the newly born. They have a common table; but not a common bed. They are in the flesh, but do not live according to the flesh. They dwell on earth, but their citizenship is in heaven. They obey the laws, and with their lives surpass them. They love all, and all persecute them. They are unknown and yet condemned. They

are killed and they give life. They are poor, and yet enrich many. They lack all, and yet have all.[4]

This depicts the paradoxical situation in which Christians have had to live, not only during the first centuries of the Christian era, when they were persecuted, but throughout history. One side of the paradox is clear: Christians are not plucked out of their culture and their ways of understanding the world and organizing life simply because they now believe in Christ. Christianity may reject some elements and practices in a culture and may succeed in eradicating them among the faithful, and perhaps even from the culture itself. A clear example is the ancient practice of abandoning unwanted newborn children to die of exposure, be eaten by beasts, or be raised as slaves. Christians objected to this, as the passage just cited declares. They did not do it themselves, and they eventually succeeded in eradicating it from the culture. Yet, this does not mean they did not retain much of their ancestral Greco-Roman culture. This in turn points to the other side of the paradox: even though they may differ from much in their own cultures, Christians still belong to those cultures and therefore understand and practice their faith within the context of that culture. Most of the same Christians who objected to the practice of exposing children accepted the rest of Greco-Roman culture with little or no qualms. Most of them accepted the views of that culture even on matters such as the practice of slavery, or the traditional order of a Roman household, in which women were often oppressed and children exploited.

Thus, the immediate downside of the doctrine of the Logos is that it tends to obscure the difference between Christianity and culture. One of the points at which Christians made most use of the work of earlier philosophies was the doctrine of God. Indeed, much of what many Christians have taken for granted as part of the doctrine of God comes not from biblical sources, but rather from the Greek philosophical tradition. This was certainly the case with the manner in which the doctrine of the Logos was applied in discussions about the nature of God. In the next chapter we shall see some of the problems this created.

Yet, on the other side, there is much to be said in favor of this doctrine—or of one like it. Having rejected the theories of Marcion and of others who saw no connection between creation and redemption,

Christians could not now claim that all that had gone on in creation apart from the advent of Jesus Christ had nothing to do with God's purposes of love. If the Creator God is the Redeemer God, and if all that exists is God's creation, one cannot simply say that entire sections of that creation and its life have nothing to do with God or with God's love. Today, many theologians express this point by refusing to speak, as many did in the past, of a "salvation history" apart from or parallel to the history of the world. There is certainly much that has gone awry in creation, in history, and in the cultures that humankind has developed within that history; but even so, history and culture exist within the realm of God's creation and under the umbrella of God's love. Not all that goes on in them is evil. God is active in them. It behooves Christians to discover and to accept this action of God in history and in cultures, for otherwise theirs is a partial God, the God of a particular religion or of their church, but not the God of all creation.

Debates over the Value of Culture

Many have objected on philosophical grounds to the doctrine of the Logos as originally expressed by the Christian apologists of the second century. Such objections are valid, for the Platonic outlook that stands behind the original statements regarding the Logos now has few followers. At any rate, the theory of the Logos is not, and never has been, official Christian doctrine. It has been rather a means whereby Christians have expressed three points that are part of Christian doctrine. The first of these is that the Redeemer God is none other than the Creator God; that the same love stands behind creation as stands behind redemption—as we saw in chapter 2. The second, a more precise consequence of the first, is that Jesus Christ, while being a historical man who lived in a particular time, is the goal to which all people in all times and places are called. The third, a consequence of the second, is that as Christians look at non-Christian reality, they are to seek and to find in it the work of the creating and redeeming God and are to judge all that happens in that reality on the basis of what they know in Jesus Christ.

Although these points are fairly simple to state in the abstract, they are much more difficult to apply in concrete cases. Both Justin, who proposed and defended the value of Hellenistic philosophy, and Tertullian (ca. 160–ca. 220), who bemoaned the influence of philosophy on the church, would subscribe to them. The difference is that Justin would go much further than Tertullian in his positive valuation of the surrounding culture, and Tertullian would go much further than Justin in his insistence on the negative effect of culture on Christianity. If we imagine a dialogue between them, Tertullian would probably tell Justin that he was emphasizing the continuity between creation and redemption to such a point that he risked losing the uniqueness of Christianity. Justin would probably reply that Tertullian was stressing the discontinuity to such a point that he was approaching Marcionism—even though Tertullian wrote five extensive books against Marcion.

The debate has continued through the ages, whenever the issue of Christianity and culture has emerged. Since this issue often comes to the foreground when the faith itself crosses into a new culture, the debate has been particularly lively in the international missionary enterprise. In India, for instance, the Roman Catholic Portuguese missionaries of the fifteenth century seem to have thought that conversion implied the acceptance of most of Portuguese culture. Hence their insistence that, upon being baptized, converts were to receive a new "Christian" name—by which they meant a Portuguese name. They justified this practice by pointing out that many Indians were named in honor of the gods of the land, and that therefore a rejection of such gods implied a rejection of their own names. Still, as Indians saw that their Christian neighbors now were named João, Carlos, Maria, or José, they had reason to feel that in order to become Christians they had to abandon their culture and tradition.

The opposite tack was taken in the next century by Italian Jesuit Roberto De Nobili, who felt that it was necessary to make it clear that Christianity was not an instrument for the Europeanization of India. He learned Sanskrit and Tamil, studied the sacred books of Hinduism, and adopted the dress, customs, and diet of India's "holy men." Much like Justin centuries earlier, he saw the action of God in the culture in which he was living and sought to affirm that action and to connect it with the life of the church. It was only in matters of religion that he and his fellow workers were to try to change the customs and the views of people in India.

Once again, the matter was not so simple. A fundamental element of Indian society was the caste system, determining the ways in which people related to one another. De Nobili decided that this was a cultural, and not a religious issue, and he therefore determined that he would work with the higher castes and build churches among them, while other missionaries would work with the lower castes and build churches for them.

Needless to say, this created quite a debate. There was, first of all, the question of ecclesiology. Is it legitimate to have different churches for people of different castes? Is this not a denial of the love that stands at the center of the gospel? The matter soon reached Rome; and in 1623, Pope Gregory XV authorized De Nobili's methods.

Something similar was happening in China at about the same time. There, another Italian Jesuit, Matteo Ricci, learned and took the ways of the ancient Confucian sages and thus was able to penetrate a land that had long been forbidden to Christian missionaries. In this case, the initial issue debated was the Chinese veneration of their ancestors. Ricci and the other Jesuits following his lead declared that this was a purely cultural matter, that it did not constitute idolatry, and that therefore it could and should continue to be practiced by Chinese converts to Christianity. Other Christians, upon hearing this, declared that the Jesuits had given up on an essential tenet of the Christian faith by allowing and sometimes promoting the continuation of what were pagan and even polytheistic practices. This led to bitter conflicts between Jesuits and Dominicans—the Dominicans often envying the position of privilege of Jesuits, who were allowed into high places in Chinese society, including on occasion the imperial court, while they were not. Eventually the conflict centered on the issue of how to translate "God" into Chinese. As is so often the case in matters of translation, there were two main alternatives for "God" in Chinese. Each had its advantages, and each had its shortcomings. One side argued for one, and the other for the other. Eventually, this and other matters in what was called "the controversy of the Chinese rites" were settled by Rome in 1742.

The very fact that both of these controversies were finally settled by Rome shows how difficult the matter of Christianity and culture is. The controversies had to do with Christianity and the cultures of India and China. Yet they were not officially resolved by Indian or by Chinese Christians, but by popes in Rome who had very little idea what was at stake. One sympathizes with the angry reaction of the Chinese emperor, who is said to have declared that a barbarian in Rome had no right to tell the Chinese how to speak their own language. Obviously, in spite of the most sincere efforts on the part of the missionaries, Christianity remained a Western religion, for it was up to Western authorities to determine how it was to be understood and practiced throughout the world.

Although the two examples just given come from the Roman Catholic tradition, the same issue has been present in Protestant missionary efforts. Thus, in the American West the question was often asked and debated, is the corn dance a purely cultural tradition, or is it so connected with the ancient religion that it ought to be banned among Christian converts? What about worship with fire? Are sweat lodges a purely hygienic and social custom, or are they a religious ritual? In Africa, the matter of polygamy has been hotly debated. Is it just a social custom, perhaps regrettable, but still acceptable? Should churches baptize polygamous converts? Should such converts be forced to set aside all but one of their wives? What is to happen then to those who have been set aside? Both in Africa and in Asia the matter of ancestors and the veneration due to them has been another cause for debate. In Asia, Protestant missionaries rejected the Indian custom of *suttee*—the burning of widows on their husband's funeral pyres—and the Chinese custom of foot binding. In Confucian lands, some missionaries sought to build bridges and connections between Confucian wisdom and Christianity, while others felt that Confucianism was too rigidly structured and too oppressive of women and should be criticized and rejected on this score.

In general, these various debates were grouped under the common heading of "accommodation"—to what extent, and how, should Christianity "accommodate" itself to the cultures and practices of new lands—or of "inculturation"—the need for missionaries to adapt themselves and their message to the recipient culture. In more recent times, missiologists prefer to speak of "acculturation"—the process whereby Christians within the culture, often unconsciously, develop forms of Christianity that are deeply rooted in their own cultural traditions. This shows a clearer understanding of the way cultures work, of how difficult it is for someone from outside a particular culture to penetrate and understand it, and of the new reality, in which the vast majority of Christians belong to non-Western cultures.

Still, however, no matter whether the adaptation takes place consciously and on the part of outside agents—such as in the cases of Ricci and De Nobili—or unconsciously and on the part of Christians within the culture itself—as in acculturation—the same issues and principles remain. Given their understanding of creation and its connection with redemption, Christians must affirm the action of God in every culture even before the gospel is heard in it. When the gospel comes to any culture, its followers must both recognize God's action in the culture itself and correct the shortcomings and injustices within their own culture, which they should now see more clearly in the light of the gospel.

When Christianity Becomes a Matter of Culture

While all of this appears most clearly in what has traditionally been called the "mission field," it is also present, although most often unnoticed, in those cultures in which Christianity has long been established. In those cultures, precisely because the initial shocks and differences have already been negotiated, it is much more difficult to see how the culture affects one's understanding of Christianity. As we shall see in the next two chapters, this was already the case of Christianity in Greco-Roman culture by the fourth century—and even more in the fifth. Even though the state had persecuted Christianity until a recent date, and even though there had been many pagans who insisted on the chasm between the new faith and the ancient culture, by the fourth century, Christians—and most particularly Christian theologians—had convinced themselves not only that they were entitled to speak of God in the terms of Greek philosophy, but even that this was the best way to speak about God. Tertullian's word of caution was hardly heard, and the result was that the church lost much of its sense of a need to critique the culture in which it lived.

Other examples abound. The most egregious and disastrous probably took place in Germany during the twentieth century, although the stage was already being set a century earlier. Germany had been generally Christian ever since the Saxons were forcibly converted by Charlemagne. It had been a center of Christian learning since the thirteenth century, when Albert the Great taught Thomas Aquinas in the University of Cologne. In the sixteenth century, it became the center of a great reformation that, under Luther's leadership, swept through Northern Europe. In the period immediately after the Reformation, its universities became centers of Protestant theologians who were training to serve and to promote Protestantism throughout the world. When the Enlightenment began asking questions about Christianity, doubting its validity for the modern world and its credibility for the modern mind, it was German scholars who responded most creatively to those challenges, mostly by restating Christian belief in such a way that it was not only compatible with, but even the best expression of, modernity.

It was German theologians who developed an entire series of systems that made it possible for Protestantism to present itself as both the forerunner and the epitome of modernity. Friedrich Schleiermacher proposed an alternative that placed Christianity above the philosophical fray of the time by arguing that religion, rather than being a system of doctrines or of ethics, is a "feeling"—in the case of Christianity, a feeling of absolute dependence before God. Wilhelm Friedrich Hegel developed a system for understanding history and all of reality in which these unfolded much as thought does, by a process in which a thesis is challenged by an antithesis, the challenge leads to a resolution in a synthesis, this in turn becomes a new thesis, and so on. Toward the end of the century, Adolf Harnack carried the historical study of Christianity to new heights, and summarized his views in a series of lectures in which he claimed that both Roman Catholicism and Eastern Orthodoxy had missed the essence of Christianity, which now remained in Protestantism—and, even though left unsaid, in German Protestantism as he knew it.

The wide variety of theological systems, however, obscured what they had in common. All of these systems, while contradicting one another, agreed on the usually unacknowledged assumption that the best way to understand Christianity was from the perspective of the new Germany. This was mostly an industrial society in which the old aristocracy of land and titles was being supplanted by a new aristocracy of investment and entrepreneurship. For this society, the new was better by definition, and history was a linear progression in which the future could only bring greater riches and more abundant blessing. Germany, as the leader in science and technology, was also the nation of the future, and therefore God's chosen instrument to bring this future about. Within that social and cultural context, most German theology in the nineteenth and early twentieth centuries had little difficulty convincing itself that Christianity, as it was interpreted and practiced in Germany at the time, was the highest possible form of Christianity and a beacon for the church worldwide.

When the sense of German superiority that had been fostered through much of the nineteenth century was challenged by a newly emerging international order, and quite dramatically by the First World War, many Germans were ready to allow themselves to be led by a man, a party, and a philosophy that proclaimed German superiority over all other nations and all other races. When that man and that party came to power, it was difficult for the church to resist them or to oppose their plans and actions of ethnic cleansing and supposed national restoration. It was difficult in part because great pressure was brought to bear on the church and its leaders. But it was also difficult for a much deeper reason: for over a century most German theology had so tied Christianity to the national culture, that it was only natural for the movement of "German Christians" to arise. This was a movement that saw Nazism, and the German quest for world dominion, as the natural outcome and expression of the faith of the German nation—which, after all, was supposed to be the highest expression of Christianity.

What was played out here—played out with tragic consequences—was the downside of efforts similar to Justin's early work in bringing together Hellenistic culture and Christian faith. The culture had been so integrated into the faith that when society and its culture went awry, Christians had little to say against it.

Fortunately, this is not the whole story. Even before the advent of Hitler, there were German theologians who were questioning the close connection between faith and culture—as well as between church and nation—that the dominant theological systems took for granted. Foremost among these was Swiss Karl Barth (1886–1968), then working in Germany, who insisted on the presence of sin in every human enterprise, thus relativizing nation and culture, and making it clear that the relationship between creation as it now exists and redemption is not one of simple continuity. Significantly, when Barth's theology first gained notoriety, Harnack, one of the last survivors among the great voices of the previous century, is said to have commented, *"Wieder Marcion"*—"Marcion all over again." (Remember that in our fictitious dialogue between Justin and Tertullian, Justin would have accused Tertullian of coming dangerously close to Marcion.) As time went by, however, it was Barth and a number of Christian leaders profoundly influenced by him who gave shape to the *Barmen Declaration* (1934), which clearly laid out the contrast between the Christian faith and any system or political agenda that usurps God's place by claiming absolute authority, and which became the foundational document for the "Confessing Church" in its opposition to Nazism.

Faith and Culture Beyond the Realm of Doctrine

All of this points to one of the great and often unnoticed shortcomings of Logos theology—and of much other theology. The issues of Christianity and culture are not played out only in the realm of ideas or religious doctrines. Although in theory the notion of Logos has to do with all of creation and its order, in practice it tends to focus on the rational and, in the case of faith, the doctrinal. Thus when looking for signs of the Logos in other cultures, theologians and missionaries have usually asked questions about their religious ideas. Do they hold to the existence of God? Are they monotheistic? Do they have a concept of life after death? What do they believe as to the origin of the world?

While these issues are important, focusing attention only on them is ignoring the wider connection between creation and redemption—and therefore between Christianity and culture. In the Fourth Gospel, the Logos or Word of God is not only the One who enlightens everyone, but also the One through whom all things are made. The Word or Logos of God, the One incarnate in Jesus Christ, is not only the teacher of truth, but also the creator of good and the designer of beauty. If so, when we look for signs of the Logos, we ought to look not only at truth, but also at goodness and beauty. In looking at a culture, we may discover signs of the Logos, not only in its religion, but also in its practice of justice, in its social order, in its family structure, as well as in its art, in its music, and in its ancient legends and myths.

This is also true of the other side of the coin. When Christians ask what there is in a culture that needs to be judged or changed, they must look not only at its religion, but also at the injustices in its social order. The caste system and the burning of widows in India, as well as the practice of foot binding in China, were not peripheral issues to be ignored as long as people believed Christian doctrine. They were denials of the Logos of God, just as much as atheism and polytheism were denials.

This in turn leads to the realization that no matter what the theory might be regarding the Logos, in actual practice it is greatly dependent on the convenience and interests of those applying it or not. Some of the early Christians developed this doctrine in order to be able to cope with the dominant Hellenistic culture of their time, and it was amply employed during the next few centuries. But when European Christians—Spanish, Portuguese, and British—came to the Western Hemisphere and met peoples whom they could conquer with relative ease, the theory of the Logos was generally forgotten. Apparently the Logos had not been at work among the original inhabitants of these lands, for the prevailing attitude of most European Christians was that the cultures they encountered here were at best primitive and expendable, and at worst the result and the expression of demonic powers. Many convinced themselves that in destroying ancient Mayan writings they were doing God's work. It is true that in some circles there was a much more positive attitude toward the native cultures and their social organization; but these were the exception rather than the rule. Similar attitudes developed vis-à-vis Africans and their cultures and societies—particularly as the slave trade made it increasingly profitable to claim that there was no Logos among Africans, and even in some cases that they had no soul.

Contemporary Relevance

Although most of the foregoing might seem to refer to issues now left behind, and of little importance for those of us who live in traditionally Christian cultures, that is not the case. Indeed, the issues of Christianity and culture will probably dominate much of Christian theology and debate for decades to come. This will be so for two main reasons.

The first of these reasons is the momentous demographic change that took place in the course of the twentieth century. Most Western

Christians are only remotely aware of what has happened in the course of their own lives. The numeric bulk of Christianity, as well as most of its growth and vitality, is no longer in the traditionally Christian nations of the North Atlantic. While the vast majority of Christians at the beginning of the twentieth century were white, today, at the beginning of the twenty-first century, the vast majority are not white. Within Roman Catholicism, the service that was almost always in Latin forty years ago is now celebrated in practically every language in the world. As for Protestantism, it is no longer a form of Christianity confined mostly to the nations of the North Atlantic. On any given Sunday at the beginning of the twenty-first century, there are more Protestants in church in Latin America than in the United States. And there are certainly more Anglicans in Africa than there are in England itself.

This means that Christianity will constantly have to ask itself how it can be one and at the same time be incarnate and expressed in so many and diverse cultures. For those of us in the traditional centers of Christianity, it will also mean that we shall often be reminded of the issues of Christianity and culture—and particularly of the tension between the two—by our Christian brothers and sisters in other cultures.

The second reason issues of faith and culture will be so important during the decades to come is that culture is also changing in the traditionally Christian nations. In the thirty-five years I have lived in the American South, in what is called the Bible Belt, I have seen radical changes in this respect. Rightly or wrongly, when I first moved to Atlanta, my neighbors generally took for granted that they lived in a Christian society. Certainly, church attendance and many traditional Christian practices and values were strongly supported by the general cultural environment. Today that is no longer the case. Christianity is still strong, and church attendance continues; but all will agree that Christianity is no longer as central to Southern culture as it used to be.

Christians within cultures that have traditionally considered themselves Christian tend to react by rather futile calls for the restoration or the preservation of the passing order. This is natural, and there is certainly much in the traditional culture whose passing we must bemoan. Yet, there is always the danger that we may confuse the particular shape that Christianity has taken in our culture with Christianity itself. Our nations and cultures have dominated the life of the Christian church for so long, that it may be difficult for us to realize that there are other ways of being Christian, and that our particular way, just as much as any other, is the result of cultural, economic, and other social forces affecting the life of the church.

A case in point is the much-debated issue "family values." Certainly, the family is important for all Christians, since it is important for every society, and the God who created us made us in such a way that we cannot flourish or even survive alone. Yet the "family" that is so threatened in Western culture, and to whose defense many Christians are rallying, is just one of the ways in which families—even Christian families—have existed. In fact, the nuclear family—a family formed by parents and children, and usually no others—is a relatively recent result of the Industrial Revolution, modern mobility, and a view of life in which "success" is too often understood in individualistic and economic terms. The result is that we tend to go to battle to defend "the family," without realizing that the more traditional and much more stable extended family—a family including all sorts of relatives—has been undercut for a long time by some of the very cultural values that we now think we can harness to "save the family." Perhaps the problem is deeper than we suspect or can even discover as long as we remain within our own limited cultural perspective.

This is just one example of many. The main point is not about family values and their defense, but rather about the need to pose anew the questions of faith and culture in ways that Western Christianity has not posed these questions for over fifteen hundred years. Just as much as those second- and third-century Christians who asked about the connection between Hellenism and Christianity, we shall have to face the urgent—and much more complex—question of the connection between our faith and our evolving cultures.

It is at this point that being part of a worldwide church and listening to our sisters and brothers in other cultural contexts may be of great help to believers in traditionally Christian cultures as we try to rediscover our role, and the role of faith, within our own evolving cultures. While we might wish that our nations and the churches in our nations were still at the forefront of the Christian movement, the very fact that we are not may be a blessing, allowing us to look afresh at issues of faith and culture in ways that we would not or could not under different circumstances.

The task is vast, and there will be no easy answers. Just as Justin and Tertullian disagreed on the use of Greek philosophy, today's Christians will disagree on a thousand issues—issues of medical ethics, sexuality, economic policy, war and peace, and so on. Yet, even though disagreeing on such issues, the same points that were shown to be crucial for the early discussion of faith and culture are still crucial today. No matter what answer we give to specific issues, as Christians we hold, first, that the Redeemer God is none other than the Creator God; that the same love stands behind creation as stands behind redemption; second, that Jesus Christ is the goal to which all people in all times and places are called, our salvation and the fulfillment of all that exists; third, that as we look at reality around us we are to seek and to find in it both the work of the creating and redeeming God, and what it lacks from fulfilling the purposes of God for all creation.

For Further Reading

On Christianity and culture in general:
Niebuhr, H. Richard. *Christ and Culture.* New York: Harper and Bros., 1951.
Sanneh, Lamin. *Religion and the Variety of Cultures: A Study in Origin and Practice.* Valley Forge, Pa.: Trinity Press International, 1996.

On the issues in the early church:
Chadwick, Henry. *Early Christian Thought and the Classical Tradition.* New York: Oxford University Press, 1966.
Fox, Robin Lane. *Pagans and Christians.* New York: Knopf, 1987.
Wilken, Robert L. *The Christians as the Romans Saw Them.* New Haven: Yale University Press, 1984.

Notes

1. Pliny, *Epistles,* 10.97.
2. Justin, *First Apology,* 46,3.
3. Ibid., 7 (*Ibid.,* 3:246).
4. *To Diognetus,* 5.1-13.

4.

GOD

I am the LORD your God...you shall have
no other gods before me.
Exodus 20:2-3

The very first Christians did not have to develop a doctrine of God. Since they were Jews, they simply took for granted the basic tenet of the faith of Israel, that there is only one God. This they bequeathed to other generations of Christians, both Jewish and Gentile. As a result, monotheism has always been a fundamental tenet of Christianity, a permanent feature of the Christian faith even as it passed from one generation to another, from one land to another, and from one culture to another.

Since monotheism was part of the faith inherited from Israel, the doctrine of God was not a subject of much debate among early Christians. When it was debated, it was most commonly in the context of the questions discussed two chapters back—questions having to do with the nature of the world and its relationship with God. It is for this reason that, although logically it would seem best to discuss the doctrine of God before the doctrine of creation, a chronological approach led us to look first at the doctrine of creation, then at the relationship between faith and culture, and only now at the doctrine of God.

As in many other cases, this particular doctrine developed under two impulses. On the one hand, Christians seeking to communicate their faith to others, or to defend it before their pagan critics, began thinking about ways to express their view of God in terms that were compatible with that audience. This aspect of the development of Christian thought about God is simply a specific instance of the issues discussed in the last chapter—how Christianity and its teachings relate to the culture in which they live. On the other hand, the very fact of the advent of Jesus Christ, and the church's convictions about him and his relationship to the divine, led to debates as to the nature of the Godhead. If Jesus Christ was at the center of Christian worship, this obviously posed some difficult issues regarding the relationship between him and the divine, particularly in view of Christian monotheism. In this chapter we shall begin by looking at each of those two impulses, in that order.

A Platonic View of God

In the last chapter we saw that, even before the advent of Christianity, Jews had begun to seek ways to build bridges between their faith and the best of pagan culture and philosophy. In Alexandria, a center of such attempts, a contemporary of Jesus, Philo of Alexandria, had taken great strides toward a Platonic interpretation of the faith of Israel. We also saw that in the second century, several Christian writers, following an approach similar to that of Philo, sought to show their pagan audiences that Christian monotheism was perfectly compatible with the most respected philosophical traditions of the Hellenistic world—particularly the Platonic tradition.

In that philosophical tradition, many had spoken of a being above every other, from which all others derive their being. Again, some Platonists spoke of all of reality as emanating from that first being, the One, and Christians soon felt the need to reject such notions, which would otherwise lead to pantheism and consequently to idolatry. In spite of this, the notion that there is one being above all others was quite attractive to Christians trying to counteract and to refute the polytheistic views of the surrounding culture.

To their neighbors, Christians appeared as simply impious and incredulous. Where were their gods? How can one worship a god one cannot see? To the popular mind, Christians were atheists. Indeed, there is a document from the second century in which a mob, seeking the death of a Christian bishop, shouts, "Down with the atheists!"[1] Faced by such a challenge in the interpretation of their faith, it was natural for Christians to turn to a tradition in which many had severely criticized the ancient gods for their vices and their pusillanimity, and one of whose greatest heroes, Socrates, had been condemned to death on a similar charge of atheism.

That tradition had reflected on the perfections of the primal and supreme being ever since the times of Parmenides of Elea (sixth century B.C.E.), one of its pre-Socratic forerunners. Parmenides and his long line of followers had generally agreed on some of these perfections. These perfections of the Supreme Being, as understood by Parmenides and most of the Platonic tradition, were often adopted, with very little change, by Christian theologians seeking to show that their faith was not as irrational as some claimed and that, far from being atheistic innovators, they were bringing the best of classical philosophy to fruition. Since these have become part of the common Christian inheritance when speaking and thinking about God, they should be mentioned, however briefly.

First of all, this being must exist in and of itself. It cannot owe its existence to any other being, for this would be an imperfection. From this view, Christian theologians came to speak of the "aseity" of God, meaning that the God's being is not derived from or dependent on any being other than God. They also spoke of the contrast between God and creatures as the difference between the one and only "necessary" being—a being whose nonexistence is inconceivable—and the rest as "contingent"—beings that can be or not be.

Second, since change is an imperfection, this being must not change. Hence the attribute of "immutability" that Christian theologians soon came to ascribe to God. There can be no change or shadow of change in God, who is one and always the same. Furthermore, since movement is a sort of change, and in any case God is everywhere—is "omnipresent"—God does not move.

A particular aspect of God's immutability, according to this tradition, is "impassibility," which means that God is never passive vis-à-vis other beings. No other being can affect God in any way. If it were not so, God would be moved by such an outside and contingent being, and it is inconceivable for the contingent to affect the necessary—which would make the necessary depend on contingent beings, and therefore no longer absolutely necessary.

In the Platonic tradition, ideas are more real than their concrete, physical expressions in things, and an idea that includes others stands above them in the hierarchy of being. In consequence, the supreme being, which is also the supreme idea, includes within itself the ideas of all things existent or even possible. Actually, nothing can exist or come to pass without having been eternally in the mind of God, who therefore knows all things, not only things existent, but even things possible. This eventually came to be known as God's "omniscience"——God's knowing all things.

Finally, nothing can limit the power of this being, God. Otherwise that which limits God's power would be greater than God. Therefore, Christians began speaking of God as "omnipotent" or "almighty"—capable of doing any and all things.

All of these "attributes" of God have much to commend them. Certainly, the Bible speaks repeatedly of the great power of God, of God's steadfast and changeless love, of God's knowledge of our innermost thoughts, on the one hand. On the other hand, the Bible also speaks of a personal God, a God who relates directly with creation and with the people of God, a God who listens to prayer, who intervenes in history, who suffers with the pain of creation. Thus, much of the later debate regarding various aspects of the doctrine of God stems from this tension between the biblical view of an active, sovereign, and loving God, and the apparently but not really compatible philosophical view of an immutable, impassible One. In other sections of this chapter we shall see a number of instances in which these tensions came to the foreground.

Difficulties in Such a View

While this understanding of God on the basis of the Platonic tradition has much to commend it as a way of building bridges with Hellenistic culture, it also made it difficult to explain how God relates to the world. In many ways, this was similar to an enduring problem in the Platonic philosophical tradition, which always had difficulty explaining how individual and material things participate of the eternal and immutable ideas that are the source of their being (what philosophers called "the problem of participation"). Now these Christians of Platonic inclinations who were defending the faith by means of this philosophical tradition were forced to ask how the immutable One whom they declared to be God could relate to the mutable realities of this world, which they said God has created and still governs.

74

This was not an easy question. Eventually it would lead to bitter controversies that dominated much of the life of the church in the fourth and fifth centuries, and which have erupted again throughout history.

In the second century, Christians of Platonic inclinations responded to this question by means of the doctrine of the Logos or Word—the same doctrine that helped them build other bridges between their faith and their culture. Plato had spoken of a "demiurge" who made this world of passing, sensible reality by copying the eternal ideas in the purely intelligible world. The Fourth Gospel begins by speaking of the divine Word "through whom all things were made, and without whom not one of the things that exist was made." Therefore, just as they had equated the Word of God in John with the Logos who is the source and the reason behind all knowledge, these theologians—usually in an effort to defend the Christian faith against the criticism of outsiders—equated the Platonic demiurge with this Logos or Word of God who was incarnate in Jesus Christ.

In this view, the Logos is an intermediary being between the immutable God and this mutable world, which the Logos has created and governs. The Supreme Being is immutable; everything in the world is mutable; and between God and the world stands the Logos or Word of God. Not being immutable, this being is not equal to the Supreme Being, and therefore both Justin Martyr early in the second century and Clement of Alexandria (ca. 150–ca. 215) half a century later speak of the Logos of God as a separate divine being in phrases that would raise many an eyebrow and were soon discarded.

The value of this doctrine of the Logos was that such a being could relate to the world in an active fashion that was not possible for the immutable and impassible Supreme Being. Thus, when Justin read in Scripture that God gave the commandments to Moses, or that God freed Israel from the yoke of Egypt, or that God punishes evildoers, he understood this to refer not to the Supreme Being—which Justin calls "the Father"—but to the Logos or Word of God. One could still attribute to the Supreme Being all the philosophical predicates such as impassibility and immutability, and still speak of a God who relates to the world and acts in it.

Another asset of this view was that it made clear the continuity between creation and redemption, as well as between the faith of

Israel and the faith of the church. The one who created the world is the same Word who is now incarnate in Jesus. The one who spoke to Israel is the same one who spoke in Jesus. There is no room here for Marcionism, nor for any other theory that interprets the Gospel as the message of a God alien to the world.

However, this view also presents serious difficulties. As the phrase itself, "another God," makes quite clear, this position risked contradicting Christian monotheism. It did not imply the sort of "conflict of the gods" that was typical of much polytheism, for the Logos—like the Platonic demiurge—was understood to do only that which was inspired by the Being of the Father. But still, it did posit a second though lesser divine being next to the Supreme One.

Thus, there were important latent problems in this entire approach to the doctrine of God. However, since the writings in which such teachings appeared were addressed mostly to readers and objections from outside the church, most Christians—even those who were aware of them—did not consider such problems a serious or urgent matter.

The apologetic bridge, however, bears traffic in both directions. What was originally devised as a means to show the Hellenistic intellectual elite that Christian doctrine was reasonable—that it was, as some of these apologists would say, the "true philosophy"—soon became the standard way for Christian intellectuals to think about God. During the second century, the influence of Platonic philosophy on Christian theology was just beginning, and several of the divine attributes mentioned above—omnipotence, impassibility, and so on—were not fully integrated into Christian thought. However, the notion was rapidly developing that philosophical discourse about God was better than the apparently more anthropomorphic language of Scripture and faith. By the end of the second century, what had begun as a means to communicate the faith, and to defend it before outsiders, became for many the preferred way to speak about God and to conceive the divine nature. Clement of Alexandria, for instance, declared that in interpreting the Bible "nothing must be said of God that is unworthy of God" [2]—by which he meant, nothing that appeared to contradict God's immutability, impassibility, or omnipotence.

By the fourth century, this way of thinking about God was hardly ever questioned. Those who did question it were considered ignorant. God was the immutable, impassible, omnipotent Being. This was the proper way to speak about God. However, some considered speaking about God as loving, as suffering, or as responsive to human need, to be unsophisticated—a view good for the masses, but not for the enlightened. (At this point, it may help to remember that the entire philosophical tradition that stood behind these views was an essentially aristocratic one, distinguishing between those few with real understanding and the many who are ignorant—*hoi polloi.*)

The Worship of the Church

There was, however, another factor that could not be ignored: the faith and the worship of the church. From a very early date, Christians began calling Jesus "Lord"—*kyrios*, the same title that the Septuagint gave Yahweh. Also from a very early date, Jesus was at the center of Christian worship, not just as someone calling the church to worship and to obedience, but also as someone receiving the worship and the obedience of the church. That this was the case, we know not only through ancient Christian writers, but also through a letter from the Roman governor of Bithynia, Pliny the Younger, to Emperor Trajan—the same letter that led to Trajan's response mentioned at the beginning of chapter 4. Pliny was concerned about the basis on which to apply the existing laws against Christians and ordered an investigation regarding Christian practices. In his letter, he reports that Christians gather the first day of the week and that there they "sing hymns to Christ as to God," among other things;[3] Christians were used to addressing Christ in prayer. For them, Christ was not only a mediator for their worship, but also the object of their worship.

In addition, although perhaps in the very early days several different formulae were employed in baptism, very soon the standard practice of the church was to baptize "in the name of the Father, the Son, and the Holy Ghost." Thus, in its life of worship, the church confessed, proclaimed, and sought to obey a God who could somehow be spoken of as "Father, Son, and Holy Spirit." There was little attempt to determine exactly what was meant by these words, which seemed to imply a multiplicity within the Godhead, and would therefore stand in tension with the philosophical conception of God as the Ineffable One.

The tensions between the more philosophical view of the Logos of God and the life and worship of the church did not come to the foreground for some time. Justin himself—the same second-century writer who seems to have been the first to refer to Christ as "another God"[4]—placed Christ at the very center of his faith and eventually died as a martyr for Christ. However, when one looks back at his own thought and that of other early Christian Platonists, the tensions seem obvious. On the one hand, one speaks of God as impassible, immutable; on the other, one worships and prays to God as a responding and active being. One says that the Logos incarnate in Jesus is a secondary being, not quite as high as the Supreme Source of all things; the other, while still insisting on monotheism, worships this Logos and praises Jesus for one's salvation. Such tensions, at first unrecognized or at least pushed aside, could not but come to the foreground as soon as conditions were ready for an attempt to clarify these points.

The Arian Challenge and the Council of Nicea

Conditions were ready once Emperor Constantine put an end to the persecution of Christians (313). Theological differences that until then had paled in the context of the need to respond in unity to the threat of persecution now came to the foreground. Furthermore, as Christianity increasingly became the religion of the population at large, what earlier might have been a debate resolved within the confines of the church, mostly by means of discussion until a consensus was reached, now became matters of public and even political interest. Constantine himself hoped that Christianity would be the cement holding his disparate empire together, and to that end he needed a church in which there was clear agreement on matters of doctrine, rather than one in which different and perhaps even contradictory positions were allowed to exist side by side. Bishops became public officials, respectable leaders in their cities, whose opinions and disagreements were studied and discussed by the newly converted masses.

The controversy finally erupted in Alexandria, in a disagreement between the bishop of that city, Alexander, and one of his presbyters, Arius. Arius was a learned man—probably more learned than Alexander. He had studied in Antioch under one of the most famous Christian teachers of his time, Lucian of Antioch. Lucian himself had been profoundly influenced by Hellenistic philosophy and was convinced that in order to preserve both Christian monotheism and the impassibility of God it was necessary to make clear that the one incarnate in Jesus is not God in the strict sense. These views were embraced by Arius and by those he called his "co-Lucianists"—that is, his fellow students under Lucian.

In Alexandria, someone raised the question, whether the Word or Logos of God—the one who is incarnate in Jesus—is eternal. Alexander took the position that the Logos, being divine, must be eternal. Arius rejected this position, declaring that only the Supreme God is eternal and that the Logos was created within time. When Arius insisted on his position, Alexander declared him deposed. Arius then appealed to two groups. First, since he was popular as a preacher among the crowds in Alexandria, these crowds soon came to his defense. Someone composed what could be termed ditties or hymns that people sang on the streets. The most common of these, "There was when He was not," expresses the Arian position in a nutshell: there was a time when the Word was not. The Word is not eternal but is a creature of God—certainly, the first creature, and the one through whom all things are made, but still a creature, created within the framework of time, as are all other creatures. Second, Arius appealed to his "co-Lucianists." Some of these were now respected teachers and bishops in important positions. Foremost among them was Eusebius of Nicomedia, who was related to the emperor and whose see (the city where a bishop resides), Nicomedia, was Constantine's summer residence, across the Bosporus from Constantinople. These Lucianists protested. They wrote letters condemning the theology and the actions of Alexander. Constantine tried to heal the growing breach within this church that he hoped would be the cement of his empire. When this failed, he called for all the bishops to meet in the city of Nicea—also across the Bosporus from Constantinople.

At this imperial summons, more than three hundred bishops gathered in Nicea in the year 325. To sense the mood of this gathering, it is important to remember that many of these bishops who now traveled at imperial expense had been under threat of martyrdom a few years before. Some still bore the physical marks of torture and maiming. All were agreed that God was doing a great thing in their newly found favor with the emperor, and all were enormously grateful to the emperor for their changed circumstances and for the peace that the church now enjoyed. They rejoiced particularly in this unprecedented opportunity to meet other bishops from distant regions, many of whom were famous for their wisdom and their faithfulness during more difficult times.

It was at this gathering—eventually called the First Ecumenical Council—that the Arian issue was discussed. There were other items on the agenda, having to do mostly with attaining greater uniformity in the practices of a church that had never been able to gather as it was now doing. Still, it was the Arian controversy that soon came to the foreground as the burning topic of the day. Since Arius was not a bishop, he was not present at the Council; but his views were presented and defended by Eusebius of Nicomedia.

Being sure of the intellectual power of his position, Eusebius expounded it clearly, showing its stark contrast with what Alexander held. The Word that is incarnate in Jesus Christ, he declared, is not God, and is not divine, but is a creature. Certainly, no other creature was made before this one, and it was through the Word that all other creatures were made; but the Word is a creature, made within time, and not eternal.

The reaction of the vast majority of the Council was one of astonishment and scandal. For generations, as far back as they could remember, the church had worshiped Christ and prayed to him. Within their own memory, many had suffered tortures and death because they had refused to curse Christ. And now Eusebius and his party declared that in so doing they were worshiping a creature! That the martyrs had died in the service of a creature!

The bishops' reaction was understandable. They must make it clear that this was not the faith of the church. After many attempts at finding a formula to that effect, they settled on a creed that was modeled after some of the creeds that were employed in baptismal services, but with the addition of some formulas that would not be susceptible to an Arian interpretation. Thus, the Creed of Nicea declared that the Son is "begotten, not made"—is not a creature, nor even the first of all creatures. And it further stated that the Son is "God from God, light from light, true God from true God."

Although any of these phrases would serve to exclude Arianism, interest soon focused on the declaration that the Son is "of the same substance"—*homousios* (in some modern translations, "of one being with")—as the Father. Apparently this particular word was suggested by Constantine himself; but no matter what its origin, it soon became the hallmark of Nicene orthodoxy.

The Council adjourned after having come to this decision; but the debates continued. There were many who, while not agreeing with Arianism, were afraid that the claim that the Son is "of the same substance" as the Father could be understood to mean that there is no difference between the two. For a long time, the church had been struggling against some within its ranks who held that the Son is the same as the Father, just performing a different function or presenting a different face. For a number of reasons, among them the baptismal formula of long-standing, most Christian leaders felt that the three persons of the Trinity should not be reduced to three faces, aspects, or "modes" of God, as if God were first Father in creation, then Son in the incarnation, and now Holy Spirit—a position called "modalism." Such a position would imply that when God is present in Jesus, this presence is all there is to God; or that when God is present in the church as Spirit, God is no longer present in Jesus. Now many were afraid that to declare that the Son was "of the same substance"—*homousios*—as the Father would lead precisely to an obliteration of the distinction between the two—in other words, to modalism.

For a while, most of the emperors after Constantine supported Arianism, whose hierarchical understanding of the divine, with the Father standing in absolute aloofness from the world, seemed congenial to their own view of the world, in which they stood at the apex and related to society through an ordered hierarchy of intermediaries. At least it certainly was much better than the notion that a crucified carpenter was "of the same substance" as the Eternal! (A carpenter who had been crucified by their predecessors, even though there was now a generalized attempt to blame the Jews, and not the Romans, for the crucifixion of Jesus.)

For these reasons, the debate regarding the decisions of Nicea was long and bitter. The defenders of Nicea were often persecuted and exiled. Some theologians began proposing a compromise, suggesting that the Son is "of a similar substance" as the Father. Since in Greek "similar" is *homoios*, they suggested substituting *homoiusios* for the Nicene *homousios*—thus prompting some nineteenth-century historians to quip that the entire debate was about a mere *i*, an *iota*. The more radical Arians rejected even this compromise, insisting that the Son is lesser than and completely different from the Father. To complicate matters, some jumped into the fray agreeing that the Son was of the same substance as the Father, but that they were not ready to say the same about the Spirit.

Eventually, more than half a century after Nicea, the bishops who gathered in Constantinople in 381 reiterated what had been decided at Nicea. The Council of Constantinople (now known as the Second Ecumenical Council) also reissued the Creed of Nicea with some additions; and this creed, commonly called the Nicene Creed, but which is in fact the result of both Nicea and Constantinople, became—and still is—the most commonly used creed throughout the Christian church.

The Point of the Debate

What was this debate all about? Was it simply, as some have stated somewhat cynically, about an *iota*? Was it just the result of feverish minds trying to penetrate the mysteries of the divine? As we seek to respond to these questions, we may find guidance in the arguments of Athanasius, who had attended the Council of Nicea as a young man and, later, as bishop of Alexandria, became one of the foremost defenders of its decisions.

Athanasius argued that the notion of the Logos or Son of God serving as an intermediary between the mutable and aloof One and this mutable world in fact solves nothing. If it is true that the immutable cannot communicate with the mutable, then a mutable Logos such as the one proposed by the Arians would not be able to communicate with the immutable. Given such premises, it would be necessary to posit a further intermediary between the Logos and God, and then another between this one and God, and so on into infinity. Therefore, even on purely logical or philosophical terms, the Arian understanding of the Logos or Son as a lesser being that serves as a bridge between the One that is divine and the many of this world, is quite unsatisfactory.

Athanasius's main arguments, however, were religious rather than philosophical. While he used the dominant philosophical tradition of this time to refute Arianism—which used that tradition to an even greater degree—his concern was primarily how to reaffirm and understand the view of the Godhead that was expressed in the worship of the church and how to understand the presence of God in Jesus in such a way that one could truly say that Jesus is Savior. As to worship, it was clear that the church had long worshiped Jesus, praising him, thanking him, praying to him. If the Arians were right, the church was worshiping a creature, and Christianity should be abandoned altogether, for Christianity is inconceivable without having Christ at its center. As to salvation, the Arian position would make it appear that we owe our salvation not to God, but to a lesser being. In contrast, Athanasius was fond of saying that our re-creation is no less a work than our creation and that God—and not a secondary being—must be credited with both. He also insisted that the presence of God in Christ, as the presence of God in creation, is what makes creation and life holy, often using the illustration of a king visiting a city and how that visit bestows royal honor on the entire city. The one whom we worship as the source of all things is God; the one whom we thank for our salvation is God; and we are able to do this because the one who dwells in us as the Spirit is God.

These arguments, as well as many others of a similar nature, led to the final rejection of Arianism. Yet, while the position of Athanasius and the Nicene party ultimately prevailed, the central issue was not resolved. If to be divine means to be immutable, impassible, and therefore aloof, this creates a barrier between the divine and all of creation, and such a barrier is a radical contradiction of much that is crucial to the Judeo-Christian tradition. As we shall see when we return to the person of Jesus Christ in chapter 6, the manner in which theologians had come to define God in terms of static and immutable perfection would pose other serious problems for Christian theology.

Thus, there is much that was amiss in the fourth-century discussion of the Trinity and its final formulation. Yet, if we remember what was said before as to the nature of doctrines, we will see much value in what was done then. If doctrines are not an actual description and sharp determination of what must be believed, but are rather fences or foul lines that allow us to see the pitfalls of the positions that the doctrine denies, then the doctrine of the Trinity, rather than an attempt to describe the inner workings of the Godhead, is a reminder of a number of possible pitfalls and a warning against them. First, in affirming the oneness of God, the Trinity stands firmly within the Jewish and Christian traditions and their rejection of polytheism. Second, in affirming the full divinity of the Incarnate One, as well as of the Spirit that dwells in the people of God, the Trinity affirms that it is possible to address them as God, and yet not as a different God than the One who is above all. Third, in affirming the distinction between the three, the Trinity reminds us that there is mystery in God that goes beyond what we may grasp of God in Jesus or in the Spirit—that the presence and action of God in Jesus or in the Spirit does not exhaust the presence and action of God. Fourth, and perhaps most important, the Trinity reminds us that our common, overly simplistic understandings of what it means to be "One" may need to be corrected—a point to which we shall return toward the end of this chapter.

Later Developments

After the doctrine of the Trinity was formulated in Nicea (325) and Constantinople (381), it was generally accepted by most believers. During the time of Arian ascendancy, some of the neighboring Germanic tribes had been converted to Christianity and had therefore become Arian. When they later invaded the Western Empire, they brought their faith with them, and as a result Arianism, which had never had much influence in the West, was now introduced into that section of the empire. But it did not last long, and the last Arian king (the Visigothic Recared, in Spain) accepted the Nicene faith in 587. After that time, and throughout the Middle Ages, there were few who questioned the doctrine of the Trinity—and those who did were quickly suppressed by the authorities. Thus, throughout the Middle Ages there was little debate on the Trinity, and much of the debate that existed took the form of polemical writings against Judaism or Islam. When the time came of the great *summas* of theology, beginning in the thirteenth century, it became customary to begin them with a discussion *De Deo trino et uno*—On God Three and One. In these discussions, much use was made of previous attempts to define such terms as "person," "substance," "hyposta-sis," and so on; but in general there was little debate on the Trinity.

The one exception was the debate, beginning late in the eighth century and in some ways continuing to this day, on the word *Filioque*, meaning "and from the Son," which was added to the Nicene Creed in the West. Thus, where the original creed professed faith in the Holy Spirit, "who proceeds from the Father," the new version said, "who proceeds from the Father *and the Son*." Quite possibly this word was first added in Spain, simply for reasons of meter when singing the Creed; but it soon became common through-out the Latin-speaking West. Eventually it became established in the kingdom of the Franks, where it was used in Charlemagne's chapel. When the Greek-speaking East learned of this addition, there was much protest for what was clearly an unauthorized change in the creed that had become the symbol of Christian orthodoxy and unity. Charlemagne and other Western leaders considered this protest an affront to their own authority, and therefore insisted on the *Filioque*. There had always been a slight difference of emphasis between the trinitarian doctrine of the East and that of the West. In the East, it had become common to say that the Son is begotten from the Father and that the Spirit proceeds from the Father, "through the Son." In the West, St. Augustine (384–431) had declared that the Spirit is the bond of love between the Father and the Son, and this had led to an understanding of the Trinity in which both Father and Son are the source for the Spirit. These were matters of emphasis that had never come to the foreground of theological debate. But now, in the heat of the controversy over the addition to the Creed, and involved as they were in matters of international policy, those differences were explored and underscored, so that the debate over the *Filioque* took the form of a debate over the Trinity and eventually became so bit-ter that it was one of the main reasons—still, more an excuse than a real reason—for the final break between East and West in 1054.

Although, apart from the matter of the *Filioque*, there was little debate over it, trinitarian doctrine and devotion did play an impor-tant role throughout the Middle Ages. If God is triune, then this tri-unity of God must be reflected in all of God's works. Hence, it behooves believers to see in all things the imprint of the Trinity—

vestigia Trinitatis, as such signs of the triune Creator were called. Augustine argued that the Trinity is like the human mind, in which there is memory, intellect, and will. These three are different. The will is not the intellect or the memory. The memory is neither the will nor the intellect. The intellect is neither memory nor will. And yet there is only one mind. Soon an entire system of such vestiges developed. Each being is true, good, and beautiful. These three are not the same. Yet the whole thing is true, the whole thing is good, and the whole thing is beautiful. Out of these and similar considerations, an entire tradition developed, which sought to contemplate the mystery of God in the mystery of God's creatures and in the manner in which they reflect the divine Trinity. Typical and foremost of this sort of devotion is Bonaventure's (1221–1274) *Itinerarium mentis in Deum*—The Mind's Road to God.

Although most of the Protestant Reformers adhered to the traditional doctrine of the Trinity, the ferment of which they were a part, and the eventual breakdown of the grip of the church over people's minds, opened the way for renewed debate on the Trinity. In the sixteenth century itself, Servetus was condemned for his anti-trinitarian views, first by the Spanish Inquisition and then by Calvin's Geneva—where he was burned as a heretic. The Socinians, who eventually found refuge in Poland, also rejected the doctrine of the Trinity. From that time on, the doctrine was questioned ever more frequently, as various forms of rationalism came to the conviction that it was an unwarranted attempt to describe the inner workings of the Godhead, that religion should be kept as simple as possible, and that this and many other doctrines were relics of a bygone age when thought could be controlled by authority. In New England, this gave rise to Unitarianism and the Unitarian Church. In Germany and other theological centers, many liberal theologians either dispensed with the Trinity altogether, relegated it to a doctrine of secondary importance, or turned it into a symbol for deeper realities. Hegel, for instance, saw in it the expression of the inner and constant working of the universal Mind—the three persons being the thesis, the antithesis, and the synthesis that are present in all thought.

By introducing the process of thought into the very nature of the Ultimate, Hegel was foreshadowing a number of new philosophical departures that would seek to free philosophy from the static and essentialist inheritance it had received from Parmenides, Plato, and

Aristotle. Existentialism—which was born in part as a reaction to Hegel's rationalist essentialism—questioned much of the received metaphysics, and particularly the notion that perfection consists in the changelessness of an essence. Process philosophy, under the leadership of British philosopher Alfred North Whitehead (1861–1947), proposed reality, not as a fixed essence, but as a process. His colleague at Harvard, Charles Hartshorne (1897–2000), worked with him on the implications of process philosophy in the field of theology, and thus gave rise to the entire theological school of "process theology," whose many adherents seek ways to conceive of God beyond the static ways of traditional philosophy and theology, speaking of God as being also in process. At the same time, theologians in various quarters were reclaiming the biblical notion of an active God who relates with creation, and speaking even of "the pain of God" (Japanese theologian Katzeo Kitamori). All of this has opened the way for new discussions, not only on the nature of God, but also on the Trinity and its significance.

This new interest on the Trinity is exemplified by Karl Barth (1886–1968), who deliberately began his monumental *Church Dogmatics* with a discussion on the Trinity, relating trinitarian theology to the very nature of revelation. From that point on, there has been a revival of interest on the Trinity, no longer as a strange doctrine or theory that Christians have to explain or for which they should apologize, but rather as central to the Christian faith and its understanding of God.

Contemporary Relevance

This renewed interest in the Trinity has led many to suggest that the doctrine of the Trinity, rather than simply posing the difficulty of how three can be one, should invite Christians to rethink what they mean by "one." What is the nature of this "oneness" in which threeness is also central? Already in 1903, George A. Gordon, in a book entitled *Ultimate Conceptions of the Faith*,[5] declared, referring to the significance of the Trinity: "The contest today is between God as an eternal egoist and God as an eternal socialist. If God is an eternal egoist, he is the contradiction of humanity;... If God is an eternal socialist, he is in himself the ground and hope of humanity." Much later in the twentieth century, Roman Catholic bishop Christopher Mwoleka of Tanzania wrote:

> I think we have problems understanding the Trinity because we approach the mystery from the wrong side.... The right approach to the Trinity is to *imitate* the Trinity....
>
> God does not reveal himself to us for the sake of speculation. He is not giving us a riddle to solve. He is offering us life. He is telling us: "This is what it means to live, now begin to live as I do."[6]

Thus, the doctrine of the Trinity is leading many today to question what it is that we mean when we say that God is one. Do we mean that God stands in supreme solitude, and therefore that perfection, and the goal of all beings as they are perfected, is solitude? Or do we mean that true oneness, true wholeness, is always oneness and wholeness in love, in interchange, in relationships? Theologians have long agreed that when we say that we believe in a "personal" God, we are referring not to the three "persons" in the Trinity, but to the very being of God. To say that God is personal is to say that God relates to us and to the world in much the same way as a person relates. Can we now add that the difference between a purely mathematical monotheism, in which God is one in solitude, and the Triune God is parallel to the difference between an "individual" and a "person"? That God is one, not in solitude, but in relational inner community? Can we say that the old Christian assertion that "God is love" means not only that God loves us and all of creation, but that in the very inner being of God there is love, and that this is the meaning of the doctrine of the Trinity? This is one of the themes that is being discussed today by Christians throughout the world, as they seek new and deeper understandings of the Godhead and of trinitarian theology. We are not done yet with trinitarian thought!

For Further Reading

Boff, Leonardo. *Trinity and Society*. Wellwood, Kent: Burns & Oates, 1998.

Grenz, Stanley J. *Rediscovering the Trinity in Contemporary Theology*. Minneapolis: Fortress Press, 2004.

Prestige, G. L. *God in Patristic Thought*. London: S.P.C.K., 1956.

Welch, Claude. *In This Name: The Doctrine of the Trinity in Contemporary Theology*. New York: Scribner, 1952.

Notes

1. *Martyrdom of Polycarp*, 9.2.
2. *Stromateis*, 2.16.
3. *Epistles*, 10.96.7.
4. *Dialogue with Trypho*, 56.11.
5. George A. Gordon, *Ultimate Conceptions of the Faith* (Boston: Houghton, Mifflin, 1903). Quoted by Claude Welch, *In This Name: The Doctrine of the Trinity in Contemporary Theology* (New York: Charles Scribner's Sons, 1952), 33.
6. Quoted in Gerald H. Anderson and Thomas F. Stransky, eds., *Mission Trends No. 3: Third World Theologies* (New York: Paulist Press, 1976), 152-53.

5.

HUMANKIND

What are human beings that you are mindful of them,
mortals that you care for them?
Psalm 8:4

We come now to what has traditionally been called the "doctrine of man," or, in less gender-specific terms, "Christian anthropology." Note that in this context the meaning of the word "anthropology" is different from its more common meaning in everyday language, as a discipline that studies human beings, their traits, cultures, and so on. Theologians often use the word "anthropology" in a specific theological sense, as that part of theology that deals with the nature, powers, and calling of human beings. This is much simpler and stylistically less awkward than "the doctrine about human beings."

The Beginnings of Christian Anthropology

As Christianity began to make its way into the Greco-Roman world, it did not see itself as a new way of understanding what it means to be human. Christians were not particularly concerned, for instance, about whether a human being is composed of body and soul, as some held, or of body, soul, and spirit or mind, as others—the majority in that culture—thought. Later theologians have discussed endlessly whether there are two or three constituent parts to a human being—in technical terms, some have held to the "dichotomist" position, and others to the "trichotomist." The reason for this is that, both in the New Testament and in other early

91

Christian literature, one can find references to "body and soul" as well as to "body, soul, and spirit [or mind]."

The very fact that both views appear in early Christian literature—and sometimes in a single writer's work—should serve as an indication that this was not a matter of contention or of great interest for early Christians. Indeed, those who even today insist on making this a crucial issue usually understand the term "soul" in a very different way than it was understood by most ancient trichotomists. When, in the ancient world, philosophers and others referred to "body, soul, and mind [or spirit]," what they usually meant by "soul" was simply the power that gives life to a body. In this sense, animals have souls, for their bodies are alive—indeed, the very word "animal" means a being that has a soul, an *anima*. Furthermore, even plants have such a soul, for without it they would be just dead wood. Above this, there is the "intellect"—*nous*—"spirit," or "rational soul," which is the center of consciousness distinguishing humans from other beings. In general, Christians accepted the notion that a human being has both a body and a "soul"—although by this they usually meant not primarily the power that gives life to a body, but rather the mind, the intellect, the "rational soul." The other, the "soul" in the sense of the life-giving element, they quite often simply took for granted—in which case they would use "trichotomist" language—or merged with either the body or the "rational soul" or "spirit"—in which case they would use "dichotomist" language.

In conclusion, the issue that has long occupied some Christians in more recent times, regarding the number of parts coming together to form a human being, was not a primary concern of early Christians, who simply adopted the language of the culture of which they were part. That language seemed to suffice for expressing their understanding, and they did not seek to change it.

The Nature of the Soul

This did not mean, however, that they were ready to accept all that Hellenistic culture taught regarding human nature and destiny. For a long time, in much of the Mediterranean basin and far into the Near East, people had held that the soul or human spirit is divine in a sense in which the body is not. Some of the ancient Greek philosophers had taught that the soul is immortal and that the body is a prison in which the soul is temporarily held. According to a common play on words in Greek, the body is a sepulcher. Plato taught that before being born into this world, souls had existed in a higher world of ideas, that from that higher world they fell into this physical world of appearances, from which they will eventually be delivered so they may return to their original and happy state as disembodied intellects. This is why Socrates could face death with great aplomb—he was convinced that by dying he was simply being born into a fuller life. In Persia, there was a strongly dualistic tradition that held that the world is composed of two elements, one spiritual and the other physical, one good and the other evil, one light and the other darkness. Human beings are a mixture of these two elements, of a good spiritual reality and an evil physical body. In Egypt, there was a long tradition of providing for the life of the soul in the afterworld. Although in ancient Egyptian religion this was closely connected with the preservation of the mummified body, in Hellenistic times this connection with the body was lessened, and the cult of Isis and Osiris, as it spread throughout the Mediterranean world, was a means to ensure the happiness of the soul after it was freed from the body. As we have seen, Gnostic dualism took up these traditions, claiming that the soul is part of the higher realm—the *pleroma* or fullness—that has somehow fallen to be entrapped in this lower world of matter and bodies.

From a very early date, Christians rejected such views. The soul, they said, is not divine. The soul is a creature, just as everything else is a creature. When Christians affirm that they believe in God, "maker of heaven and of earth," or "of all things visible and invisible," this includes the soul. The soul is not a bit of God living in a human body and waiting to be freed from its imprisonment. The soul is a creature and, like every other creature, owes its existence not to itself, but to God.

Surprising as this may seem to many Christians today, this means that the soul is not immortal. The soul depends on God, not only for its origin, but also for its continued existence. Just as no other creature can subsist in and of itself, but has to be sustained in existence by God, so does the soul. The life of the soul, just as much as the existence of a stone, is totally dependent on God. The soul continues living after death, not because it cannot be destroyed, but because God grants it continued life.

This relates to what we saw in the last chapter regarding the eternity of the Word of God. One way in which orthodox Christians expressed that eternity was by affirming that the Word is of the substance or nature of God, and not the result of God's will. What they meant by this is that everything else that exists apart from God is the result of the divine will of creation. In this context, Christians would say that the soul is the result of an act of creation, the product of God's will, and therefore is neither eternal nor by nature immortal—even though God can grant it immortality. Furthermore, Christian hope goes beyond the expectation of the continued life of the soul after death and includes the expectation of the soul being united again with a body, for a soul by itself is not a full human being. It is for this reason that the Apostles' Creed affirms that Christians believe "in the resurrection of the body."

The creeds that we studied earlier, and the doctrine of creation they convey, also hold for human beings. We, too, are creatures. We are not divine. Thus, the first "fence" or "foul line" that Christians drew in their theological anthropology is simply this: human beings, including human souls, are created by God and are dependent on God for their existence.

One way this was expressed was by showing the contrast between the attributes of God—as they had come to be understood, in large measure due to the influence of Greek philosophy on theology—and human nature. God is infinite, omnipotent, omnipresent, omniscient, impassible. Humans are by nature finite, weak, limited to a particular place, and carried to and fro by others—particularly by our passions.

Created in the Image of God

There clearly is something special about human beings as compared to the rest of creation. Humans are called to a particular sort of communion with God. Humans have the freedom to obey and to disobey. Humans have an intellect that allows them to understand the world around them. Humans have control over much of that world. Humans are qualitatively different from the rest of creation.

The early church, picking up on earlier Jewish thought, spoke of this unique character of humankind by referring to the creation stories in Genesis and particularly to the "image of God"—*imago Dei*—after which humankind is created. Genesis declares that God made humankind "in our image, after our likeness." There was much discussion in the early church as to whether the "image" and the "likeness" are two ways of saying the same thing or refer to different ways in which humans were created like God. Some felt that one of these gave Adam and Eve powers that they lost when they sinned, while the other still remains. This, however, need not detain us here. The crucial point is that the early church affirmed that, although humans are creatures and in that sense are distinct from God, they also have a special relationship with God. Some believed that the *imago Dei* was a physical similarity. Others said it was an inclination to approach God, and that it is for this reason that only humankind among all creatures was made to walk erect. In general, most held that the image of God in humans consisted either in one or in several of the following: (1) Rationality: Humans alone, among all creatures—except the angels—are given the ability to reason. (2) Authority: By being created in the image of God, humans are to govern the rest of creation in the name of God, and in representation of God's will. (3) Freedom: Humans have been given the Godlike capacity to make decisions—even decisions against the will of God. (4) Virtue: Humans are made in such a way that when they are what they are supposed to be they reflect God "like a mirror," particularly in goodness and love. (5) As an announcement of the incarnation: While today we tend to think of the incarnation as God's response to sin, many in the early church, reminding their readers that according to Paul, Jesus is the image of God (Col 1:15) and Adam was a "type" or "figure" of Christ (Rom 5:14), believed that the incarnation—an intimate relationship with humanity—was God's goal for the creation of humankind, and that the model that God used in order to make humankind was none other than Jesus incarnate, whom God foresaw.

Leaving aside such matters, on which the church never made an official decision, it is important to point out that the practically universal emphasis on the *imago Dei*—the image of God in humans—serves a balancing purpose vis-à-vis the insistence on humans being part of creation. If one clear fence was that humans are not divine, another clear fence is that humans are not entirely like all other creatures. Humans are made for communion with God. They are made for love. They should represent God's governance over the rest of creation. Over the centuries, Christian anthropology has held these two in tension—the limits of the human being as a creature on the one hand, and that creature's high nature and calling on the other. In general, during the early centuries of Christianity, Western, Latin-speaking theologians tended to emphasize more the first of these two aspects, and Eastern, Greek-speaking theologians stressed the second. The result is that Western theology has a history of being less optimistic about human abilities than its Eastern counterpart.

The Origin of the Soul

Granted that the soul is distinct from the body, what is the origin of individual souls? In the early church, four options were open. Two of these were soon rejected, the third tended to fade away, and the fourth generally prevailed. First, souls could be part of the divine substance. This position was readily rejected as a denial of the doctrine of creation. Second, it is possible to hold that souls exist before they are born into a human body. This was Plato's position, and therefore it had significant appeal for those who were inclined toward the Platonic tradition. Its most significant Christian proponent was Origen (ca. 185–ca. 254), who held that souls were fallen intellects for whom God had created this temporary abode that is the physical earth. [1] In this he was followed by very few, and eventually the Second Council of Constantinople (Fifth Ecumenical, 553) declared the theory of the preexistence of the souls to be anathema. The reasons for this were several. Foremost among them were the clear implications that souls are eternal—which Origen did hold—and are therefore divine, and that life in this world is a punishment for previous sins—which Origen also held. A third option was to see an individual soul as being begotten and transmitted just as bodies are. This position, called "traducionism," was held by many in the second through the fifth centuries. Foremost among them was Tertullian, who believed—as many did—that the soul is corporeal. This view had the advantage that it made it easier to explain original sin—to which we shall come later in this chapter. Just as we inherit our physical traits, so do we inherit a soul tainted by sin.

Finally, a fourth position was that each soul is created individually and directly by God—usually at conception or, if not, at the time of "quickening." This position, supported by Augustine (354–430), is called "creationism." Augustine believed that the soul is incorporeal and therefore cannot be transmitted as the body is. Although at first there was strong opposition in some quarters to this notion that the soul, in contrast to the body, is incorporeal, after the fifth century—and even earlier in the Eastern church—creationism became the usual way to understand the origin of individual souls.

(An unfortunate consequence of this is that, following Augustine, many theologians, as well as popular piety, have tended to connect original sin with sex. Since, given his creationist stance regarding the origin of individual souls, Augustine could not explain original sin as a direct inheritance from one's forebears, he claimed that original sin is transmitted through "concupiscence." Concupiscence consists in looking to the creature rather than to the Creator. As a result of sin, the act of procreation and the passions connected with it are concupiscent, and those who are thus begotten—no matter how saintly their parents may have been—are begotten in sin.)

Augustine and Pelagius

It was in the late fourth and early fifth centuries that the most important controversy arose regarding the human creature—a controversy that has marked Christian theology, particularly in the West, to this day. It had to do with the extent to which humans are able to please God and to work out their own salvation.

Long before this time, the Latin-speaking church of the West had begun to differ from the Greek-speaking church on the capabilities that each attributed to the human creature. The Eastern church, with its more mystical inclination and its emphasis on God having created humankind with a goal of communion with the divine, was much more optimistic than the Western church about human capabilities. In the East, there was a long tradition—going back at least into the second century—that spoke of Adam and Eve having been created "as children." In that tradition, rather than emphasizing how far humankind had been corrupted as a result of Adam's sin, there was a tendency to see the Fall as an unfortunate interruption in what would have been a long process even apart from sin. When Eastern theologians discussed the effects of sin on human free will, they would agree that sin had weakened the will, but not that it had made it incapable of choosing the good. They certainly agreed with Western theologians that salvation is unattainable by human effort and that God works in the believer so that the believer may come into closer communion with God. Yet they would always be careful not to conclude that this renders humans incapable of doing what is pleasing to God.

In the West, on the contrary, there was another long-standing tradition, going back to the end of the second century and the early years of the third, that tended to think of Adam and Eve as somehow superhuman. They were much better than we are. They had strength, knowledge, capabilities—and, according to some, even physical size—that we can hardly imagine. The Fall is much more than an interruption or a detour in God's plans. The Fall is the loss of much that was good. Tertullian, one of the earliest exponents of this view, had declared that, as a result of sin, "our entire being was changed from its original wholeness to a rebellion against the Creator." [2] Toward the middle of the third century, Cyprian, who called Tertullian "the Master," also insisted on the corruption of human nature as a result of sin.

When the controversy broke out, early in the fifth century, the most influential theologian in the Western church was St. Augustine, the bishop of a relatively small city in northern Africa, and a man much admired by his contemporaries for his holiness, intellectual insight, and publications. Augustine had come to Christian faith through a long and tortuous path. His mother had been a Christian, and therefore he had known—and in a sense also believed— Christian doctrine from his childhood. Yet he had difficulties, both intellectual and moral, before he could truly believe and live by such beliefs. For a while, he was a skeptic; then he became a Manichean; then he found in some Neoplatonic doctrines the beginning of his way back to the Christian faith. (Neoplatonism made it possible for him to conceive of immaterial realities such as God and the soul, and also to deal with evil, not as a bad substance—as the Manicheans did—but rather as a privation of good.) Yet, even after he was convinced that Christianity was true and that he should follow it, he had found himself incapable of taking the decisive step toward full belief.

He tried to lead his will in the right direction but discovered that he could not. As an example of his wretchedness and his inability to turn his will to the good, he later wrote that at this time he would pray, "Grant me chastity; but not yet." [3] He was at the brink of despair when, in a way that he could only attribute to God's grace, his will was made capable of accepting and following Christianity. When he became a bishop and a theologian, he kept that experience at the center of his theology—an experience of having been incapable to do or even to will the good until God intervened. His most famous book, the *Confessions*, is mostly a hymn celebrating God's grace that brought him to salvation. There he speaks of the pleasure he took, even as a child, in what he knew was evil, and of how he has seen the same in other children. There he rehearses his long path to faith—a path in which he repeatedly went astray by his own willfulness and pride. There he confesses—hence the title, *Confessions*—and praises God's great gift of grace that saved him even without his willing it, for his will was corrupted by sin. For Augustine, were it not for the power of God's grace, he and all humankind would be nothing but a "mass of damnation."

The controversy broke out when another famous teacher and saintly man, Pelagius, read some words of Augustine that he considered intolerable. Pelagius was a respected Christian teacher who had come from Britain to Rome, where his teaching emphasized spiritual and moral discipline, and the task of pleasing God by means of a life of purity and obedience. Quite likely, he had been aware for some time of the differences between himself and Augustine; but what led to the controversy was a line that he now read in which Augustine prayed to God: "Give what you command, and command what you will"—*da quod iubes, et iube quod vis.* [4]

Pelagius correctly understood Augustine to be saying that it is God who makes it possible for humans to obey the commandments; that without such help, obedience is impossible; and that with such help, obedience springs from the soul. As Pelagius saw matters, this would undercut the very heart of Christian faith and life, making it all rest on the gift of God's grace, and thus excusing sin and disobedience as a lack of help from God. Although he criticized Augustine's words, little came of it until the approach of the Goths led Pelagius and his disciple Celestius to flee from Rome to North Africa. Celestius remained there, and Pelagius moved on to the East, where he sought support for his teachings and against those of Augustine.

Pelagius's teachings were based on his pastoral concern, that people be encouraged to obey God and to do good works. According to him, although the Fall stands between creation and the present state, this does not mean that humans are no longer free or able to do good. Adam's sin was his own, and not ours, and to claim that we are damned by it is to accuse God of injustice. The devil is certainly powerful, and if we are not watchful we shall fall into his snares. But even so, we certainly have the freedom and the capacity both to sin and to refrain from sinning—*posse peccare*; *posse non peccare*. However, this does not mean that humans can do anything apart from God's grace. On the contrary, God's grace is seen everywhere. First of all, there is the "grace of creation," which allows us to live and to understand the world around us. This by itself preserves the freedom of the human will and makes it possible to please God. Then there is the "grace of revelation," by which God tells us what is good and calls us to do it. Finally, there is the "grace of forgiveness," by which God forgives the sins of those who repent from their evil and move on in good works. In short, Pelagius believed that our very freedom is a gift of God's grace and that grace in no way acts on the will, except by teaching and exhortation, for the will by itself is capable of doing what God wishes. Any theory or doctrine that does not allow for this free action and decision of the will relieves humans from their responsibility before God and must be rejected.

Augustine could abide none of this. His own experience was that God had saved him, not so much because of Augustine's will, but in a sense even against it. The will, and not only individual actions stemming from the will, has been corrupted by sin. Were one to say that one believes because one has freely decided to do so, and that others are condemned by their own fault in not deciding or doing what they could have decided and done, this would lead to an arrogance that in itself is contrary to Christian faith. No! The corruption brought about by sin is such that infants are already born with it—a view that had become generally accepted doctrine, particularly in the West, and which Pelagius denied. It is true that in Eden Adam and Eve had the freedom not to sin—*posse non peccare*—as well as the freedom to sin—*posse peccare*. But once humankind opted to exercise this second sort of freedom—in the Fall—the first was lost. Fallen humans are still free, but all their options, even those seemingly most virtuous, are tainted by sin and are the result of sin, for all that is available to them is the freedom to sin—*posse peccare*. They can choose among various degrees of evil; but all choices will still be sinful. Negatively stated, this means that they cannot not sin—*non posse non peccare*. It is only after conversion, when one is saved by the grace of God and the merits of Christ, that humans once again have the freedom not to sin, although they remain free to sin—both *posse peccare* and *posse non peccare*. Finally, in the end, when we are in the presence of God, our freedom not to sin will remain, but we shall no longer be free to sin—*posse non peccare* and *non posse peccare*.

The disagreement between Augustine and Pelagius is partly based on a different understanding of sin and how it affects humans. For Pelagius, a sin is an action against the will of God. Sin, even though it may affect the will by becoming a habit, does not affect human nature to such an extent that it incapacitates it for doing good. For Augustine, although actions against the will of God are certainly sinful, sin is much more than an action or even a series of actions. Sin is also a condition. Once humankind has opted for sin, its own will and nature have been tainted, and this to such a point that all the options left are sinful—not that there are no options, or that the will has no freedom, but that all decisions are made in a state of sin and are therefore sinful. (Perhaps a good example would be to imagine that humans at some point had wings and therefore were free both to fly and to walk. Now, having lost our wings, we are still free. We still have options. But none of our options goes beyond walking, and no matter how hard we try, we remain unable to fly. While we retain our freedom as far as walking is concerned, all our decisions will still keep us bound to earth.)

However, the matter does not stop there. If it is impossible for humans not to sin, how is it that they can accept the grace of God and become believers? Such a step cannot be sin and therefore falls beyond the range of options open to fallen humans. How can it happen? Only by the grace of God. Even before we will it, and quite apart from our willing, grace intervenes, restoring our will, our freedom to love and to serve God. As Augustine would put it, grace is not the result of the will. Grace moves the will—even though this is done in a sort of "soft violence" in which the will is turned, while at the same time it is not coerced. [5]

What then about those who do not believe? Did they simply resist the grace that was given to them? Although such an explanation may seem attractive at first, it implies that those who believed did so out of a different attitude or decision on their part, and this in turn leads us back to attributing salvation to an act of the will rather than to God's grace. The only possible solution is to rest the matter entirely on the grace of God, and not on human acceptance of or resistance to that grace. Grace must be irresistible, for if it were only up to it, the human will would certainly resist grace and insist on sin. God has granted this irresistible grace to some within this "mass of damnation" that is humankind.

This seems to lead inevitably to the doctrine of predestination. Augustine did not derive his views on predestination only from the apparently inexorable logic of his position regarding the consequences of human sin. As a student of Scripture, he had to account for the many biblical passages and arguments that support predestination. As one who had been brought into the fold by no doing of his own, he had to attribute his salvation to a divine, and not to a human, decision. As a grateful believer, his theology was mostly a song of praise to the God who had saved him through grace. But his doctrine of predestination—which he would have held anyhow as an act of giving God the glory—certainly came to the foreground in the context of his controversy with the Pelagians and is thus intrinsically bound with that controversy. According to Augustine, God grants grace—irresistible grace—to those whom God has chosen. These are predestined to salvation. The rest are simply left to remain part of the human "mass of damnation." Furthermore, God has not made such choices on the basis of what God knew beforehand would be the responses or the actions of each person. Predestination is not the result of human action even in this way. Rather, human action for salvation is the result of predestination—of a predestination decided by God on the basis of God's own counsel.

After the Death of Augustine

These were the main points at issue between Augustine and the Pelagians. After a brief sojourn in North Africa, Pelagius continued traveling to the East, where he correctly felt that Augustine's pes-

102

simistic view of human capabilities would not find much support. Even though some did lend him an ear, even in the East his atomistic view of sin, as a series of actions rather than a state, was not very congenial to Eastern theology. Celestius remained in North Africa, where he became Augustine's main opponent in this controversy. Finally, the Third Ecumenical Council (Ephesus, 431) rejected the views of Pelagius—although not necessarily endorsing those of Augustine.

As to Augustine's views, they have had a curious history. While he was still living, there were many who questioned his strong emphasis on the absolute primacy of grace to the point that it seemed to exclude the role of the will in conversion and faith. In the East, the very theologians who rejected Pelagianism were not too comfortable with doctrines that seemed to view the relations between God and humans as a sequential series of events, and which therefore tended to discount the reciprocity of love. In the West, there were many—particularly some very respected monks in Southern France—who rejected the notion that the beginning of faith—the *initium fidei*—is only up to God's grace, and not to human freedom. While these have traditionally been called "Semipelagians," it would probably be more exact to call them "Semiaugustinians," for they agreed with Augustine that grace has the primacy in salvation and that believers have no right to boast for their decision to believe, but were not ready to carry Augustine's logic to the point at which salvation is brought about by divine predestination and irresistible grace.

The result of this resistance is that, while Western theologians have repeatedly rejected Pelagianism and have declared themselves to be Augustinian, very few have followed him to the ultimate consequences of his views. This may be seen in the decisions of the Synod of Orange (529), which are usually said to have put an end to the Pelagian and the Semipelagian controversies by endorsing Augustine's views. Most of what that synod expressed as true Christian doctrine was taken from the writings of Augustine and certainly rejected the views of both Pelagians and Semipelagians. Thus, according to the Synod, the beginning of faith—the *initium fidei*—is not in human nature, but in grace. The grace of God does not come from our willing; rather, our willing comes from the grace of God. While Adam abandoned his state of grace by his sin, his descendants can leave their state of iniquity only by the grace of God. Apart from such grace, all human action is sin. However, the Synod did not draw from these points the conclusion that grace is irresistible or that predestination is the result of a sovereign decision on God's part—although the Synod did declare that any who held that God predestines some to damnation should be anathema. Its declarations seem to equate baptism with grace, which shows the discussion had moved on to other issues. No one can do any good without grace; but grace is conferred unto all at baptism. The will needs to be restored by grace; and that restoration takes place at baptism. Augustine had argued against Pelagius that if human nature has not been tainted by sin there is no point in baptizing infants; but he had not concluded that the irresistible grace of which he wrote was granted at baptism. Thus, what in Augustine was intended as a hymn of praise to divine grace, and as a warning against believers claiming that they were saved by their own meritorious decision, had been coopted into a sacramental system in which grace was almost mechanically infused through baptism, and then again in the other sacramental acts of the church. Grace, rather than an expression of the sovereign freedom of God, had become a fluid necessary for Christian living that was mostly under the control of the church that controlled the sacraments.

The history of Augustine's views on these matters has been one in which three general tendencies, all claiming to follow Augustine and all opposing one another, have often clashed. The first tendency, and by far the dominant one, has been a mitigated Augustinianism after the style of the Synod of Orange. Every Western theologian during the Middle Ages claimed to follow Augustine—and probably most were convinced that they did. Yet this was not the Augustine who felt the impulse to attribute his salvation only to God; nor was it the Augustine of irresistible grace and unconditional predestination. It was rather a mitigated Augustine who was made to fit into the sacramental system of the church, and who therefore was often interpreted in such a way that the grace of baptism came to play practically the same role that Pelagius attributed to the "grace of creation"—a grace universally bestowed, allowing people to respond to God out of their own free will. It was for this reason that Luther felt that practically all medieval theologians were Pelagians.

A second and much better option has been to reaffirm Augustine's views, not so much as part of a system, but rather as a way of expressing and proclaiming the experience of salvation as an unexplainable and unmerited act of God's grace. It was thus that Luther, after his own experience of justification by grace, came to a renewed appreciation for what Augustine had taught regarding grace and predestination. The same is true of Calvin, who discussed predestination not as a logical consequence of divine omnipotence and omniscience, or even as a crucial point of orthodoxy, but rather as an expression of the experience of salvation, not by our own merits and decisions, but by the grace of God alone.

Third, and unfortunately quite often, there have been repeated moments in Christian history in which someone has rediscovered the teachings of Augustine and has sought to revive or to sustain them; but this has been done in such a way that what comes forth is the harshness of predestination and irresistible grace, rather than Augustine's hymn of praise for the love and grace of God. In the ninth century, a monk by the name of Gottschalk, after a careful study of the writings of Augustine, concluded—correctly—that what the church was teaching was not what Augustine had taught, and he set out to restore the fullness of Augustine's doctrines regarding grace and predestination. Commenting on Gottschalk and his work, I have said elsewhere that

> One must say in his favor that he certainly had a clearer understanding of Augustine's doctrine of predestination than did his opponents. But one must add that the manner in which he understood and expounded that doctrine was so severe that it became inhuman. His is not the constant hymn of gratitude which the Bishop of Hippo sang in his doctrine of predestination, but rather an obsession that sometimes seems to turn into morbid joy over the condemnation of the reprobate.[6]

He actually rejoices that those who disagree with him must be among the reprobate, destined to eternal damnation.

Similar views developed after the Reformation, particularly in the seventeenth century. Among Roman Catholics, Cornelius Jansenius (1585–1638), a professor of theology at the University of Louvain, spent twenty years studying Augustine's doctrines of grace and predestination. His book *Augustinus*, published eleven years after his death, was a strict, rigorous restatement of Augustine's views on these matters. Like Gottschalk before him, Jansenius was correct in his rendering of what Augustine had written. But, once again, this was not the Augustine of the *Confessions*, singing the praises of God who had saved him. It was a strictly systematized and harshly cold Augustine. For Jansenius and his followers, Augustine's doctrines of predestination and grace were to be held, not because they expressed the joyful experience of salvation by God's loving grace, but simply because they were Augustine's, and because the church had become too lax in its interpretation of Augustine.

Among Protestants, roughly at the same time as Jansenius was writing his book, a later generation of Calvinists sought to express and to defend what Calvin had taught. They systematized what Calvin—and to a large extent Luther—had said about grace and pre-destination. Some of them turned the doctrine of predestination into a corollary of God's foreknowledge and omnipotence, which Calvin would not have done. While Calvin had discussed grace and predes-tination under the heading of salvation, as an expression of the joyful experience of salvation, these later Calvinists turned the doctrines of grace and predestination into a test of orthodoxy and drew from them the most extreme consequences. In the Synod of Dort (1618–1619), they systematized this into five points that bring forth the harshness of the most extreme Augustinianism and Calvinism: (1) Not only is humankind a "mass of damnation," as Augustine had declared, but even more, all of humankind is totally depraved, so cor-rupted by sin that it would resist grace if it could. (2) God's election is totally unconditional, based solely on God's own hidden counsel, and not on any foreknowledge that God may have of future human decisions or actions. (3) Grace is irresistible, for if it were not, sinful humans would resist it, and none could be saved. (4) Since it would be blasphemous to suggest that the sacrifice of Jesus has failed in its purpose, one most conclude that his atoning work is limited and intended only for the elect. (5) Since salvation is by grace and only for the predestined, the saints can never "fall from grace," but will per-severe until the end. All of this was decided as a response to the teach-ings of Arminius and his followers, who were also Calvinists in everything except the doctrine of predestination, which they sought to make less harsh by speaking of a "preventing" or "prevenient" grace, given to all and allowing all to accept or to reject saving grace. Thus, both sides of the debate turned the matter of salvation into a rather mechanical, orderly system of doctrine—in which, although calling themselves "Calvinists," they in fact departed from the spirit of Calvin's affirmations regarding grace and predestination.

In brief, this third option, both among Protestants (strict Calvinism) and among Roman Catholics (Jansenism), is the typical result of later generations seeking to interpret what great teachers (in this case, particularly Augustine and Calvin) had said earlier, and in the process turning it into a strictly logical, rational, systematic, cold set of principles rather than an expression of the joy of God's saving grace. Even further, those principles now served as narrow criteria to which all who expect to experience that grace must agree.

It would thus seem that the best alternative is the second option: looking at grace, rejoicing in it as God's unmerited gift, and not attempting to turn God's free action in grace freely given into a system of doctrine, or into a program determining the way in which God must act. Although this option has not found frequent expression in Christian theology—preoccupied as theology often is with logical coherence and consistency—it has long and often been an important element in the piety of countless Christians whose purpose is not so much to express their views in strictly logical fashion, but rather to express their gratitude to God for their own salvation. This is certainly true of much Christian hymnody. A well-known example is the popular hymn "Amazing Grace," in which with very little thought to irresistible grace or to predestination, worshipers proclaim that their salvation is not due to them, but rather to the amazing grace of God; that without such grace they were wretched; that they were blind; that it was not they who found grace, but rather grace that found them. Thus, once again, Christian theology is closely entwined with worship, which often finds ways to express in poetry, in symbol, and in gesture what theologians fail to express in words and systems.

Contemporary Relevance

Christian doctrine regarding grace, predestination, and free will has never been formally defined by the church at large. Or rather, a number of churches have defined what they consider to be orthodox doctrine, and none of them has succeeded in being generally accepted by Christians at large. And yet, even out of these inconclusive and sometimes divisive debates, there are some "fences" or "foul lines" that emerge. As in other such cases, they do not tell us exactly what to believe; rather, they point to the dangers of a number of positions and assertions. First, there is a fence that tells us, as Augustine quite clearly told his contemporaries, that God's grace is freely given—*gratia gratis data*. Christians have no right to claim that God has accepted them because of something they have done or something they have decided or a point of doctrine they have believed. God's grace is God's to bestow, and not ours to handle. Second, while we cannot claim credit for having believed, neither can we blame others for not having believed. The difference between faith and unfaith is not in some human action or decision. It is this that the doctrines of predestination and of irresistible grace seek to remind us. This is important in our day, when believers are so often tempted to take the title of "Christian" as a sign of special virtue, or of something we have done, and when as a result we judge others who disagree with us with what amounts to a most unchristian spirit. Third, we must affirm that humans are endowed by God with freedom of the will and that we are therefore responsible for our actions. Fourth, and probably most important, we are incapable of bringing together the three previous points into a coherent and logical whole, and to do this in such a way that does not do violence to one of them. How they come together is for God to determine. Ours is a limited vision and understanding. We are like a person looking out of a window and seeing an eave pointing in one direction, and then looking out of another window and seeing an eave going in a different direction. We know that these somehow meet. We know it because the roof that we see so imperfectly somehow keeps the rain out. Yet exactly how and where they meet must be left for another time when we are able to stand outside and look at the whole house from a perspective that for the present time we cannot have.

For Further Reading

Anderson, Ray S. *On Being Human: Essays on Theological Anthropology.* Grand Rapids: Eerdmans, 1982.
Brunner, Emil. *Man in Revolt: A Christian Anthropology.* New York: C. Scribner's, 1939.

Burns, J. P., ed. *Theological Anthropology*, in the series *Sources of Early Christian Thought*. Philadelphia: Fortress Press, 1981.
Moltmann, Jürgen. *Man*. Philadelphia: Fortress, 1971.
Niebuhr, Reinhold. *The Nature and Destiny of Man*. Louisville: Westminster John Knox Press, 1996.

Notes

1. *On First Principles,* 1.5; 2.1
2. *On Spectacles,* 2.
3. *Confessions,* 8.17.
4. *Confessions,* 10.29.
5. *Sermon* 131.
6. *A History of Christian Thought,* vol. 2 (Nashville: Abingdon Press, 1987), 113.

6.

CHRIST

In Christ God was reconciling the world to himself . . .
2 Corinthians 5:19

As was the case with most other doctrines, the church long believed about Christ, and expressed in worship, what it eventually sought to clarify in doctrine. Even the earliest Christian writings, first the epistles of Paul and later the rest of the New Testament—and early Christian literature after that—are unanimous on the point that Jesus of Nazareth is the Christ, God's anointed One, the Messiah, and also that it is through him that believers are redeemed. Later developments of doctrine would revolve around these two points: first, who Jesus is; and, second, how he saves. In more technical language, these two general themes are often called the "person" and the "work" of Christ. Since the matter of the "person" was the subject of debate long before the "work," in this chapter we shall look first at the person, and then at the work of Christ.

The Person of Jesus

As far as anyone can tell, the earliest preaching of the new movement that eventually came to be known as "Christianity" focused on Jesus of Nazareth as the fulfillment of the hope of Israel, that God would send an "anointed one"—in Hebrew, the Messiah—to redeem the nation. This was the point at issue between the more traditional Jewish leaders and the preachers of the new sect. They agreed on the Scriptures of Israel, and many believed that the Messiah would come—and even that he would come soon. Where they disagreed was on the claim of this new sect, that Jesus of

111

Nazareth, whom the religious leadership in Jerusalem had turned over to the Romans, and whom the latter had crucified as a common criminal or a subversive, was the long-awaited Messiah. This disagreement—and its possible political consequences if Rome became convinced that Judaism, like Jesus, was subversive—was the main reason the religious authorities in Jerusalem tried to suppress the new sect. Partly as a result of that attempt, however, the new sect expanded first beyond the confines of Palestine and then even beyond the confines of Judaism itself, making converts among the Gentiles.

In that mission to the Gentiles, the missioners of the new sect had to use mostly the Greek language, which was the common tongue of trade and communication throughout the Eastern portion of the Roman Empire. In Greek, "anointed" or "Messiah" is *Christos*, and therefore an important part of the message of the new sect was that Jesus was the anointed, the *Christos* of God. This was such an important element in their proclamation, that very soon they came to be known as "Christians," that is, followers or servants of the *Christos*. According to Acts, this new name was first given to them in Antioch, where some Jewish followers of the new sect—what Acts calls "the way"—began preaching to the Gentiles. As a result, it became customary for Christians to speak of their Savior as "Jesus Christ"—Jesus the anointed. Very soon what had originally been an adjective or a participle, "Christ," became a name, so that people began referring to Jesus simply as "Christ." As has already been mentioned, early in the second century pagan governor Pliny wrote that Christians gathered, among other things, "to sing hymns to Christ as God."

Thus, Christians were very clear that there was something special about Jesus and that this was from God. However, exactly how this was to be understood was not altogether clear. On this matter, there were two extremes that the early church soon rejected. On the one hand, there were those who said that Jesus was a mere human, much like the prophets of old, in whom the Spirit of God had dwelt, and that, apparently by reason of his faithfulness, God adopted him as Son. These were called "Ebionites," from a Hebrew word meaning "pure," because they taught that Jesus was a great teacher of purity and that to follow him was essentially to be pure like him.

On the other extreme, there were those who claimed that Jesus was a purely celestial or spiritual being and that he only seemed to be human and to have a body. These were called "Docetists," from a Greek word that means "to appear," because they taught that Jesus was human only in appearance. Obviously, such views tended to agree with the notion that God had not created the material world. If matter is evil, it makes sense to claim that the Savior did not have a physical body. It is probably against such notions that the Old Roman Symbol—an earlier form of our Apostles' Creed—insisted on the true sufferings of Jesus: "suffered under Pontius Pilate, was crucified, dead, and buried."

As a result of their struggle with these two extremes, Christians were soon convinced that it was necessary to affirm both that Jesus is fully human and that he is more than human. Returning to what was said earlier, to the effect that doctrines are like foul lines in a playing field, not attempting to determine exactly what is to be said, but warning about dangers or unforeseen consequences that may follow from certain positions, the church had very early determined that two of these fences were, first, that Jesus of Nazareth was truly and fully human; and, second, that he could not be described merely in terms of his humanity, for God was present in him in a unique way. Exactly what this meant was not the focus of major debate until the fourth century, when the conversion of Constantine and most of his successors put an end to persecutions. Even then, for the first few years theological debate centered on the matter of the divinity of the Word that was incarnate in Jesus, as we saw in chapter 4. That controversy led to the declaration (in the councils of Nicea, 325, and Constantinople, 381) that the Word or Logos who was incarnate in Jesus is not a lesser being, but is "true God of very God." Now another foul line was drawn: Jesus must be said to be not only fully human, but also fully divine.

All of this meant that, once the matter was settled of the full divinity of the Word of God, theologians would necessarily turn to the question, which flows almost inevitably from the previous controversy, of how the divine and the human are united in Jesus—in other words, how it is possible to speak of a God-human.

What made this question particularly difficult was that, following the lead of Greek philosophy, the church had come to think of God in terms that are incompatible with a human being. On the one hand, God is omnipotent, omniscient, omnipresent, immutable, and so on. Being human, on the other hand, implies the opposite. Humans are limited in their power and in their knowledge. Humans are also limited in that they cannot be in more than one place at a time. And, in contrast with the immutability of God, for a human being to live is to change. The incarnation of God in a human being, which in any case would have been a mystery, was turned into a logical contradiction. To ask someone to explain how it is that the divine can be human was like walking up to a soda fountain and asking for hot ice cream!

Two Schools of Thought

Thus the stage was set for bitter controversies. To summarize the development and outcome of these controversies, one may say—at the risk of some oversimplification—that they took place mostly in the Greek-speaking East, which was divided into two camps, and that the Latin-speaking West, less inclined to theological speculation and more concerned with the actual life of believers, took an intermediate position between the two eastern camps. Thus, while the two schools prevalent in the East vied with each other for supremacy, the West, under the leadership of Rome, played a moderating influence, with the result that when the conflicts were eventually settled, Rome had gained great prestige, while the traditional centers of Christian theology in the East had lost much of theirs.

The two prevalent and competing approaches in the East centered on the cities of Alexandria and Antioch, and therefore historians speak of an "Alexandrine" and an "Antiochene" theology—a contrast that has often been exaggerated, but which nevertheless helps illuminate the issues at stake.

Alexandria had long been a center of learning and of philosophical inquiry. By the time of the advent of Christianity, it had clearly superseded Athens in that role. While the city and its schools were places where religions and philosophies from all over the Mediterranean world, and even from Persia, met and mingled, the dominant philosophy in Alexandria was Neoplatonism, which was actually born in that city with the teachings and writings of Plotinus (205–270). As a result, Alexandrine Christian theologians were inclined to interpret Christianity in terms of Neoplatonic philosophy—much as Jewish philosopher Philo of Alexandria had sought to interpret Judaism in terms that were compatible with the prevailing Platonism of his time. Since to them Jesus was first and foremost a teacher, a guide into the heavenly realities, what was important to them was that Jesus be truly a representative from on high, that he be truly and fully divine. For them, the humanity of Jesus was the means whereby he accomplished this, his means of communicating with us. Therefore, if the difficulties implied in the notion of a God made human required it, they were more willing to sacrifice some elements of the humanity of Jesus than to distinguish between the divinity and the humanity in such a way that the latter could not be a true instrument for communication of the former. For this reason, historians often describe Alexandrine Christology as "unitive"— insisting on the real union between the divine and the human. When faced with the question of how the humanity of Jesus could be preserved without being swallowed up in the divinity, the Alexandrines would tend to speak of Jesus having all the components of a human being, without the limitations. (Coming back to our image of hot ice cream, they would tend to list the ingredients of ice cream, put all or most of them in a bowl, and heat the result, claiming that they had produced hot ice cream.)

For their part, Antiochene theologians also showed signs of being influenced by their environment. Antioch, in Syria, was closer to Galilee and to the historical sites of the Jewish tradition. People traveled from Antioch to Palestine regularly. They saw the actual places of which the Gospels speak. The large Jewish community in the city had close contacts with Palestine, and therefore so did the Christian community. The city was also a center of historical and literary studies. As a result, Antiochene Christian theologians were much more interested in the actual history of Jesus of Nazareth than their Alexandrine counterparts. For them, the humanity of Jesus—the humanity that walked in the well-known roads of Galilee and Judea—was not to be denied or diminished. First and foremost, one must affirm that Jesus was fully human. Still, as most in their time, they had accepted the notion that the best way to speak of God is as impassible, immutable, and so on. How can such a God be truly human, when to be human implies a series of characteristics that are diametrically opposed to all that is to be said about God? (Once again, the problem of hot ice cream!) The Antiochenes sought to respond to this question by proposing positions in which, while Jesus is both divine and human, the divinity is not allowed to impinge on the humanity. The two are joined, but in such a way that the divine does not affect the human, or vice versa. Thus, historians who describe Alexandrine Christology as "unitive" refer to its Antiochene counterpart as "disjunctive." In the context of our metaphor of "hot ice cream," it would seem that the Antiochenes have solved our difficulties: baked Alaska! The secret of a baked Alaska is to put the ice cream on a layer of cake, cover it with a thick layer of meringue, and then place it in a very hot oven. The outside comes out hot and even toasted, while the ice cream does not melt. The two go together. They are indissolubly bound to each other—as are the components of a baked Alaska. Yet, the two are still two, and not really one.

In the West, the christological debate was never the burning issue that it was in the East. At the time when the East was discussing Christology, the West was much more interested in the issues posed by the debate between Augustine and Pelagius that we saw in the last chapter. For a long time, Western theologians had affirmed that Jesus is both divine and human and that these two are united in one. Around the year 200, two centuries before the controversy erupted in the East, the first major Christian writer in Latin, Tertullian, had spoken of Jesus as having "two natures" in "one substance." Exactly what Tertullian meant by that is not clear. His formula was generally forgotten until Augustine revived it. Yet, significantly, this was very close to what eventually became the formula of orthodox Christology: "two natures in one person." In any case, it is clear that the West was not particularly interested in the matter of how the divine could become human. It felt the need to affirm—as Tertullian had done before, and as had become the common view of Christians everywhere—that Jesus is both fully divine and fully human, and that these two are united in such a way that they cannot be separated. Thus, Western Christology had some of the "unitive" emphasis of Alexandrine Christology, but it was not ready to allow this to diminish the full humanity of Jesus.

One of the first to offer a solution to the problem of the incarnation of God in a human being was Alexandrine theologian Apollinaris of Laodicea. Apollinaris began with the commonly held notion that human beings are composed of three constituent parts:

the body, the "soul"—by which he did not mean what today we call "soul," but simply the element that gives life to a body, which may be human, animal, or even plant—and the "rational soul"—which was what today is commonly known as the mind. According to Apollinaris, Jesus has a human body and "soul," but not a human rational soul. While the body of Jesus and the principle that gave it life were human, his mind was divine. In proposing this, Apollinaris was simply stating clearly and bluntly what some other Christians had thought before him—and what many still think—although they had never given much thought to the matter and its consequences. However, once this view is expressed as clearly as Apollinaris expressed it, immediate problems arise. Can one really say that Jesus was human if he had no human mind and never thought like a human? If Jesus became human in order to free humankind from its sins, how could he do that if he did not assume a full human being? Is it not in the mind or soul that most sin resides? Does the soul not need to be saved? What difference, then, does an incarnation make that does not include a full human being?

Were we to look at Apollinaris's position on the basis of our earlier metaphor of hot ice cream, it is as if a full serving of ice cream consisted of a scoop each of vanilla, strawberry, and chocolate. Apollinaris would solve the problem of hot ice cream by serving us a scoop of vanilla and a scoop of strawberry, but then substituting a scoop of hot chocolate syrup for the third scoop. It may sound good, but it is no longer a full serving of ice cream. Something of the ice cream has been lost in order to be able to claim that it is hot.

Apollinaris put forth this view toward the end of the Arian controversy (see chapter 4), resulting in the Council of Constantinople in 381—the same council that reaffirmed the decisions of Nicea and that therefore marks the end of the Arian controversy—rejecting it, affirming that Jesus did have a human "rational soul." Thus what would have seemed a fairly simple solution from the Alexandrine side of the debate was rejected, and it seemed that Antiochene theology had won the upper hand.

However, things changed early in the next century. In the year 428 Nestorius, who was patriarch of Constantinople, came to the defense of some Antiochenes who had declared that Mary should not be called "mother of God," but only "mother of Christ." Although it may seem to us today that this had to do mostly with Mary's special role—and it probably did in the minds of many of the faithful—what was at stake in the ensuing debate was not so much who Mary is, but who is this Jesus who is also said to be God. Following the traditional Antiochene "disjunctive" Christology, Nestorius declared that there are certain things that may be said about Jesus as human, and certain things that may be said about him as divine. It was the man who walked in Galilee, wept on the death of Lazarus, and suffered thirst on the cross. Therefore, it is incorrect to say that God walked in Galilee or that God wept or that God suffered or—and this was the crux of the controversy—that God was born of Mary's womb. In the Savior, there are not only two natures, divine and human; there are also "two persons" (two subjects of predication), and one must attribute some things to the divine person, and some others to the human. These two must be kept distinct and even separate, for if the union is too close, the divinity will eclipse the humanity, and rather than God made human, we would have God obliterating the human. Nestorius's solution to the christological dilemma is to protect the full humanity of Jesus by isolating it from the divinity, just as in a baked Alaska there are certain things one can say about the inner core of ice cream and others one can say about the heat outside.

This was pointed out by Nestorius's main opponent, Cyril of Alexandria, patriarch of that city and a staunch defender of the traditional Alexandrine Christology. According to Cyril, if there are some things that can be said of the divinity in Jesus, and some things that can be said of his humanity, then we have two different subjects, and there is no real union. The union in Christ must be more than "moral"—a phrase that Nestorius had used. In Christ there is only one subject, and whatever is said of him is said of him as a single person, and not of part of him. To use Cyril's phrase, there must be a "sharing of predicates"—the traditional theological phrase is *communicatio idiomatum*. Without such sharing, one cannot really say that God came to us in Jesus, nor that his sufferings have any particular significance beyond the tragedy of the sufferings of a good man.

The debate grew increasingly bitter and even malicious. Each side collected all its resources, theological as well as political. The emperor became involved. In the year 431, the Council of Ephesus sided with Cyril against Nestorius, who was deposed; but a rival—

although much smaller—council took the opposite position. Seeking to bring some sanity into the matter, the authorities had both principals arrested. Eventually, mostly through imperial pressure, an uneasy compromise was reached—although Nestorius was never restored to his see.

The unstable truce did not last. Less than two decades after the compromise, both sides were at it again. Now the issue was the doctrine of a monk named Eutyches, whose theology was clearly Alexandrine, but whose exact position is not clear to this day. Apparently, he held that in Jesus are all the components of a human being, but that he had never been a man, for these components existed only in their conjunction with the divine. He clearly held that in the Savior there is not only one person, but also "one nature." This is typical Alexandrine Christology, in which the "hot ice cream" problem is solved by mixing all the ingredients of ice cream and bringing them to a boil, but never freezing them.

Intrigue prevailed once again. The palace chamberlain, who practically ran the empire for the weak and incompetent Theodosius II, was bought with Alexandrine gold. A council was called in 449, and the Antiochenes were not even allowed to express their views. From Rome, Pope Leo (known as Leo the Great) sent a letter that was not allowed to be read. All the Antiochenes were declared heretics and deposed. In Rome, Leo fumed against what he called the "robbers' synod." Then the emperor died in an accident. His successors, Pulcheria and Marcian, heeded the protests of the pope and many others, and a new council was called.

This council (now recognized by most churches as the Fourth Ecumenical Council) met in Chalcedon, a city across the straits from Constantinople, in 451. There was ample discussion of the issues. Most of the leaders of both the Antiochene and the Alexandrine parties expressed their opinions. The letter from Leo was read. (Leo himself was not present.) In the end, the Council decided to issue *Definition of Faith*—not a creed, for they felt that there should be no other creed than the Nicene. This is very far from being a creed, or even a statement that could really be used in worship—as the Nicene has been to this day. *Definition*'s purpose was rather to set the bounds of orthodoxy. This it did with words that excluded both the Antiochene and the Alexandrine extremes: "we jointly declare it should be confessed that our Lord Jesus Christ is one and the same

God...of one substance to us as to his humanity; in all things except sin like unto us...one and the same Christ, Son, Lord, Only-begotten, manifested in two natures without confusion, without change, without division, without separation...the difference of natures not disappearing because of the union...not divided into two persons."

This may sound like pure mumbo jumbo; and, if taken as an attempted explanation or description of the incarnation, that is exactly what it is. But the purpose of the *Definition* of Chalcedon is not to explain the incarnation, nor even to propose a particular solution to the problem being discussed. It is rather to set the boundaries for discussion. Looking again at our metaphor of doctrines as foul lines on a playing field, or fences atop a mesa, what Chalcedon did, rather than describe the incarnation or determine the exact content of Christian belief on the matter, was to set a number of fences beyond which an important aspect of the faith was denied. (Etymologically, the word "definition," which was part of the title given to their decision, actually means "to set limits.") These limits are essentially three: Jesus is fully human ("of one substance to us as to his humanity; in all things except sin like unto us"); Jesus is fully divine ("one and the same God"); Jesus is one ("not divided into two persons").

After Chalcedon

As could be expected, the decisions at Chalcedon did not put an end to the discussion. Even apart from purely theological matters, there was too much dissension within the Eastern Roman Empire, and this dissension often took the form of theological disagreement. Yet, even though the debate persisted for some time, the *Definition* of Chalcedon held, and its "fences" have been respected by most Christian theologians since that time. There were a number of churches that broke away from the rest of the church, refusing to accept the Chalcedonian formula. Such are, for instance, the Church of Ethiopia, the Coptic Church, and the Syrian Jacobite Church. Yet, even in these cases, the disagreement was more with imperial policy than with doctrine, and many today believe that the christological differences among these churches are verbal rather than substantial.

After that time, there were still significant differences among theologians as to how the incarnation was to be understood. Luther, for instance, tended to stress the unity of the Savior, much as the Alexandrines had done before, although always remaining within the Chalcedonian limits. (Also, in contrast with the ancient Alexandrines, Luther's emphasis on the unity of the Savior did not lead him to question or to limit his full humanity. Luther was convinced that the best way to know God is not through some preconceived philosophical notion of the divine, but rather to see God in the sufferings and humiliation of the cross.) In contrast, Calvin leaned more toward the Antiochenes, making the distinction between the divine and the human more marked than did Luther.

It was, however, in the Modern Age that the decisions of Chalcedon were more severely criticized. The notion that a human being could also be divine in a unique sense was not acceptable to modern rationalism. Therefore, liberal theologians, while disagreeing widely among themselves, generally agreed that Christology had to be revisited, and new ways had to be found to speak of the uniqueness of Jesus and his centrality for Christian faith. Thus, various liberal theologians spoke of Jesus as a great moral teacher, as a man of profound insight into the crux of the religion of Israel, as a harsh critic of that religion, as a man of unequaled charisma whose very presence awed those around him, as a man of compassion, and so on.

This process crystalized in the "quest for the historical Jesus," in which scholars sought to discover, behind the Gospels and other documents expressing the faith of early Christianity, the historical and purely human figure of Jesus as he would have appeared to those who met him. In this endeavor, they claimed and were convinced they were using the most sophisticated, objective, and "scientific" methods possible. And yet, as one now looks at their findings, it is clear that the Jesus these scholars discovered was very much a reflection of the ideals of the society in which they lived. Thus, Alsatian theologian Albrecht Schweitzer, after a careful review of the work of these scholars, concluded:

> It is a good thing that the true historical Jesus should overthrow the modern Jesus, should rise up against the modern spirit and send upon the earth, not peace, but a sword. He was not a teacher, not a casuist; He was an imperial ruler.

121

He comes to us as One unknown, without a name, as of old, by the lakeside. He came to those men who knew Him not. He speaks to us the same word: "Follow me!" and sets us to tasks which He has to fulfill for our time. He commands. And to those who obey Him, whether they be wise or simple, He will reveal Himself in the toils, the conflicts, the sufferings which they shall pass through in His fellowship, and, as an ineffable mystery, they shall learn in their own experience Who He is.[1]

Shortly after Schweitzer wrote these words, a revival of theology commonly associated with the name of its initiator, Karl Barth (1886–1968), began seeking to recover the value and the significance of the decisions of Chalcedon and the other early councils. Eventually, this revival of Chalcedonian orthodoxy spread throughout most of the Christian community—although often seeking to respect and affirm the "fences" set up by Chalcedon without using its metaphysical presuppositions or its exact formulations. Typical of this new movement was Dietrich Bonhoeffer, who commented that even though the nineteenth century set out to depict Jesus in purely human terms, it actually turned him into some sort of a superman, a supposedly human being that could not have existed in the first century, and that in so doing, rather than depicting Jesus as human, the effect was exactly the opposite.

Jesus as Savior

Just as Israel knew God first as Redeemer and then as Creator, so did the early church first know Jesus as Lord and Savior, and then begin thinking about what this meant in christological terms. Thus, in the order of Christian experience, the "work" of Christ precedes all debates about his "person." Certainly, from the very beginning the church proclaimed Jesus as its Savior, and in the patristic age there had been a variety of views as to how Christ saves sinners. But the matter of the "work" of Christ—how it is that Christ saves us— did not become a subject of significant theological debate until the twelfth century.

As one looks back at the patristic age, it becomes apparent that each of the various christological positions outlined in the first half of this chapter is most amenable to a particular interpretation of the work of Christ. Thus, if one believes that the main work of Christ consists in bringing wisdom or illumination to the world, one will emphasize his divine origin, and his body will be only the means whereby he accomplishes his mission. This was clearly the position of the Docetists, whose teachings the church rejected quite early, and also of the Alexandrines, who could not understand why their Antiochene critics were so concerned about affirming the full humanity of Jesus. Apollinaris, for instance, was satisfied that his proposal, which deprived Jesus of a human mind, did not really threaten anything important, for such a Jesus could still communicate the message of love and invite sinners to follow him. If one believes—as did many Antiochenes—that what Christ does is to become the head of a new humanity, to assume humanity so that it can be brought back to God, then it is of paramount importance that he be fully human. As some of the opponents of Apollinaris would say, if Jesus did not have a human soul, how can his incarnation save our souls?

These differences regarding the work of Christ remained in the background of theological debate, and once the parameters of orthodox Christology were settled at Chalcedon, there was no need to discuss them or to seek a consensus on them.

It was as a result of an intellectual renaissance that took place in Europe beginning in the eleventh century, but flourishing in the twelfth, that the work of Christ became a subject of controversy. Before the controversy broke out, and to a measure providing the background for the controversy itself, Anselm of Canterbury (1033–1109) wrote a book asking himself why God had become human—*Cur Deus homo?* Anselm had no doubts regarding the incarnation or Christ's saving work; but he felt that when one really loves, one seeks to understand the beloved. Thus, his book was not one of theological controversy, nor even in the strict sense, of theological construction; it was rather a book of theological devotion. Anselm began from the proposition that since God is the Creator of all, all owe God all that they are or can be, as well as all that they have or can have. Humanity owes its all to God, so that all we can do, even at our very best, is render to God what is already due to God. What, then, if we commit a sin? How can we ever pay, if all we have we already owe to God? To make matters worse, sin is an offense against the infinite Almighty, and therefore even the slightest sin is an infinite offense. How can we, finite beings as we are, ever pay the infinite debt we have contracted with God? Obviously, the only one who can pay such a debt to God is God, who alone is infinite. But it is not fitting for God to pay a debt that is in reality a human debt. It is for this reason that God has become human, so that by the sacrifice on the cross the God-man Jesus can make an infinite, yet human payment for the debts of all humankind.

Anselm's theory of atonement has often been called the "juridical" theory, for the obvious reason that it is based on notions of debt and payment, honor and offense. It is also called "substitutionary atonement," for Jesus saves believers by taking their place in the payment for sin. In this view, the saving work of Christ takes place mostly at the cross, and Jesus Christ is the victim in a cosmic sacrifice.

A few decades after Anselm, Peter Abelard (1079–1142) also considered the matter of how it is that Christ saves us. His response, however, was very different from that of Anselm. What Jesus has done, Abelard would say, is to give us an unforgettable lesson in love and an overwhelming sign of God's love for us. The cross saves us because it draws us away from our own petty concerns and our fears of God's wrath—which leads us to hide from God—and brings us back to the love of God. God did not need to be reconciled. God did not demand payment for a debt. God has always loved us. We are the ones who forget or doubt that love, and who therefore need to be reminded and shown that God is indeed loving, and all we have to do is return that love.

Abelard's theory of atonement has often been called the "subjective" or "moral" theory of atonement, for it is not based on the objective work of Christ on the cross, as is Anselm's, but rather on the moral effect that the cross and the entire life of Jesus make on believers. In this view, the saving work of Christ takes place mostly at the cross, but also throughout his life and teachings; and Jesus is seen primarily as an example and a teacher, the visual and emotional demonstration of God's love for us.

Although there is no doubt that through the ages the church has thought of Christ as an example to be followed, it has seldom accepted this as a full explanation of his saving work. Among other reasons, to say that all Jesus does is to set an example for us, so that we may then act lovingly and be saved, implies that we are capable of our own salvation. The controversy between Augustine and

Pelagius had led the church at large to the conclusion that this is not so, that our salvation is beyond the reach of our actions or even our will to be saved. This means that we need more than an example or a teacher so that we may gain salvation. We need someone who can grant us a salvation we cannot achieve on our own. Abelard's proposal—and many other similar ones in later times—requires that we have the power to be saved if we only have the right example or the right inspiration, and this is a view that had been generally rejected since the times of Augustine, seven centuries earlier. This is why the synod that rejected the teachings of Abelard included among such teachings the notion "that free will suffices to do some good."

When Bernard of Clairvaux (1090–1153) learned of Abelard's opinions, he was shocked. Bernard himself was a saintly man, respected all over western Europe for his piety and his eloquent preaching. He was also a powerful and rather intolerant man, the great preacher of the Second Crusade, a man to whom kings and popes looked for advice and support. Bernard correctly felt that Abelard's theory strayed from the traditional teaching of the church regarding the work of Christ. It was not that the church had not seen Jesus as the great example and demonstration of God's love—which it had. It was rather that Abelard's theory reduced the work of Christ to this role as a teacher and an example and left aside other important aspects of Christian teaching on redemption.

Bernard had other reasons for enmity against Abelard, who seemed to him an extremely arrogant man, daring to question the traditional doctrines of the church, and bringing philosophy and logic to bear on religion in an illegitimate way. So Bernard had a synod called (1141), and this synod rejected the doctrines of Abelard.

Significantly, however, what the council objected to was not that Abelard denied Anselm's theory. What the council rejected was Abelard's view that "Christ did not come to free us from the yoke of the Devil."[2] This points to a third, more common view of the work of Christ. According to this view, Christ is neither the victim who pays for sin (Anselm), nor the example who shows us the way (Abelard), but the conqueror who defeats the powers of evil. As we look at the earliest Christian writings, we see that an important— probably the most important—aspect of the work of Christ is as a conqueror who defeats evil and thus breaks the bondage of humankind to evil and its powers. In those cases in which the notion of paying "ransom" appears, this is usually paid not to the justice of God, as in Anselm, but rather to the devil, who because of sin had a right of ownership over humanity. Most often, however, the imagery is one of victory. In the cross, the devil thought that he had conquered Jesus, and took him to hell as his possession; but in the resurrection Jesus broke forth, destroying the stronghold of the devil, and opening the way for those who are joined to him as his body— the church.

It was Swedish theologian Gustaf Aulén who in a famous book, *Christus Victor*—Christ the Conqueror—published in 1931, called the attention of theologians and historians to this other view, which is certainly prevalent in the early church, and which continued being the primary image for speaking of the saving work of Christ until well into the Middle Ages. It is for this reason that when Bernard had the synod of 1141 condemn Abelard, the fault they found with his doctrine was not, as we would expect, that he rejected Anselm's theory of the sufferings of Jesus as payment for sin, but rather that, according to Abelard, "Christ did not take the flesh in order to free us from the yoke of the Devil."

This third, and apparently much older, view of the atoning work of Christ, rather than focusing its attention on the payment of the cross (as did Anselm), or on the example of Jesus (as did Abelard), sees the work of Christ as beginning with the incarnation, continuing throughout the life and death of Jesus, but coming to its culmination in the Resurrection and the Ascension. Thus, while in the other two views, Christ saves because he is a victim, in this other view he saves because he is a victor—although in Bernard's devotion, even this victory of Christ revolved around his suffering and his death.

Life Reflected in Worship, and Worship in Theology

There is a connection between all of this and the worship of the church, for, once again, the development of doctrine often follows the directions and experiences of worship. In the very early church, worship centered on the Eucharist, and this was not so much a remembrance of the cross of Jesus as it was a celebration of his resurrection and of his promised return in victory. This is why the church gathered early Sunday mornings, the "day of the Lord," the day of Resurrection. The early Eucharistic services were not of lamentation or of repentance, but rather of celebration. Christians were a small and often persecuted minority in the midst of one of the largest empires the world had ever seen. In that setting, the church lived by the conviction that their Lord had conquered the greatest powers of evil and would in the end conquer every power of oppression, idolatry, and injustice.

Then, soon after the church became powerful by being espoused by the state, difficult times arrived, particularly in the West. For several centuries, it was a time of invasion after invasion, of frequent famine, and of epidemics that repeatedly decimated the population. In that setting, Christian worship focused on the need to repent for sins, and in a Jesus who had suffered just as the population at large now suffered. It was a funereal age, and as a consequence the worship of the church took increasingly funereal tones. Although the Eucharist was still celebrated on Sundays, the mood was better suited for Fridays. It no longer centered on the Resurrection, but rather on the cross. Increasingly, Jesus became no longer the Victor who conquers all evil, but rather the Victim who is offered in communion in expiation for human sin and in an effort to avert the consequences of such sin.

This was the general mood of the church during the times of Anselm and Abelard. Bernard, Abelard's nemesis, focused much of his own devotional life on the sufferings of Christ. Thus, although disagreeing radically on their interpretation of the work of Christ, all three reflected the worship of their time and thus centered their attention on the work of Christ as Victim.

It is also significant to note that each of these views reflects a different understanding of the human predicament, as discussed in chapter 5. If the human predicament is owing a debt to God, Christ's saving work will consist in paying that debt. If the human predicament is lack of will or of direction to do the will of God, Christ will be an example or a guide for doing that will. If the human predicament is one of enslavement to sin and to the powers of evil, Christ will be the conqueror who destroys those powers.

Anselm's view of the work of Christ as "substitutionary atonement" soon prevailed. Although it was not explicitly promulgated as

127

official doctrine of the church, it stands behind most of the theology of the later Middle Ages as well as of the Council of Trent (1545–1563). According to Aulén, Luther revived the view of Christ as conqueror—which is partly true. Yet very soon most of traditional Protestantism accepted Anselm's theory as the traditional, orthodox view. This was particularly true of the theologians of the seventeenth and eighteenth centuries, often called the "Protestant scholastics."

It was late in the nineteenth century, and early in the twentieth, that a number of ecclesiastical bodies, mostly in the United States, adopted substitutionary atonement as a standard of orthodoxy. This was mostly a reaction against the liberalism of the nineteenth century, which rejected substitutionary atonement in favor of Abelard's theory of atonement as moral example. Thus, when Fundamentalism arose, one of the five "fundamentals" of orthodox Christianity that gave the movement its name was substitutionary atonement. A number of church bodies—mostly in the United States—declared themselves in favor of this theory and rejected any other option as heretical. This is the reason why for many of us the "traditional" view of the work of Christ is some version of Anselm's theory.

Contemporary Relevance

In more recent times—in part as a result of Aulén's book, but more as a revival of early Christian worship and theology—the notion of Christ as the conqueror of the powers of evil has once again come to the foreground. This may be seen in many of the Eucharistic liturgies of the late twentieth and early twenty-first centuries, which rather than focusing on the cross as the place where the Victim is sacrificed for us, focuses on the resurrection as the event in which the Victor's power is manifested and works for our salvation.

This has obvious practical implications for our faith and the way we live it. If Christ saves us by being the victim in a cosmic sacrifice, then our task as Christians is also to allow ourselves to be victimized. The prevalence of this view of atonement in much of contemporary Christianity may well contribute to the passivity of many Christians before suffering and abuse. If Christ saves by taking abuse meekly, his followers should be expected to do likewise. If Christ saves us by setting an example, then our task as Christians is to improve our moral life, to follow the example of righteousness and love set by Jesus. If Christ is the conqueror over the powers of evil, then our task as Christians is to confront those powers as those who know that in Christ the ultimate victory is ours, even if it means that we must suffer in the way to it. Trusting in the power of the Victor, we may stand firm in opposition even to overwhelming evil, knowing that ultimately his victory is also ours. These various views, and their very different ways of life and attitudes toward the existing order, are connected to different styles and practices of worship and to different views of the church, to which we shall now turn.

For Further Reading

Aulén, Gustaf. *Christus Victor: An Historical Study of the Three Main Types of the Idea of Atonement.* London: S.P.C.K., 1953.

Baillie, D. M. *God Was in Christ: An Essay on Incarnation and Atonement.* London: Faber and Faber, 1948.

Barth, Karl. *The Humanity of God.* Richmond: John Knox Press, 1960.

Pelikan, Jaroslav J. *Jesus through the Centuries: His Place in the History of Culture.* New Haven: Yale University Press, 1985.

Turner, H. E. W. *The Patristic Doctrine of Redemption: A Study of the Development of Doctrine during the First Five Centuries.* London: Mowbray, 1952.

Notes

1. *The Quest of the Historical Jesus: A Critical Study of Its Progress from Reimarus to Wrede* (New York: Macmillan, 1922), 401.

2. *Mansi*, 21:568.

7.

THE CHURCH

The church, which is his body, the fullness
of him who fills all in all.
Ephesians 1:22-23

The principle that worship leads to doctrine—*lex orandi est lex credendi*—is nowhere as clear as when it comes to the doctrine of the church. From the very birth of Christianity, its followers would gather regularly for worship, and considered themselves members of a community that was somehow different from the rest of society. Apparently, for some time they did not even have a name for this community, referring to themselves as the followers of "the way." At some point—still in the first century—they began calling themselves the "assembly," the *ekklesia*. This word became such an important part of their faith and life, that when other Christians began writing in Latin, rather than translating it, they simply took the Greek word in a Latin form, *ecclesia*. Hence the Spanish *iglesia*, the Portuguese *igreja*, the Italian *chiesa*, and the French *église*. (It was in the fourth century that some missionaries among the Goths and other Germanic peoples taught their converts to refer to this body as *kyriakon*—of the Lord—and hence the English "church," the German *Kirche*, the Danish and Norwegian *kirke*, and the like.)

Clearly, the church began reflecting on its own nature and mission at a very early date, and in that sense ecclesiology—the branch of theology dealing with the doctrine of the church—is as old as the church itself. However, while there were repeated disputes as to what or who was the true church, and about its purity, its unity, its authority, its government, its relation to society, and so on, it was not until the Middle Ages that ecclesiology reached its full bloom, or at least its highest view of the church and its authority. It is for this reason that the theology of the church—which already existed implicitly in the very first community—has not occupied our attention in earlier chapters.

The Unity of the Church

Already in New Testament times, the church played a crucial role in the life of believers. The word itself, *ekklesia*, appears repeatedly in the earliest writings of the New Testament—the epistles of Paul. This referred both to the local church—as in "the Church in Corinth"—and to the global body of all these churches. Thus, in Colossians (1:18), Paul declares that Christ "is the head of the body, the church," and many similar statements appear in Ephesians. This dual use of the same word for the local congregation of believers and for the entire body of Christ is not just a matter of the same word being used for two different realities. It is rather a matter of a very real connection between the one and the other, so that believers are part of the universal church because they are also part of the local church. The one universal church, the body of Christ to which Paul refers in his epistles, is known to the Colossians, Corinthians, and others only in the local churches in Corinth, Colossae, and other places.

This poses one of the fundamental questions with which ecclesiology has had to deal repeatedly throughout the centuries: If the church is one, how does that one church relate to the many? Similarly, how does one account for the way Paul speaks of the church in his epistles to the Corinthians, at the same time that he chastises the church in Corinth for incest, idolatry, divisions, ignorance, and injustice? How can a church be the body of Christ, when in its gatherings some eat more than they should, while others go hungry?

For Paul and for the very first generations of Christians this does not seem to have been a problem. Paul himself never even raises the question of how can a sinful and contentious church be the body of Christ. About half a century after Paul, Ignatius, the Bishop of Antioch, wrote seven letters in which one still finds this dual view of the church, apparently without much of a sense of tension between the two. He certainly had a very high concept of the church—even the local church. Thus, in writing to the church in Ephesus he addressed it as "predestined before all time in order to serve forever to the glory of God," and as "chosen by the grace of the real passion [of Christ] and by the will of God the Father and of Jesus Christ our god."[1] He is also the first to use the phrase, "the catholic church."[2] He holds the church to be the body of Christ, to the point that "if any walk in a different mind than the church, they have no share in the passion of the Lord."[3] Yet he is also aware of the shortcomings of the church. Quite possibly, the reason he was on his way to martyrdom was that some from among his own congregation in Antioch had brought him to trial before imperial authorities. This is why he is insistent on the need for all Christians to be subjected to their bishop, "just as Jesus Christ according to the flesh is subject to his Father, and the apostles to Christ and to the Father and to the Spirit."[4] In this way, he declares there will be "unity both in the flesh and in the spirit."[5] In the context of the argument, this would seem to imply that there is unity in the spirit (or the Holy Spirit?) even when Christians bicker with one another, and even when they disagree in matters of doctrine—for in the previous chapter he inveighs against those who tell "old and worthless fables." Apparently, then, Ignatius understands the spiritual unity of the church to be such that human disagreements cannot break it; and yet physical and visible unity—"in the flesh"—is not to be spurned or to be considered of lesser importance.

Not quite half a century after Ignatius, Hermas, whose brother was bishop of Rome, wrote down a series of visions and exhortations that he had apparently preached in Rome. There he speaks of the church as an old lady, for "it was created before all things, and was the reason for the creation of the world."[6] But the church created before every other creature is also a great tower being built by the angels out of stones that are those who have remained faithful.[7] Since the church is the very goal of God's creation, Hermas has very little patience for those—including himself—whose sin sullies the church, and the purpose of much of his writing is to keep the church pure; yet he also realizes that there is an eschatological—a "not yet"—dimension to this purity, for he speaks of the day when "the church of God will be purified, and all those who are undeserving, and the hypocrites, and the blasphemous, and those who hesitate, and the evil ones who practice all sorts of evil, will be cast out, and then it will be a single body, a single thought, a single faith, and a single love." [8]

In short, from the very early times until well into the second century one finds a very high notion of the church as a single entity, the body of Christ, and even as the first of all creatures, the very purpose for which all things were made, existing before there were even Christians. And jointly with such views, sometimes in the same paragraph, one finds a very realistic understanding of a church that exists in dozens of local churches—a church often divided, whose members are not as pure as they should be. How are these two to be reconciled? Already in Ignatius one finds a hint of a distinction between the unity of the church "in the spirit" that cannot be broken, and a unity "in the flesh"—that is threatened when people bicker among themselves or disregard the direction of their bishop or hold strange opinions. Hermas struggles with the two realities of a church created before the foundation of the world in order to be holy, and the very same church as composed of people like himself, much too inclined to sin.

Thus, while Ignatius was very disturbed by divisions in the church, and particularly by doctrinal differences, Hermas was equally disturbed by the persistence of sin within the church. These two, the doctrinal unity and the moral purity of the church, in tension with its disunity and its impurity, would give rise to many a debate and would be the occasion for much ecclesiological reflection.

Unity and Heresy

The doctrinal unity of the church became a burning issue during the second half of the second century, when Gnosticism was making such headway that there was real danger that Christianity would be swallowed in a flood of Gnostic views. The importance of this challenge was such that we have referred to it in the context of many other issues—the canon of Scripture, creation, the relationship between faith and culture, the notion of the soul, and so on. The church responded by insisting on the multiple witness of the evangelists, by developing creedal formulas such as the "Ancient Roman Symbol" (from which the later Apostles' Creed developed), by stressing the authority of bishops as teachers of truth, and in general by paying much attention to the refutation of "heresies" and to the theological formation of all its members. The challenge, however, also had to do with the very reality of the church. The Marcionites as well as most Gnostics created their own communities. Sometimes they called them churches, and sometimes schools; but for all practical purposes they were actually rival churches—sometimes even with rival bishops, a rival baptism, and their own written gospel. Thus, in the late second century the challenge came to a point where new arguments were needed. It no longer sufficed to point to the bishops and their authority, or to the Scriptures and their authority, for these groups did not acknowledge either, with the result that the faithful were constantly forced to decide which bishops, which church, and which Scriptures were true.

It was at this point that the notion of "apostolic succession" developed as an argument supporting the "true church"—the church at large, whose bishops were in communion and general agreement among themselves—and the various groups or churches that made similar claims. The principle of apostolic succession, as first developed late in the second century and early in the third by theologians such as Irenaeus (?–ca. 202) and Tertullian (ca. 155–ca. 220), was quite simple. Marcion claimed that what he taught was the pure and original teaching of St. Paul. Many of the various Gnostic schools claimed that they were continuing the more advanced teaching that Jesus had passed to one of the apostles in secret and that they had somehow received from that apostle.

What can one respond to such a claim? Simply, that whatever Jesus had to teach he taught to the same apostles to whom he entrusted the preaching of the gospel and the founding of churches. And that, if these apostles had received any secret teaching from Jesus, they would have entrusted it to the same people to whom they entrusted the churches they founded. This second generation would have done likewise; and so on, until the present—that is, the late second century or early third. The argument then continued: if you look at the churches founded by the apostles—churches such as Antioch, Rome, and Ephesus—it is reasonable to expect that, if there were any such secret teaching, it would be known by the current bishops of those cities, who can trace a direct line from the apostles to themselves. Yet these bishops agree that there is no such secret doctrine. Furthermore, these churches were not all founded by the same apostle; and still they agree not only on rejecting any notion of a secret doctrine, but also on the essence of what they teach as the gospel. Thus, in cases of doctrinal disagreement—and specifically cases in which people claim that what they are teaching they have received through a secret tradition passed on by some apostle—all one has to do is look at the churches that can claim apostolic succession and see whether they teach this particular doctrine or not.

At first, the notion of apostolic succession did not mean that every bishop or presbyter in every church had to be in a direct line of succession from the apostles. Tertullian clearly stated that those churches that could not claim direct apostolic succession were nevertheless apostolic inasmuch as they agreed in doctrine with the strictly apostolic churches. [9] This was important to him, for he was a Christian in Carthage, where no apostle had even been; and in any case the vast majority of churches in his time could not claim to have been founded directly by an apostle. Yet he also offers another reason for declaring those churches apostolic: even though not founded by an apostle, they are all "the offspring of apostolic churches," either directly or indirectly. [10] Thus, to the question of how these many churches in various parts of the world can be the one church of God, the body and the bride of Jesus Christ, Tertullian would respond that, while existing in different places, they were all joined in the one faith, and that this was the faith of the apostles.

However, the notion of apostolic succession, adduced by Irenaeus and Tertullian as a means to preserve both the purity of doctrine and the doctrinal unity of the church, was the beginning of a process in which apostolic succession, originally a matter of agreement in doctrine, became a matter of an uninterrupted succession by the laying on of hands. This process was reinforced by the practice—existing even before Tertullian—whereby a bishop duly elected by his church, and after sharing his faith with neighboring bishops, was consecrated by a delegation from among those bishops. Slowly, the notion developed that in order to be a proper bishop one had to be consecrated by bishops and that the validity of these other bishops was grounded on their unbroken line of succession from the apostles. Now apostolic succession became not only a matter of agreement in faith, but also a matter of an uninterrupted chain, so that any who could not claim such a chain could not claim a valid ordination.

This became the generally accepted view of apostolic succession, to the point that even at the time of the Reformation many still held

136

that such succession was physical and that ordinations within a church were valid only if those performing such ordinations could claim to be in the direct succession of the apostles. In the Roman Catholic Church, this soon became an argument for its claim that it was the only true church and that Protestant ministers were not properly ordained—which in turn meant that their Eucharistic celebrations were not valid. Calvin rejected such views, declaring that "nothing is more absurd than to lodge the succession in persons alone to the exclusion of teaching. Nothing was farther from the minds of the doctors ... than to prove absolutely, as if by right of inheritance, that the church exists wherever bishops succeed one another." [11] Yet not all Protestants discounted the significance of a physical chain of succession. Several Lutheran bodies—notably the Church of Sweden—whose first bishops had been Catholic bishops before becoming Protestants, long boasted that they had retained apostolic succession. The same claim was made by the Church of England—although insisting, in contrast to the Roman claim basing its authority on Peter, that true apostolic succession was derived from all the apostles. This stress on physical apostolic succession was so strong that in the eighteenth century John Wesley, pressed by believers in North America to send them ministers, did so only on the basis that in the early church there was no distinction between presbyters and bishops, and that therefore he, being an ordained presbyter within the line of apostolic succession, could take on episcopal functions and ordain others to serve in America. Needless to say, this was one of the crucial steps leading to the permanent breach between Methodism and the Church of England.

Unity Through Worship

Still on the subject of how the church can be one at the same time that it is many churches, existing in various parts of the world, it is important to point out that in the early church there was another focus of unity beyond doctrinal agreement. This was the worship of the church. As we shall see in the next chapter, the very heart of that worship was the Eucharist. Although today we tend to think that it is the church that celebrates the Eucharist, in the early church it was also true that it was the Eucharist that creates the church—the church is not a body that decides to worship, but is rather a body created and sustained by its very act of worship. The church is one because it shares the one meal pointing to the final meal at which the whole church will be present. Christians could be scattered over the face of the earth, but in communion they were reminded of the hope expressed in one of the earliest Eucharistic prayers recorded: "As this bread was scattered over the mountains, and gathered has been made one, so may your church be gathered from the ends of the earth into your Kingdom."[12] This unity was symbolized in rituals, both positive and negative. On the positive side, when the church in Rome became too large and too widespread to gather every Sunday in a single place, pieces of bread from the bishop's Eucharist were taken to every other communion service in the city, as a sign that the church is indeed one. Also on the positive side, it was customary to pray in each Eucharistic service for the rest of the church and its leaders. On the negative side, when differences among the churches and their leaders led to a breaking point, that breach was signaled by erasing the names of those with whom one disagreed from the list for the Eucharistic prayers of intercession. Unity was not essentially—as it is for many today—a matter of organization, but rather a matter of worship that was then reflected in the organization of the church.

The Holiness of the Church

The question of how one can claim that these many local churches are indeed the one body of Christ had another dimension beyond the doctrinal and the organizational. This had to do—and still has to do—with the holiness of the church: how can the bride of Christ be pure and immaculate, when sin persists in the local churches? There is no doubt that, even after their conversion and baptism, Christians continue sinning. The early church was well aware of this, and for this reason Christians were often exhorted to repent for their sins, to pray for forgiveness, and to pray for others and to forgive them.

There are, however, sins that put in doubt the holiness of the church. In the second century, Hermas was preoccupied over his own lust, but especially over the sin of those who abandoned or denied the faith under pressure. By the end of the second century, most Christian writers seem to agree that there are three major sins that cannot simply be forgiven on the basis of private repentance and prayer. These are homicide, fornication, and apostasy. The first includes any taking of human life, no matter whether legally or illegally—one of the main reasons Christians frowned on military service. The second includes any disorderly or extramarital sexual activity. The third, denying the faith in any way, particularly by burning incense or otherwise adoring the gods or the statue of the emperor. Although apparently Hermas had thought that there was opportunity for one more act of repentance after baptism, by the beginning of the third century many felt that those who committed any of these three great sins could not be restored to the communion of the church. Perhaps they could be forgiven through an action of martyrdom or by acts of penance carried faithfully until their death. But in any case the purity of the church required that such people be permanently excluded.

There were those, however, who felt that such moral rigor was a denial of the forgiving love that stands at the heart of the gospel. While not saying that such sins were not serious, they argued that Christians can never give up on people, just as God has never given up on them.

The tension between these two principles—the holiness of the church and the call to forgive sinners—has been and still is at the heart of many debates about the nature of the church and how that nature is to be reflected in its life. Already in the first half of the third century, this led to a conflict between two leaders of the church in Rome, Hippolytus and Bishop Callistus. The latter offered those who had been guilty of fornication the opportunity to be restored to the communion of the church—after a long process of repentance and penance. Hippolytus, who represented the more rigorist position, attacked Callistus's stance, and the result was a schism in which both men claimed to be the legitimate bishop of Rome. From North Africa, Tertullian, who also was a rigorist and who eventually left the communion of the church because he felt it was not sufficiently demanding of moral purity, wrote against Callistus, although without mentioning him by name. The schism lasted for some time, until persecution forced the church to deal with more urgent matters. Both Callistus's successor and Hippolytus himself were exiled to the mines, and we are told that they were eventually reconciled. In any case, the schism was soon resolved, and the Roman church came to consider both Callistus and Hippolytus as saints.

A similar schism that arose shortly thereafter, once again in Rome, lasted much longer. In this case, the issue was apostasy rather than fornication. On the rigorist side stood Novatian, whose main opponent was Bishop Cornelius. In the end, Novatian became a rival bishop of Rome, and the schism that ensued lasted well into the fifth century. In North Africa similar debates took place. Roughly at the same time as Novatian, some of those who had endured persecution and stood firm—the "confessors"—felt that bishops such as Cyprian, who had fled and hid during the time of persecution, had no right to restore sinners to the communion of the church, and that it was they, the confessors, who had such a right. In other regions similar issues were debated, frequently resulting in other schisms.

The most significant of these many episodes, however, was the Donatist schism. This emerged in the fourth century, when Constantine put an end to persecution. The last persecution had sought to destroy all copies of Scripture, and a number of bishops and other leaders had complied by handing over the sacred texts. Their opponents called them *traditores*—those who had "turned over" the Scriptures. Once persecution passed, some declared that bishops who had obeyed the decree to turn over the Scriptures were unworthy and that therefore their ordinations and sacraments were invalid. The result was a schism that received the name of "Donatism" after one—or perhaps two—of its main leaders. Soon the theological debate was complicated by ethnic and cultural tension. The more extreme Donatists took up arms against the authorities, who supported the larger church. The schism, that would last until the Muslim invasions, was a very live issue when Augustine became bishop of Hippo, and therefore it was mostly in refuting the Donatists that Augustine developed his ecclesiology.

The Church Visible and Invisible

Augustine understood the church to be central to the gospel. He agreed with Cyprian, bishop of Carthage a century before Augustine's time, who had declared that "outside of the church there is no salvation" [13] and that whoever does not have the church as mother cannot have God as father. [14] By this Cyprian had not meant that one had to obey the dictates of the church, but simply that the Christian faith is communitarian and that therefore the church is an indispensable part of it—that whoever decides to be a Christian alone has embraced an impossible task and that those who simply leave the church because there is something in it they do not like are leaving not only the church, but Christianity itself.

When Augustine took up the challenge of refuting the Donatists, others had done it before him, and therefore much that he said was simply a repetition and an expansion of older arguments. He could also draw on the affirmation of the Nicene Creed—as amended by the Council of Constantinople in 381—that the church is "one, holy, catholic, and apostolic." Indeed, one could say that Augustine's refutation of the Donatists revolves around these four points that eventually came to be called "marks" or "signs" of the church.

Essentially, Augustine and the Donatists agreed that the church is one and that it is holy. They differed as to which of the rival churches was the true one, and also as to where the holiness of the church lies. As in earlier theology, Augustine sees the unity of the church, not so much in organizational terms, as in the sharing of a common Eucharist, during which the church in each place prays for the church elsewhere. He then bases his defense of what he considers to be the one true church on two points, the catholicity and the apostolicity of the church. By "catholicity," he understands the presence of the church everywhere—its universality. Donatism is essentially an African movement, with a few supporters elsewhere. If, in contrast, one looks at the church that the Donatists reject, one sees that this other church—the true church—is present everywhere. By "apostolicity," Augustine means that this church of which he is a part, and which the Donatists reject, can claim an uninterrupted chain of succession linking it to the apostles. In earlier times, this apostolic succession was primarily a matter of agreement in doctrine. However, since in their basic doctrines the Donatists agreed with the faith of the entire church, Augustine tended to understand this apostolicity in terms of physical succession, and of being in communion with a church all of whose leaders could claim that succession.

However, the point at which Augustine most influenced later ecclesiology was in his defense of the holiness of the church, which he based on a distinction between the visible and the invisible church. Cyprian and others had argued that the present church is like a field in which weeds are growing together with the wheat. It is not for us to pull the weeds, but for the Master of the harvest, who in due time will reveal who among those now in the church are truly part of the harvest and who are not. Augustine now systematized and defended this way of understanding the holiness of the church, not as an actual, visible reality, but rather as a reality visible only to the eyes of God. The church we see now is not exactly what the church really is. The church is the company of the elect—remember Augustine's view on predestination—and exactly who these are will be revealed only in the end. The visible church may be riddled with sin; but the invisible is holy.

The Augustinian distinction between the visible and the invisible church has been used by some—particularly some medieval mystics, and later some Protestants—to claim that the visible church is of little or no importance. What is important is not that one be part of the visible church, but rather that one be part of the invisible. Although Augustine would agree with this statement, he would add that the only way people can be part of the invisible church is by being part of the visible. While the two are distinct, there is a clear connection between them. The invisible church exists on earth only as the visible church.

However, during the Middle Ages this Augustinian distinction most often led in the opposite direction. If the church is corrupt, if it does not practice what it preaches, this does not diminish its authority, for the invisible church is still holy and pure. Sin was seen as an unavoidable reality in human life and therefore also in the life of the visible church. All that the church could do was develop a system whereby sinners could repent, be forgiven, and be part of the communion of the church without thereby tainting it with their sin. This is the origin of the penitential system of the medieval church, whose abuses eventually led to the Protestant Reformation—a matter to be discussed in the next chapter.

The emphasis on the distinction and connection between the visible and the invisible church was closely linked to a philosophical development that was taking place precisely as Augustine wrote but that would gain momentum in the next two or three centuries. Augustine himself and many others of his more intellectual contemporaries were profoundly influenced by Neoplatonism. These theologians were attracted to that philosophical school mostly because it spoke of invisible realities beyond the reach of the senses, and also because it made it possible to speak of incorporeal realities, such as the soul and God. Yet we have already seen in the chapter on creation that Neoplatonism also had a strong tendency to see all reality as hierarchical.

Augustine's distinction between the visible and the invisible church made it simple for theologians to think of the invisible church as a reality existing above the visible, untouched by human sin, and communicating with the visible reality of the church by means of a celestial hierarchy. The earthly ecclesiastical hierarchy is a reflection of the celestial hierarchy and therefore is legitimately charged with governing and regulating the life of the visible church, as a reflection of the invisible and of the heavenly hierarchy. As a result, it is possible to characterize most medieval ecclesiology as a reflection on, and defense of, this hierarchical view of the church.

The Church Defines Itself in Its Worship

Doctrines, however, seldom emerge from pure thought or from philosophical speculation. In this case, the emerging view of the church, grounded to an extent on Augustine's distinction between the visible and the invisible church, and on a Neoplatonic view of hierarchy, was also propelled both by worship and by new social and political circumstances.

The worship of the church had been profoundly affected by the new policies set in place by Emperor Constantine and by the resultant new status of Christianity as the religion of the empire. From the fourth century on, there was a marked tendency to make worship more and more elaborate, sometimes imitating the pomp of the imperial court. Bishops and other officers wore rich vestments. The Eucharist ceased to be a celebration by the people, who increasingly became spectators to the holy mysteries performed by the clergy. Eventually people became accustomed to attending worship as spectators, believing that mere attendance gained them the benefits of worship. As worship came to rest more and more on the shoulders of the clergy, so did the church become a clerical institution, to the point that phrases such as "the church teaches" or "the church says" really came to mean "the hierarchy teaches" or "the hierarchy says."

143

Social and political circumstances changed drastically in the fourth and fifth centuries. Shortly after the empire became Christian, the Western portion of the empire collapsed before the invasion of a number of Germanic peoples who sought to settle on imperial lands and to draw the benefits that imperial order seemed to grant, but who had very little idea of what that order entailed. Schools and centers of learning almost disappeared. The collapse of imperial government brought about the loss of many of those elements of Roman life that the invaders had craved. In such a situation, it was the church—more precisely, the learned and organized hierarchy of the church—that became the main avenue for the preservation of an order that seemed to be constantly collapsing. In the city of Rome, for instance, Pope Gregory, often known as Gregory the Great (r. 590–604) took up the responsibilities of the civil administration of the city—the care and rebuilding of the aqueducts, roads, and drainage ditches; the procurement and distribution of food; the care of the sick; and so on. He also worked to preserve life and order throughout much of Western Europe.

Since I have just referred to Gregory as "Pope," this may be the place for a word regarding the origin of that title. "Pope," or *Papa*, was originally a term of endearment and respect given to bishops whose position seemed to merit it. Thus, in the fourth century people spoke of "Pope Athanasius" in Alexandria. In the West, although it had also been used for other respected and loved bishops, it slowly came to be reserved for the bishop of Rome.

Thus the hierarchical view of the church, supported by an increasingly elaborate liturgy, gained further impetus as leaders of the church—particularly the bishop of Rome—took on greater duties in civil administration and therefore also greater authority within the church.

The Church Becomes a Hierarchy

As this hierarchy became increasingly identified with the church—and certainly with the government of the church—it also became the actualization on earth of the invisible church, and even the bridge that allowed the sinful multitudes in the visible church to gain access to the invisible, and thus to life everlasting. The result was a series of

144

actions and declarations on the part of the hierarchy, leading to a growing tension between the ecclesiastical and the civil authorities. It is in this context that one should understand the clashes late in the eleventh century between Pope Gregory VII and Emperor Henry IV—clashes that continued under their successors. By the thirteenth century, under Innocent III (r. 1198–1216), it seemed that the popes had won the struggle, for Innocent was able to determine who was the rightful emperor in a disputed succession, and he intervened in similar fashion in several of the most powerful kingdoms of Europe. By the end of that century, Boniface VIII (r. 1294–1303) issued the bull *Unam Sanctam,* which may be seen as the high point of papal claims. On religious matters, the bull declared that "it is absolutely necessary for salvation that all humans be under the Roman pontiff." On civil government, it stated that God has ordered two powers to which all are subject, the "earthly"—meaning civil—and the "spiritual"—meaning religious. If the former errs, the latter can intervene and correct it; but if the spiritual power errs, only God has the authority to intervene. [15]

Boniface's claims, however, rang hollow, for shortly after this bull was issued he was seriously humiliated by agents of the French crown, and the papacy never recovered the power it had under Innocent III. From that point on, and for two centuries, the papacy became increasingly weak and corrupt, often serving as a tool of French policy, particularly when it left Rome and resided in Avignon (1309–1377), then for a long time (1378–1423) being disputed among rival popes—usually two, but at times three—and finally becoming more devoted to Italian politics and to the embellishment of Rome than to its spiritual and religious functions.

The conciliar movement arose as a response to such decay in the papacy. This movement sought the reformation of the church by calling a series of councils to end the struggle between rival popes and by issuing a series of reforming decrees. It was grounded on a different ecclesiology than what had become dominant at the high point of papal power. In general, the leaders of the conciliar movement argued that the church is not the pope, but the entire body of believers, and that therefore a council of the whole church, representing that whole body, has authority over the pope. It was on this basis that a series of councils gathered in order to end the strife surrounding the papacy and to reform the church, as they said, "root and branches." Eventually, the conciliar movement produced its own demise, by finally appointing popes who could once again lead the church with a strong hand—and several of them committed to the moral reform of the church.

However, the truth is that even the conciliar movement still saw the church as composed essentially of the hierarchy. The councils that claimed to represent the entire church were councils of bishops, not of the faithful nor of their representatives. Indeed, the view of the church as a hierarchy continued prevailing within Roman Catholicism until the Second Vatican Council (1962–1965), which turned to more inclusive language, such as "the people of God" and "the pilgrim people of God."

The Reformation

The ecclesiology of the major Protestant reformers followed the general outlines of Augustine's ecclesiology, particularly in the distinction between the visible church and the invisible. Most Anabaptists rejected this distinction, insisting on the need for the visible church to manifest its holiness in the visible purity of its communal life. But the other reformers did accept Augustine's distinction, while insisting that this is not a reason to abandon the visible church, for the invisible is available to us only in the visible. They saw it rather as a way of distinguishing between the church as it gathers on earth and the company of the elect—for on the subject of predestination both Luther and Calvin agreed with Augustine. The church is one, not because it has a single head on earth, or a single organization, but because it is the one company of the elect. Luther had little difficulty with the holiness of the church, for—as we shall see in chapter 9—he did not believe that the holiness of believers lies in their actions, but rather in their being accepted by God even while they are and remain sinners. Calvin, while not rejecting the four traditional marks of unity, holiness, catholicity, and apostolicity, preferred two other marks: the preaching of the Word and the administration of the sacraments: "Wherever we see the Word of God purely preached and heard, and the sacraments administered according to Christ's institution, there, it is not to be doubted, a church of God exists." [16]

146

Contemporary Relevance

In more recent times, ecclesiology has lost interest among many Christians, for the notion has become common that the church is an institution that believers create in order to support each other in their faith, and perhaps to engage in mission jointly. As earlier ecclesiologies reflected their social and cultural circumstances, this more recent ecclesiology reflects the individualism that is prevalent in Western culture—an individualism that sees society as a conglomeration of individuals, rather than individuals as members of a society. From this perspective, it is believers who create the church, and not vice versa.

This is a valuable corrective to the medieval notions of the church as a heavenly hierarchy represented on earth by an earthly hierarchy. It is precisely the demise—or at least the waning—of the vision of the church as a hierarchy representing God on earth that has made it possible for many previously excluded or marginalized people—women, racial and ethnic minorities, believers in poor nations—to reclaim their place in the church and to begin the process of reinventing the church in ways that are more just. As we shall see in chapter 11, these current movements are movements of power and of hope. In brief, the modern individualistic correction is calling the church to new obedience and has opened possibilities that would not exist otherwise.

Yet in this correction much of the ancient view of the church is lost. The church is no longer an essential part of the gospel and is therefore dispensable. It is possible to be a Christian without church. Churches are to be created, divided, and abandoned at will, and often for as trivial a cause as not liking a preacher or preferring a different choir. Churches vie with one another for members, much as commercial franchises vie for customers—indeed, there are churches in which believers are seen, treated, and pampered as customers. In such a situation, could it be that some of the more ancient views of the church have something to teach us? Is there a sense in which it is not us who give birth to the church, but the church who gives birth to us? Is there a sense in which the church is and can only be one, in spite of all our divisions and our bickering? How is that unity related to the one bread that we break? All these are questions that become increasingly urgent as the twenty-first century progresses and as Christians discover that the notions and experiences of church that have prevailed since the end of antiquity no longer serve.

For Further Reading

Evans, Gillian R. *The Church and the Churches: Toward an Ecumenical Ecclesiology.* Cambridge: Cambridge University Press, 1994.

Kärkäinen, Veli-Matti. *An Introduction to Ecclesiology: Ecumenical, Historical & Global Perspectives.* Downers Grove: InterVarsity Press, 2002.

Nygren, Anders. *Christ and His Church.* Philadelphia: Westminster Press, 1956.

Volf, Miroslav. *After Our Likeness: The Church as the Image of the Trinity.* Grand Rapids: Eerdmans, 1998.

Welch, Claude. *The Reality of the Church.* New York: Charles Scribner's Sons, 1958.

Notes

1. *Ep. to the Ephesians*, 1
2. *Ep. to the Smyrneans*, 8.2.
3. *Ep. to the Philadelphians*, 3.3.
4. *Ep. to the Trallians*, 13.2.
5. Ibid.
6. *Vision* 2.4.1.
7. *Vision* 3. Cf. *Similitude* 9.
8. *Similitude* 9.18.
9. *On Prescription against Heretics*, 32.
10. Ibid., 20.
11. *Institutes*, 4.2.3 (Philadelphia: Westminster Press, 1960), 1045.
12. *Didache*, 9.4.
13. *Epistle* 73.21.
14. *On the Unity of the Church*, 6.
15. *Corpus of Canon Law*, 2.1245.
16. *Institutes*, 4.1.8, 1023.

8.

THE SACRAMENTS

*He took bread, blessed and broke it, and gave it to
them. Then their eyes were opened, and
they recognized him.*
Luke 24:30-31

If it is true that doctrine is formed mostly within the context of worship, then the sacraments stand behind practically every Christian doctrine, for since the earliest date, and in most churches until now, the sacraments have been the very heart of worship. Thus, baptism in the name of the Father, the Son, and the Holy Spirit was the general practice of the church long before there was much discussion on the doctrine of the Trinity—and the doctrine of the Trinity may be seen, in part at least, as the result of reflection on the baptismal practice of the church.

Given that reality, it may seem surprising that during the early centuries of the life of the church there was little debate on the meaning of the sacraments. When the sacraments were an occasion for debate, the disagreement usually had to do more with their administration—who is to be baptized, who is to be admitted to communion, and so on—than with their meaning. However, upon further reflection this may not be so surprising after all. What a group does repeatedly as part of its usual practice is seldom a subject of debate. In many churches we stand for singing and kneel for prayer, but we seldom discuss the meaning of these various positions. The early church gathered for worship. In that worship they broke bread. Those who wished to join the church were baptized. By baptism one became part of the body of Christ. By communion, one was nourished as part of that body. It was simply done, with little discussion or disagreement as to the meaning of these practices—

149

what is the efficacy of the sacrament, what actually happens when it is administered.

The Meaning of the Word "Sacrament"

The word "sacrament" stands for the Latin *sacramentum*, which is the way Latin-speaking theologians usually translated the Greek *mysterion*. This Greek word, translated as "mystery," means something secret or hidden, and most often something hidden because it is inscrutable and may only be known—if at all—through its own disclosure. It is thus that the New Testament uses it when referring, for instance, to "the mystery hidden for ages and generations, but now made manifest to his saints" (Col 1:26; cf. Rom 16:25-26). Thus, when Greek-speaking Christians spoke of any of their rites—and particularly of the Eucharist—as a *mysterion*, they were indicating that the rite pointed beyond itself, that there was in it a content beyond the visible, that it acted upon believers—and perhaps also upon the world at large—in unknown ways. The term itself would seem to discourage much speculation on what it is that actually takes place in the celebration of the rite; and it is significant that most of what early Greek literature remains regarding the Eucharist has a distinctly poetic and metaphorical tone, precisely the tone one would normally employ to refer to any reality beyond words.

The Latin *sacramentum* sometimes has the same connotations of a hidden and inscrutable mystery; but in common Latin usage it also meant an oath, particularly an oath of service to another. In this sense, it often referred both to the oath itself and to the rites by which the oath was expressed and sealed. Thus, Roman soldiers expressed their commitment to the emperor by means of a ceremonial oath or *sacramentum*. Likewise, the rites of initiation into a religion or into a guild were often called *sacramentum*—or, in the plural, *sacramenta*.

Given these different connotations of *mysterion* and *sacramentum*, it is not surprising that Latin-speaking Christians were more likely to inquire into the exact nature, validity, and efficacy of the sacraments than were their Greek-speaking counterparts, and that as a result it is the Western church that has most debated these matters—with the Eastern church often agreeing to some of the Western definitions, but seldom being embroiled in the controversies regarding the sacraments that often engaged Western theologians.

The Nature of a Sacrament

Most later medieval theologians, in discussing the sacraments, began with a section often called *On the Sacraments in General*, in which they discussed the very notion of sacrament, including what it is that makes a rite a sacrament, the efficacy of sacraments, and their number. Here, I shall follow roughly the same order: first, the notion of sacrament; then, the efficacy of sacraments; finally, their number. After that, we shall consider the sacraments separately.

In discussing the nature of a sacrament, medieval theologians would begin with the definition, stemming from St. Augustine, that a sacrament is "a visible form of an invisible grace."[1] Expanding on the notion of "visible sign," they emphasized the material aspect of a sacrament, often as a way of refuting an extremely mystical piety that claimed direct, spiritual revelation from and communication with God. Without denying the possibility of such direct communication, medieval sacramental theology repeatedly reminded the faithful that God speaks and acts through the physical creation, and in particular through these material elements—water, bread, wine—that God has set apart as the specific sacramental signs, occasions, and channels of God's grace.

In the twelfth century—a time of significant theological activity and creativity—Hugh of Saint Victor (ca. 1095–1141) wrote *On the Sacraments of the Christian Faith*, in which he affirms that anything that serves to know God and that serves the sanctification of the soul is a sacrament. According to Hugh, sacraments are material elements that "by similitude represent, by institution signify, and by sanctification contain, a certain invisible and spiritual grace."[2] These four points—materiality, representation, institution, and consecration or sanctification—appear repeatedly in later treatises on the nature of the sacraments. That sacraments are material implies that, although the grace they confer is invisible, they themselves are visible and material. Good sacramental theology, these theologians would insist, does not fall into the Gnostic trap of imagining that spiritual, invisible communication with God can ever be a substitute for the

151

material and visible signs that God has chosen. The point regarding representation should be obvious. The water of baptism represents cleansing; the bread and wine represent the body and blood of Christ. They have been chosen by God to do this because there is in them a certain "similitude" with what they represent. The "institution" refers to the action of Christ in directing that this rite be celebrated. Christ instituted communion at the Last Supper, and baptism when he sent his disciples to baptize. Finally, the "sanctification" is crucial. Bread and wine may be material signs representing the body and blood of the Savior, but what gives them their sacramental power, according to medieval theology, is the words of consecration pronounced over them, thus sanctifying them and making the sacrament possible. When all of this happens, Hugh affirms, these material elements, that by their similitude represent certain things, become true channels that contain and confer "a certain invisible grace." (Remember that St. Augustine had spoken of grace as a fluid or power infused into the believer. What Hugh now declares is that the sacraments actually cause grace to flow into the believer.)

In the thirteenth century, St. Thomas Aquinas (ca. 1225–1274) developed this further, establishing more clearly and systematically what Hugh of St. Victor and others had said, and undergirding it with the Aristotelian philosophy that had recently been reintroduced into Western Europe and that Thomas thought was an ideal basis for understanding much of Christian doctrine. He agrees with Hugh of St. Victor and Peter Lombard that the sacraments are seven; that they are material things that represent, signify, and contain invisible grace; and that all of this requires the "sanctification" or consecration of the sacrament itself. On this point, Thomas would strongly affirm that the sacraments not only symbolize or represent, but actually cause or produce the grace they signify.

As to the nature of the sacraments, Thomas has recourse to the Aristotelian distinction between "form" and "matter." In a sacrament, he says, "the words are the form, and the sensible things are the matter." [3] It is for this reason that sacraments require certain verbal formulae, which act as a form upon the matter of the rite. For instance, in communion the matter is the bread and the wine, and the form is the words of institution. Likewise, in baptism the matter is water, and the form is the trinitarian formula pronounced over the person being baptized.

The Efficacy of a Sacrament

If the sacraments actually confer the grace they signify, the obvious question that follows is, What makes a sacrament efficacious? This had become an important issue for Augustine, long before the time of Thomas, in his controversy with the Donatists. The latter refused to accept the ordinations conferred by unworthy bishops—that is, bishops who according to the Donatists had faltered during the time of persecution. Their argument was simply that, since these bishops are unworthy, a rite of ordination performed by them is not valid. In consequence, baptisms performed by those bishops or by someone ordained by them, as well as the Eucharistic celebrations of the same people, are not valid. People baptized by what the Donatists consider the impure church who now become Donatists must be rebaptized, for their baptism by the hands of those unworthy ministers was worthless. Likewise, the communion offered in that church is not valid, for those consecrating the elements are unworthy and have no right to do so. This was not an entirely new issue in North Africa, for in the third century the bishop of Carthage, Cyprian, had argued that people baptized by schismatics should be rebaptized when joining the catholic church. In this he had disagreed with the Roman and other leadership, who held that any baptism done in water and in the Triune name was valid. Although Cyprian never changed his mind, after his death the church in Carthage had come to agree with Rome, that schismatics ought not to be rebaptized upon entering the catholic church. Thus, to a certain extent, the Donatist position was a revival of what Cyprian had held in the past.

For responding to the Donatists, Augustine had recourse to *Seven Books on the Donatist Schism*, by Optatus of Milevis, whose arguments Augustine repeated. Following Optatus, Augustine held that in a sacrament there are three participants: God, the recipient, and the person administering the sacrament. While all three are necessary, the validity of the sacrament depends only on the first two, and not on the third. In baptism, it is God who washes, and the baptized who receives the grace. The third element, the person who administers it, is only an instrument of God's action. This means that a sacrament is valid quite apart from the moral virtues or defects of the one administering it. While Augustine offers a number of arguments to prove his point, in the last analysis his most powerful argument is pastoral, for the practical consequences of believing that the efficacy of a sacrament depends on the person administering would be enormous. If I believe that the validity of my baptism depends on the worthiness of the person who baptized me, I shall never be certain that I am baptized. What am I to do then? Be baptized repeatedly, in the hope that one of my baptisms will be valid? Am I to check on the minister's character before receiving communion?

Augustine sees the pastoral absurdity of such a view of the sacraments and in order to deal with it distinguishes between the validity and the regularity of a sacrament. A sacrament administered by an unworthy person may be irregular. This is particularly true if it is administered by schismatics such as the Donatists. As a result, schismatics administering a sacrament may be doing this to their own damnation. If aware of the irregularity of the sacrament, those receiving it may also be working for their own damnation. But the sacrament is still valid. Those receiving a sacrament in faith—and in good faith—may be confident that the grace promised in the sacrament is indeed available and granted to the recipient. (Notice once again that in this context "grace" is a power that God infuses in the believer.) In brief, the efficacy of a sacrament depends not on the one administering it, but on the sacrament itself. The sacramental acts on its own power, and not on the merit of the minister.

While affirming the efficacy of the sacrament in spite of the unworthiness of the minister, Augustine does not seem to be quite ready to affirm that the sacrament is efficacious even if the recipient lacks faith. This seems to be implied at least in the case of infant baptism, for it is difficult to argue that an infant has faith. The result was the view generally accepted in later Catholic theology, usually expressed in the Latin phrase, *ex opere operato*. This phrase means that the sacrament is efficacious in and of itself, quite independently of both the minister and the recipient.

The Reformation reopened the debate. Luther came to reject Augustine's view of infused grace. For him, grace is not a fluid or power that God infuses into the believer, but is rather God's love. Therefore, a sacrament cannot confer grace, but only seal and confirm a person on the justifying grace of God. A sacrament does not make a person holier or more acceptable to God. What it does is claim and brand the person—and the community—as God's own. Calvin agrees, stressing the connection between a sacrament and the promises of God. The promise is already made; the sacrament confirms it, calling the believer to trust in the promise—and in a sense even giving believers a foretaste of its fulfillment. Thus, he explains:

> We understand that a sacrament is never without a preceding promise but is joined to it as a sort of appendix, with the purpose of confirming and sealing the promise itself, and of making it more evident to us in the sense of ratifying it.... Yet, properly speaking, it is not so much needed to confirm his Sacred Word as to establish us in faith in it.[4]

Both Luther and Calvin, as most major reformers, agreed that the preaching of the Word and the administration of the sacrament must go together. Medieval theology had emphasized the place of words in a sacrament. According to that view, in communion the sacrament is empowered by the words of institution pronounced by the priest: "This is my body ..." The Reformers felt that this was not enough. The sacrament must be accompanied by preaching. The words that empower the sacrament are not a magical formula that the celebrant may mumble, but the preaching that explains and confirms the significance of the sacrament in the mind of the recipients. Calvin affirms this bluntly:

> We ought to understand the word not as one whispered without meaning and without faith, a mere noise, like a magic incantation, which has the force to consecrate the element. Rather, it should, when preached, make us understand what the visible sign means.[5]

Although there were disagreements among the reformers on the meaning and efficacy of the sacraments, these were exacerbated in the seventeenth century, when Protestant scholasticism sought to work out every detail on the matter and to condemn every position that in any way deviated from the strictest interpretation of the views of the various reformers. The result was that the efficacy of the sacraments became increasingly tied to orthodoxy, to the point that it seemed it was the orthodoxy of the celebrant and the partaker that determined the value of the sacrament. Partly as a reaction, many in the revivals of the eighteenth and nineteenth centuries regarded the sacraments as aids to the inner devotional life, or as testimonials before the world, but seldom as a gift of God in which God is actively blessing the community of believers. This was later reinforced by the growing influence of rationalism and of individualism in Western society, which led both "conservatives" and "liberals" to reject any notion of a particular efficacy in the sacraments. In more recent times, in both Protestant and Catholic circles, there is a growing emphasis on the sacraments as actions of God—even though there are still wide theological differences between Protestants and Catholics, as well as among various Protestant groups. This has led to a renewal both of liturgy and of sacramental theology.

The Number of the Sacraments

As to the number of rites or practices that may properly be called "sacraments," the answer varies. It is clear that in the early church baptism and the Eucharist belonged to this category, for each of the two is repeatedly called a *mysterion* or a *sacrament*. During the patristic period, various other practices such as foot washing, making the sign of the cross, calling on the name of Jesus, and repeating the Lord's Prayer are occasionally called sacraments. It was not until the twelfth century that the Western church fixed the number of sacraments at seven. Since according to Hugh of St. Victor all of creation is geared toward its proper end of manifesting God and sanctifying the soul, the list of possible sacraments is endless. As a result, Hugh can refer to the recitation of the Lord's Prayer, to making the sign of the cross, and to dozens of other practices as sacraments. There are, however, seven rites on which he focuses his attention: baptism, confirmation, communion, penance (commonly called confession), extreme unction (or last rites), marriage, and ordination. The number seven is a sign of perfection, and therefore there is a "mystical" reason why Hugh believes the major sacraments to be seven. However, although there are reasons for the number seven, Hugh gives no real reason for this particular list, and apparently in paying special attention to these seven, he is simply reflecting what by then was the common practice of the church. Once again, worship shapes theology, much more than vice versa. Slightly later, Peter Lombard (d. 1160), in his *Four Books of Sentences*, listed these seven as the sacraments of the Christian church and also adopted a definition of "sacrament" that was very similar to that of Hugh.

156

Since the *Sentences* of Peter Lombard became the basic textbook on theology for the rest of the Middle Ages, this was the most influential step in the process of fixing the number of sacraments at seven. After him, most medieval theologians declared the number of sacraments to be the seven that Hugh of Saint Victor and Peter Lombard had listed.

It was not, however, until the sixteenth century that the Roman Catholic Church promulgated the official list of sacraments, when the Council of Trent decreed:

> If any say that the sacraments of the new law were not all instituted by Jesus Christ our Lord, or that they are more or less than seven, that is, baptism, confirmation, communion, penance, extreme unction, ordination, and marriage . . . let them be anathema.[6]

This was done in reaction to the Protestant reformation, most of whose leaders held that the sacraments were only two: baptism and communion. Luther did consider penance as a possible third, but he eventually rejected it on the grounds that it detracts from baptism. Calvin, who emphasized the teaching role of the minister, considered the possibility of including ordination, but he rejected it because a sacrament must be available to the entire church. Some of the Anabaptists added foot washing as a third sacrament instituted by Jesus. The Anglican Church took an intermediate position between the continental reformers and Roman Catholicism, declaring that there are two main sacraments—baptism and the Eucharist—and five other rites that are also sacramental in nature.

Given this disagreement as to the number of the sacraments, in the rest of this chapter we shall focus our attention on the two on which all are agreed, baptism and communion, and then look at the development of the sacrament of penance, for this is crucial in order to understand the debates at the time of the Reformation regarding salvation—to which we shall turn in chapter 9.

Baptism

From as far back as we can discern, the early church practiced baptism. Exactly what baptism meant was not altogether clear; but there is no doubt that it was considered a powerful rite. Ignatius of

Antioch, early in the second century, declared that Jesus was baptized so that "the water would be purified by his passion."[7] At about the same time, or even earlier, the *Didache* gives instructions as to how it is to be administered:

> Regarding baptism, baptize as follows: Having said beforehand all these things [the teaching of the faith], baptize in the name of the Father, and of the Son, and of the Holy Ghost in living [running] water. If you have no living water, baptize in other water; if you cannot do it with cold water, do it with warm. If you have neither one nor the other, pour water over the head three times in the name of the Father, and of the Son, and of the Holy Ghost.[8]

This shows that there was great flexibility in the administration of baptism, and therefore any description of the rite in the early church should be regarded as an example of what was done, and not as a description of a normative and universal practice. By the middle of the second century, however, some common practices had begun to emerge, and therefore it is possible to reconstruct the process for administering baptism, at least at that time.

In looking at baptism in the early church, the most important point to make is that baptism was not the mere rite of going through the waters, but was a long process for which people prepared for years—usually three years—and which continued even after the rite was administered. After being presented for baptism by a sponsor, and receiving instruction, both moral and doctrinal, for several years, the persons to be baptized underwent a special period of more intensive preparation. It was at this point that they were taught the Creed—which apparently varied from community to community, although expressing the same essential points—the Lord's Prayer, and all that had to do with communion, to which they had never been admitted. Since baptism most commonly took place on Easter, this period of intensive preparation, during which the rest of the congregation also prepared for the renewal of its baptismal vows, is the origin of Lent. On Easter Eve those to be baptized gathered at the place where the rite was to take place—originally a river, but soon a pool especially constructed for this purpose. There they were baptized nude, first the children—for at least by this time children were baptized—and then the adults, men and women separately. If a child was too young to respond to the questions, the family would do so in the child's name. Before being baptized, the person had to renounce the devil and all his works—usually three times, facing West, which is where the sun sets. They then turned to the East, where the day dawns, and declared their faith in Jesus Christ, the Sun of justice, reciting words similar to our present Apostles' Creed. Most commonly, baptism was received by entering into the water, kneeling in it, and having water poured over the head three times, in the name of the Father, of the Son, and of the Holy Ghost. Upon coming out of the water, several other symbolic actions took place: being dressed in a white robe as a sign of newness of life, being anointed with oil as a sign of belonging to a new Master to the priestly royalty, which is the people of God, receiving a lighted candle, and so on. They then joined the rest of the congregation for the Easter service, during which they partook of communion for the first time—and were given a chalice with milk and honey, in celebration of their entrance into the land of promise.

While there is much that could be said about this rite, its variations, its later development, the most important points to note are: First, that this was a communal rite. It was administered in the context of congregational worship. Even when the actual baptism took place at a different site, both because water was needed and because people were baptized nude, the entire congregation was gathered, praying for those being baptized, and the rite culminated with the joint celebration of communion. Second, baptism involved much more than the actual rite with water. It was a process that began several years before the rite was administered and, precisely because it was an act of joining the people of God, continued throughout life— much as today one becomes a naturalized citizen at a particular time, but that even is valid throughout life.

As to the meaning of baptism, the early church saw it as a multifaceted rite whose many meanings enrich and clarify one another. It was an act of grafting a new member into the body of Christ. Since it involved water, it was often seen as an act of cleansing from sin. In many cases, the shape of the baptismal pool was a reminder of one of the many meanings of baptism: a round or pear-shaped pool, resembling a womb, was a reminder that, just as all people are born through the water of the womb, Christians are born anew through the waters of baptism. A pool in the shape of a coffin pointed to baptism as dying and rising with Christ. An eight-sided pool announced that with the resurrection of Jesus a new creation had begun—a new day beyond the seven of the old creation—and that those baptized were now part of this new creation.

As time went by, however, this multifaceted view of the significance of baptism was lost. Increasingly, baptism came to be viewed as an act of cleansing from all previous sin. As a result, both the baptism of adults and the baptism of infants changed. Adults often postponed their baptism to the last possible time—sometimes in their deathbeds—to make certain that they were clean of sin when they died. As to infants, they were now baptized not because they were children of the promise, but because of original sin, which had to be cleansed through baptism. Since infant mortality was very high, the safest—and eventually the most common—practice was to baptize a child as soon as possible. (At times, children in grave danger of dying before birth were even baptized in the womb!)

Since the sacraments work *ex opere operato*, baptism became something mechanical, almost magical. The pouring of water, jointly with a fixed formula, gave the sacrament its power. There was little mention of the Holy Spirit in the process; and even then, the Spirit seemed to be controlled by the words and the actions of the person administering the sacrament.

As an act of cleansing, baptism no longer was a congregational, communal act, but a relatively private one that could be administered apart from the worship of the congregation—or, as even today is common practice in many Protestant churches, as a sort of parenthesis during worship. In some cases, the connection of baptism with Easter remained, in that the water blessed at the Easter Eve service was "holy water," employed for baptisms during the rest of the year. This led to superstition regarding the power of such water, which was used for healing the sick—or for improving recipes! For a number of reasons, the anointing with oil was separated from baptism, thus giving rise to the practice of confirmation.

However, the most important consequence of this reduction and change in the meaning of baptism was that now sins committed after baptism posed a grave pastoral problem. If baptism cleanses from all previous sin, what can one do about sins committed after baptism? This gave rise to the penitential system, to which we shall turn after looking at communion.

The reformers—particularly Luther and Calvin—insisted that baptism be restored as a congregational act. Luther saw the value of baptism, not just as the beginning of the Christian life, but as the continuing foundation for such life. Thus, when he was sorely tempted or distressed, he would remind himself: "I am baptized!" Calvin recovered the notion of baptism as being "engrafted in Christ" [9] and, like Luther, affirmed its value for all of life:

> But we must realize that at whatever time we are baptized, we are once for all washed and purged for our whole life. Therefore, as often as we fall away, we ought to recall the memory of our baptism and fortify our mind with it, that we may always be sure and confident of the forgiveness of sins. [10]

Both Luther and Calvin continued the practice of baptizing infants. Other reformers, however, insisted on the need for personal faith before baptism, and this gave rise to the Anabaptist movement—which originally was not concerned over baptism by immersion, but over baptism of believers. Eventually, Baptists took up this requirement of personal faith before receiving baptism and also insisted—as most Anabaptists did by then—that baptism should be by immersion. However, this emphasis on baptism was often coupled with the view—supported by a mixture of rationalism and individualism—that there is no power in baptism, which is mostly an act of witness before the congregation and before the world.

More recently, there has been much discussion among Protestants regarding the widespread practice of infant baptism—a practice that reflects a time when membership in the church was practically coextensive with membership in the civil society. As Christianity grows in new lands, and as its effect wanes in the traditional Christian areas, the conversion and baptism of adults is becoming increasingly common, even in those traditions that do baptize infants. Still, most traditions do not rebaptize as adults those who were baptized as infants.

Communion

The history of communion is just as old as the history of Christian baptism, for the very church that baptized its first converts also gathered regularly on the first day of the week to break bread in celebration of the resurrection of its Lord and in anticipation of his return and his rule. For this reason, in discussing communion, it is important to remember that the Eucharist was the most common form of Christian worship for centuries, and that when ancient authors refer to it they are not necessarily focusing—as we tend to do today—on the bread and the wine, but on worship itself. Thus, when Ignatius of Antioch, early in the second century, advises the Ephesians to "be diligent in gathering more frequently to celebrate God's Eucharist and give thanks to God," [11] he is urging them, not only to take the bread and the wine, but also to gather for worship, "for when you gather closely as one, Satan's bulwarks come down." [12]

At first, this worship service was a meal; but even then the bread and the wine were of special significance. At some point, apparently to avoid the sort of abuse to which Paul refers in 1 Corinthians, and also because of the pressure of increased numbers and limited space, as well as the danger of persecution, the meal was reduced to its two central components of bread and wine. The Eucharist was preceded by reading and exposition of the Scriptures—the "service of the Word"—after which those who were not yet baptized were dismissed. This dismissal was followed by the prayers of the people, for the community of the baptized saw itself as the priestly people, part of whose task is to pray for the world—including the emperors who persecuted them. This served as an opening for the Eucharistic celebration itself—the "service of the table."

As to the efficacy of the Eucharist, there is unanimity among the most ancient Christian writers. To withdraw from the Eucharist is to withdraw from God. The Eucharist is the bond of unity by which Satan is resisted and defeated. According to Ignatius, Christians ought to avoid schism by obeying the bishop and his elders and by "breaking a single loaf, which is medicine for immortality, antidote against death, and nourishment to live forever in Jesus Christ." [13] Quite clearly, for those ancient Christians, communion was much more than a symbol or a reminder of the passion of Christ. It was a celebration of the passion and resurrection and a reminder and foretaste of the final heavenly banquet.

Although there is little disagreement among historians on this last point, there is wide disagreement on the point at which the focus of the Eucharist became the bodily presence of Jesus in the bread and the wine. Some quote passages in which the "body of Christ" present in the Eucharist is clearly the gathered church. Others quote passages in which the bread and the wine are declared to be the body and blood of Jesus. To quote Ignatius once again, he declares that "the Eucharist is the flesh of our Savior Jesus Christ; the same flesh that suffered for our sins; the same flesh that was resurrected by the Father's love."[14] Perhaps all that one can honestly say is that during this early period, Christians were convinced of the efficacy of the Eucharist, but there was no discussion as to how Christ is present in it, nor as to how that presence works for salvation. To ask more than this is to project later questions into the early church, and to seek answers to questions that they did not really ask.

Soon, however, the emphasis clearly moved to the presence of Christ in the bread and the wine. In the fourth century, Ambrose believed that his brother Satyrus was able to survive a shipwreck because he had a piece of consecrated bread tied around his neck. Slightly later, Augustine still wrote about the Eucharist both in terms that make it appear as a symbolic and communal memorial of the death and resurrection of Christ and—in other passages—in terms that would seem to support the physical transformation of the bread into the body of Christ.

This latter emphasis soon became dominant. As the vast majority of the population became Christian, the gathering of the community lost much of its significance. The church was no longer a particular and different community that gathered around the table. Communion became the occasion during which the individual believer is nourished by the body and blood of Jesus by eating the bread and drinking the wine.

By the ninth century, the community celebrating the Eucharist had practically disappeared from the minds of theologians and believers alike. At that time, a monk by the name of Paschasius Radbertus wrote the treatise *On the Body and the Blood of the Lord,* in which he claimed that in the Eucharistic celebration, the consecrated bread and wine are no longer such, but become the flesh and blood of Jesus—the same who was born of Mary, was crucified, and rose again. This treatise led to a fuller discussion of the matter, with a number of scholars refuting Radbertus's claims. However, by then what Radbertus wrote probably expressed what had become the common belief of most people, and in the end of that century, people were declaring that what took place in the consecration of the elements was a change in the "substance" of the bread and the wine. In the middle of the eleventh century, controversy flared up again, this time around the teachings of Berengar of Tours, who declared that the bread and wine remain bread and wine and that the body of Christ, which is in heaven, cannot be present in a number of altars at the same time. While Berengar himself was soon condemned, the controversy continued for a long time, until the Fourth Lateran Council (1215) promulgated the doctrine of transubstantiation. This doctrine is based on the distinction in philosophy between a substance and its accidents. The accidents of a thing are its characteristics—appearance, taste, weight, shape, and so on. The substance is the reality behind the accidents, to which the latter adhere. According to the doctrine of transubstantiation, in the Eucharistic consecration the substances of the bread and the wine cease existing, and their place is taken by the body and blood of Christ, although the accidents of the bread and wine remain unchanged.

This view was scarcely challenged until the time of the Reformation. Luther held that the bread and wine remain such, but now become also the body and blood of Christ—a view often called "consubstantiation," although Luther himself did not use that term, for he felt that the very notion of "substance" in this context was an expression of theology's enslavement to Aristotelian metaphysics. According to Luther, after the resurrection the physical body of Christ enjoys ubiquity—the ability to be in several places at the same time—and this makes it possible for that body to be both in heaven and on a multitude of communion tables at the same time.

This was the main point of contention between Luther and Ulrich Zwingli, for Zwingli insisted that the presence of Christ in the Eucharist is symbolic, a reminder of the death and resurrection of Christ for our sakes. On this point, most of the Anabaptists agreed with Zwingli rather than with Luther.

In the next generation, Calvin took the intermediate position between Luther and Zwingli, declaring that the presence of Christ in communion is real, yet spiritual. The body of Christ is in heaven, and not on the communion table. But Christ is indeed present, not just in our minds or as a symbol, but because by virtue of the Spirit the worshiping community is, as it were, taken to heaven and there given a foretaste of the heavenly banquet in the presence of Jesus—a view that theologians call "virtualism." He states his position as follows:

> But greatly mistaken are those who conceive no presence of flesh in the Supper unless it lies in the bread. For thus they leave nothing to the secret working of the Spirit, which unites Christ himself to us. To them Christ does not seem present unless he comes down to us. As though, if he should lift us to himself, we should not just as much enjoy his presence! The question is therefore only of the manner, for they place Christ in the bread, while we do not think it lawful to drag him from heaven. [15]

Given the marked difference of opinion on this matter between Zwingli and Calvin, there are those within the Reformed tradition who hold to one of these positions or the other. In general, Lutherans have considered the physical presence of Christ in communion, and the bread remaining bread, a distinctive mark of their tradition, while Roman Catholics have insisted on transubstantiation, and many Protestants see communion merely as a symbol of the presence of Christ. In recent times, however, these various traditions are drawing closer, as the emphasis shifts back from the bread and the wine to the community that shares them in the presence of the risen Lord—a community that is itself the body of Christ.

Penance

Penance evolved out of the obvious fact that baptized believers still sin. This was to be expected, and for that reason, services traditionally included prayers of confession, in which those present would confess their sins to God and pray for forgiveness and amendment of life. But then there were those who committed egregious sins, and whose membership in the community seemed to be a denial of this community being "the holy people of God." In the early church, there apparently were three sorts of sin that were considered particularly grave: homicide—which included murder as well as killing in battle or in the service of the state—fornication—sexual activity outside of marriage—and apostasy—denying Christ, which was a common enough occurrence in times of persecution. Apparently any of these three required a long process of confession and penance before the person could be readmitted to the communion of the church. These acts of penance were public, although the confession of the particular sin itself was often private. According to Hermas, a Christian writer in the second century, such a penance, which normally would take years and sometimes even a lifetime, could only be granted once—after which the sinner's only hope was to be saved through the blood baptism of martyrdom. Even so, there were Christians who felt that such readmission was a concession to moral laxity—a matter that led to several schisms in the second and third centuries. By the fourth century, however, it was generally agreed that no sin is completely unforgivable. Thus, the Council of Nicea (325) established a series of rules and guidelines for the readmission into the church of those who had been guilty of apostasy during the recent persecutions. Even then, the penalties for sin were not minor. For instance, the Synod of Elvira, in the third century, prescribed an entire year of public penance for any who gambled with dice. In sixth-century France, it was customary to use monastic life as a punishment for sin, forcing sinners to live in a monastery, often for life.

By the late sixth century, Pope Gregory the Great (r. 590–604) systematized much of the current thought on penance and the restoration of the fallen. According to him, penance requires contrition, confession, and satisfaction. Although at earlier times the works of penitence demanded of believers were understood to be a sign of their repentance, by Gregory's time "satisfaction" had become undoing one's sin by means of good works. Thanks to the power granted by Christ to his apostles, Gregory would say, the church has the power to absolve sinners who repent, confess, and make satisfaction for their sins. These four—contrition, confession, satisfaction, and absolution—have remained the main constituents of penance through the centuries. By then, the old notion that there was only one opportunity for penance—at least, for penance for major sins— was being abandoned in favor of the practice of repeated acts of penance. Apparently the main reason for this was that, if repentance could only be granted once, people tended to wait as long as possible before they availed themselves of its remedy—much as at an earlier date others had postponed their baptism until they were in their deathbeds.

It was in the Celtic church that this change first took place. There it became customary for sinners to confess their sins—both major and lesser ones—in private, to holy people of their choosing. These early confessors were usually monastics—men or women—known for their holiness and wisdom. It also became customary to repeat this act of confession as often as necessary. Thus penance, which earlier had been limited to a once-in-a-lifetime process, became repeatable, to the point that many availed themselves of it periodically. Also, since confessors needed some guidance in the setting of the satisfaction due for a particular sin, a new body of literature developed. These were the "penitentiaries"—books instructing confessors how to proceed, what questions to ask, and what penalties to prescribe.

All of this was not immediately accepted on the Continent—although private confession to a monastic had been practiced in Southern France for some time. As it was beginning to be introduced, several regional synods condemned the repetition of penance. However, Celtic missionaries and wandering preachers had their effect on the Continent. First in Gaul and Spain, and later throughout the Latin-speaking West, the practice of repeated acts of confession became normative. This was officially sanctioned by the Fourth Lateran Council in 1215, which decreed that all should avail themselves of this sacrament at least once a year.

From that point on, the development and corruption of penance seemed logical and inexorable. For practical reasons, the priest would declare absolution before satisfaction was made. Even though this was theoretically a conditional absolution, dependent on the sinner's works of satisfaction, it tended to make penance more of a priestly action, dependent on the priest's words of absolution rather than on the penitent's contrition and satisfaction. Then came the question of substituting one form of satisfaction for another. If a person was supposed to go on pilgrimage, but for some reason could not, was it licit to send someone else in one's stead? What about paying for another to perform one's works of satisfaction? Thus, through an almost imperceptible development, the sale of indulgences became customary, and by the time of the Reformation it was being abused in scandalous manner—often claiming for such indulgences power beyond any officially sanctioned by the church.

Luther and other reformers objected not only to the sale of indulgences, but also to the entire penitential system and its theological underpinnings. The very notion that one can offer "satisfaction" or payment for one's sin ran contrary to Luther's own view of justification by grace—to which we shall turn in chapter 9. Furthermore, to think that sins committed after baptism require a special treatment is to view baptism as a single, passing rite at the beginning of the Christian life, and not—as Luther felt it was—as the foundation for that entire life. Baptism, Luther insisted, is valid not only for sins committed before receiving it, but throughout life—whenever faith renews confidence in the promise God has sealed at baptism. Thus, the penitential system, its theological presuppositions, and its implied view of how salvation is attained were the crucial points at issue between Luther—and eventually all the Protestant reformers—and traditional Roman Catholicism. To this we must turn in the next chapter.

Contemporary Relevance

Seeing that there is so much divergence among Christians regarding the sacraments, one may well ask, is there anything here that we may learn for the entire church? Are there any "fences" or "foul lines" that these past—and present—controversies have bequeathed to us? Although there are no "fences" beyond those drawn by each denomination or Christian tradition—that is, the specific teachings of each regarding the sacraments—there are at least some lessons to be learned from the long debates on the sacraments, and some caveats to be raised.

First, as Augustine, Hugh of Saint Victor, and many others have pointed out, the sacraments are material or visible realities. The centrality of the sacraments in Christian worship and tradition serves as a reminder that our God is the creator of all that exists—visible and invisible, in heaven and on earth—and that therefore our worship of God may not exclude visible, material, or earthly means. The water of baptism is the water of creation.

Second, communion goes one step further, reminding us that our God is not only the God of creation, but also the God of human labor—the God of history. The bread and the wine are the products of the soil; but they are also the product of human work and ingenuity. They are signs of human responsibility as collaborators with God and as stewards of God's creation.

Third, we must remember the connection between Word and Sacrament that is part of all sacramental theology, but which the Reformers emphasized and other Christian traditions—Roman Catholic and Eastern Orthodox—are emphasizing once again. If the sacraments have power, they have power because of the Word that was in the beginning, through whom all things were made, and who is now proclaimed in the human words of preaching and the human action of the sacraments. At the same time, many Protestants are rediscovering the significance of sacraments for understanding and appropriating the Word.

Fourth, no matter how we differ in our interpretation of their efficacy, we should at least agree that the sacraments are more than a human action. God is present and active in them. They work for our salvation. They point toward the final destiny of all creation. They are not just empty ceremonies by which we promote our commitment and announce our faith. The Spirit of God, who hovered over the waters of creation, once again hovers over the waters of baptism.

The fifth point is the counterpart of the fourth: although they are powerful, the sacraments are not acts of magic. Their power remains the power of God, and not ours. It is God—and not the minister or the celebrant—who invites us to the waters of baptism and to the table of communion. It is God's Word—and not our words—that gives the sacrament its power to heal and to save and to sanctify.

Finally, the sacraments—as their original name, *mysteria*, implies—are never fully transparent to us. We approach them, no matter what our theological stance, as Moses approaching the burning bush. In the end, all our explanations and theories are but approximations to what the Spirit of God is doing in the sacraments. One could even say that the sacrament is a sacrament because it is a visible yet mysterious sign of God's ultimate mystery, which is a mystery of love and of grace.

For Further Reading

Stookey, Laurence Hull. *Baptism: Christ's Act in the Church.* Nashville: Abingdon Press, 1982.

————. *Eucharist: Christ's Feast with the Church*. Nashville: Abingdon Press, 1993.

Watkins, Oscar Daniel. *A History of Penance*. New York: B. Franklin, 1961.

Notes

1. *On Teaching the Unlettered* (*De catechizandis rudibus*), 26. Similar phrases appear in several of Augustine's works, and therefore Augustine is often quoted in slightly different wording.
2. *On the Sacraments of the Christian Faith*, 1.9.2.
3. *Summa Theologica*, Part III, q. 60, artl. 7.
4. *Institutes*, 4.14.3. (Philadelphia: Westminster, 1960), 1278.
5. Ibid., 4.14.4., 1279.
6. Session 7, *proemium*. Denzinger, *Enchiridion symbolorum*, 844.
7. *Ep. to the Ephesians*, 18.2.
8. *Didache*, 7.1-3.
9. *Institutes*, 4.15.1 (Philadelphia: Westminster, 1960), 1303.
10. *Ibid*. 4.15.3., 1305.
11. *Ep. to the Ephesians*, 13.1.
12. *Ibid*.
13. *Ibid*., 20.2.
14. *Ep. to the Symyrneans*, 7.1.
15. *Institutes*, 4.17.31 (Philadelphia: Westminster, 1960), 1403.

9.

SALVATION

How can we escape if we neglect so great a salvation?
Hebrews 2:3

The God of Israel and of Christianity is a redeemer God. As we saw in the early chapters of this book, one of the common traits in much of the religiosity of the Hellenistic world was the quest for salvation. The Gnostic systems promised salvation by means of secret knowledge and passwords. Mystery religions offered salvation through initiation. Philosophers hoped to attain salvation through intellectual contemplation leading to ecstatic experiences. Into this field of competing promises and means of salvation Christianity now entered.

The Effect of the Surrounding Culture on the Christian View of Salvation

The Christian and Jewish view of salvation, however, was quite different from what these other religions, schools, and philosophers sought and promised. For these others, salvation was salvation *from* an evil world of matter, and from slavery to the body and its infirmities. However, Jews and Christians affirmed that the Redeemer God is also the Creator God and that therefore creation itself is part of God's plan of redemption. In traditional Jewish religion, the possibility of life after death was at best one of the many promises of God. At the time of the advent of Jesus, one of the main differences between Pharisees and Sadducees was that the former believed in the final resurrection of the dead, and the latter did not—which shows

171

that such a notion was not a central tenet of the Jewish faith. In the New Testament, "salvation" often refers to the healing of the body, for the two words are the same. Indeed, the famous words of Peter to the effect that "there is no other name ... by which we must be saved" (Acts 4:12) come after an act of healing, and the debate is not about eternal salvation, but about the power and the authority to heal the body. Thus, one of the main points of disagreement between Christians and other teachers such as the Gnostics and Marcion was that the latter posited a discontinuity between creation and salvation, while Christians affirmed that salvation was the very goal of creation and that the God who has made all things in the first place will eventually bring all things to their divinely appointed destination. For Christians, salvation is much more than life after death. It is becoming part of a new creation, the beginning of the restoration of a creation corrupted and enslaved by sin.

However, it was difficult to proclaim this message in a culture as concerned over salvation *from* the world as was the Hellenistic culture of the time. Gnostic teachers, Marcionite preachers, recruiters for mystery religions, and religiously inclined philosophers all thought of salvation as the continued life of the soul after death, and in many cases its return to the "plenitude" or the "world of ideas" from which it had come.

The continued life of the dead was certainly always part of the Christian view of salvation, and there were reasons to try to equate this with the more generally accepted views on the meaning of salvation. When some mocked Christians for believing that they would continue living after death, and even showing themselves ready to face death as those who know it does not have the final word, Christians often responded by pointing out that many respected figures in the Greco-Roman world—including some of its best philosophers—had taught that the soul continues living after death. This proved to be a very valuable apologetic tool, showing that Christianity was not as harebrained as its detractors claimed.

Once again, however, we are reminded that the apologetic bridge bears traffic in both directions. As Christians endeavored to show that their preaching of life eternal had good antecedents in Hellenistic culture, they slowly began to interpret their own faith on the basis of what that culture took salvation to be. They increasingly emphasized salvation as the continuing life of the soul and neglected the fuller, biblical view of salvation as God's bringing all of creation to its intended end. What now mattered most was what happens to the soul after death, and during this life as preparation for death. The point soon came at which the body and its well-being were seen as an obstacle to salvation, and people began seeking salvation by punishing their bodies—a practice that continued for centuries.

Another point at which the surrounding culture influenced Christian teaching was in the notion of the immortality of the soul. There is abundant evidence that the early Christian writers did not believe the soul to be immortal. As God's creature, the soul is perishable and continues existing only by God's sustaining power. God may certainly grant immortality to the soul—and Christians clearly affirmed that thanks to that gift of God the soul continues living after physical death. By their nature, souls are mortal; it is only by God's grace that they continue living into eternity. Yet as time progressed, Christians tended to speak of the immortality of the soul as part of its very nature, and of salvation as making sure that the immortal soul is destined to live in heaven forever. The wider notion of salvation, as involving all of God's creation, was increasingly set aside.

This process was accelerated by the conversion of Constantine and the eventual rise of a Christian Empire. The notion of a coming kingdom of God—a kingdom that is not purely spiritual, but has to do with all of creation—has obvious subversive overtones. If we are to lay our hope in that coming kingdom, what of the present one? Is it not doing what God wills? Why should we need another kingdom? Is society not ordered as it should be? Is the emperor not a proper ruler? The result of all of this was that the earlier tendency to reduce salvation and Christian hope to spiritual matters was now intensified. Thousands now came to be baptized, not as a means of becoming part of the new creation, but as a means to go to heaven—and also, obviously, as a means to join the religion of the emperors. While there was still talk of the resurrection of the body and of the future kingdom of God, this was now eclipsed by discussions on how to assure that the soul does go to heaven at the time of death.

A parallel development, particularly in the West, was the growing notion that entrance into heaven is determined by one's conduct on earth. The church had always held that conduct is important and that those who are saved must live accordingly. There is also a long-standing tradition in the Bible—in both the Old and the New Testaments—that God rewards good deeds and punishes evil ones. Yet there is also a sense that God's salvation is a free gift of grace, and not something that the people of God have earned. God chose Israel because God loved Israel, not because of something Israel had done. Paul is clear that the same is true of Christians. In the Bible, these two are kept in tension—a God who rewards and punishes, and a God who gives freely. However, as the church made its way into the Hellenistic world, the second of these two points was obscured, and preaching and teaching had to do mostly with doing the works that God will reward with eternal life.

The conflict between Augustine and Pelagius (see chapter 5) had to do with these varying views of the way salvation is attained. Pelagius, on the one hand, wished to preserve human freedom of the will, because it is only through the exercise of such freedom that people can achieve merit and thus earn salvation. Augustine, on the other hand, insisted on the primacy of grace, and in so doing sought to proclaim the principle that it is God who saves, and who does this out of love, and not out of some indebtedness to us for our good works.

Salvation as a Reward for Good Works

Even Augustine, however, had already succumbed to the notion that salvation is attained as a reward for doing good. While Protestants have been eager to claim Augustine as their forerunner because of his insistence on the primacy of grace, Roman Catholics have repeatedly pointed out that what Augustine actually teaches is that grace empowers the believer to do the works that are pleasing to God, and thus to attain salvation.

After Augustine's time, as grace became a gift granted almost mechanically in the act of baptism, the net result was that salvation became God's reward for good works. In a generally Christian society, practically everybody was baptized shortly after birth. This meant that all were supposedly enabled to do good works worthy of eternal life, and that if they did not do them, or if they sinned, ways must be found to balance the account in the sinner's favor. This was the reason the penitential system outlined in chapter 8 became so important during the Middle Ages. If salvation is attained through merit, and one has sinned, the penitential system provides the opportunity to undo the consequences of sin.

This led to a closely reasoned understanding of the path to salvation. As the doctrine of original sin teaches, all are born in sin. Yet a remedy is readily available in baptism, for when a child is baptized, the penalty for original sin—and for all previous actual sins—is erased. (Remember that by this time baptism was seen mostly as an act of cleansing of sin.) If a child is unfortunate enough to die before being baptized, that child is destined to an eternal existence in limbo—a place not of punishment, but of a shadowy existence that does not include the joy of heaven. Having been baptized, one now has the power to do good works, thanks to the very grace of baptism. When, as so often happens, the baptized sin, they may have recourse to the sacrament of penance, which, after confession, allows them to make satisfaction—payment—for their sins and to receive absolution from a priest. Even beyond the sacrament of penance, there are other ways to earn merit for the forgiveness of sins. One of these is the Eucharist, or the mass, which during the Middle Ages came to be understood as a repetition—although a bloodless repetition—of the sacrifice of Christ. Those attending mass—it was not even necessary to partake of the Eucharist—received merits that were applied to their salvation. Eventually, the practice arose of having a chaplain who would celebrate private masses for their employers, thus allowing the rich to go about their business without having to bother too much about their own good works or their personal need to offer satisfaction for their sins.

Within such a system, the question immediately arises, what about those who die without having made full satisfaction for their sins? Just as there is limbo for children who die unbaptized, there is purgatory for those who die while still owing satisfaction for all their sins. Several early Christian writers, including Cyprian in the third century and Augustine in the fifth, had suggested the possibility of such a place. By the time of Gregory the Great, early in the seventh century, the existence of purgatory had become a commonly accepted fact and a fundamental part of the medieval view of the world. Those who die in mortal sin and are destined to hell do not go to purgatory. Those in purgatory are eventually destined to heaven, but are not quite ready for it. They must first purge their sins—hence the name, "purgatory." In medieval theology, this was expressed by means of the distinction between time and eternity. Heaven and hell are eternal, and the souls in them will be there eternally; purgatory is temporal, and souls in purgatory will eventually be taken to heaven.

Those still on earth can earn merits for those in purgatory. This may be done by having masses said for their benefit. In such cases, the merits attached to the mass are credited to the dead in purgatory and hasten their rise to heaven. Gregory the Great, who was pope from 590 to 604, tells a story of a monk who appeared in a vision to tell his monastic brothers that, thanks to the masses that they had said for him, he was now in heaven.

Another way to earn merit for those in purgatory was to buy an indulgence for their benefit. Indulgences, originally intended only for those who received them—for instance, by going on a crusade to the Holy Land—came to be transferable to loved ones awaiting their release from purgatory.

All of this was justified on the basis of the "treasury of merits," whose manager was the hierarchy of the church. There have been saints who have performed more works than were required for their own salvation—works of "supererogation." These merits are stored by the church, to be applied as necessary to those who perform various deserving acts—in particular, for those who buy an indulgence. And, if any fear that this treasury of merits might be exhausted, there is no reason for such fear, for the treasury also includes the infinite merit earned by Christ on the cross.

Salvation by Faith

It was within this system that Luther was raised, and through it that he eagerly sought salvation. Eventually, it was against this system and its basic theological presuppositions that he raised his voice, thus leading to the Protestant Reformation.

Although originally impelled into the monastic life by an oath made out of fear in a thunderstorm, Luther saw the monastic life as a means to gain his own salvation. He worked hard at it, strictly following all that was required of members of his order—the Canons of St. Augustine—and making full use of the penitential system offered by the church as a means for salvation. His struggle was long and intense—not because he was a particularly hardened sinner, but on the contrary, because he was exceptionally aware of his own sin and the consequences it entailed. He believed the common doctrine of his time, that the eternal penalty for sins may be avoided by confessing them, making satisfaction for them, and receiving the official absolution from the church. He assiduously listed his sins and went to confession as often as he could. Yet, he soon discovered that, no matter how hard he worked at trying to remember all his sins, there were always some that he forgot and would remember only after confession. Aware of his distress, his confessor told Luther that it was necessary to confess only the most serious sins and those that weighed heavily on his conscience. Luther's response was that every one of his sins was grievous and that they all weighed heavily on his conscience. His confessor then recommended that he read the mystics—who at that time enjoyed great prestige in Germany. Luther did so, and for a time found some relief; but eventually he came to the conclusion that this, too, was sin, for it placed him, and not God, at the center of his devotion. He was then ordered to become a specialist on Scripture, so that he could teach at the newly founded University of Wittenberg, but apparently also in the hope that his studies would help him leave behind the self-examination and self-incrimination that allowed him no peace of mind. This he did, but the struggle continued. He became a professor of Scripture at Wittenberg, but still found no peace. He came to the place where he rebelled against the notion that he should love God, and he declared that he actually hated God, this demanding ruler who required absolute righteousness of him.

It was in the midst of these anxieties that he eventually found peace. Although it is probable that his discovery actually took some time, he describes it as the result of his struggle with Romans 1:17: "For in it [the gospel] the righteousness [or justice] of God is revealed through faith for faith." He says:

> I had indeed been captivated with an extraordinary ardor for understanding Paul in the Epistle to the Romans. But up till then it was ... a single word in Chapter 1, "In it the righteousness of God is revealed," that stood in my way. For I hated that word "righteousness [or justice] of God," which ... I had been taught to understand ... the righteousness with which God is righteous and punishes the unrighteous sinner....

> Though I lived as a monk without reproach, I felt that I was a sinner before God. . . . I did not love, yes, I hated the righteous God who punishes sinners, and secretly, if not blasphemously, certainly murmuring greatly, I was angry with God. . . .
>
> At last, by the mercy of God, . . . I began to understand that the righteousness of God is that by which the righteous lives by a gift of God, namely, by faith. . . . Here I felt I was altogether born again and had entered paradise itself through open gates. There a totally new face of the entire Scripture showed itself to me. [1]

This is what is commonly known as Luther's doctrine of "justification by faith." It is important to understand, however, that Luther does not mean by this that in order to be justified a sinner has to decide to have faith. What he means is rather that it is God who declares the sinner just, not because the sinner has done anything, but because God is gracious. Perhaps it would be better to call this doctrine "justification by grace," for in some quarters "faith" has become a new sort of work by which sinners are expected to justify themselves.

For a while, Luther was content with sharing his discovery with some of his colleagues at Wittenberg. But then an exceptional sale of indulgences came to shatter the peace. For a number of reasons—including the need of funds to complete the building of St. Peter's in Rome—a special indulgence was being sold in a nearby area. Seeking to promote their business, the sellers of this indulgence made extravagant claims as to the indulgences' power—claims that went far beyond what the church officially taught regarding indulgences. Luther was incensed. Soon he realized, however, that his discomfort was not just with the exaggerations of these particular sellers of indulgences, but with the very notion of indulgences and the theology behind them. Even then, he was not ready to start a revolt. He simply offered a series of ninety-five theses to be discussed within the academic confines of the University of Wittenberg.

Others realized the far-reaching consequences of the theses that Luther proposed, translated them from their original Latin into German, and had them printed and widely distributed. Thus Luther found himself propelled into a position of leadership in a vast reformation of the church that he had never intended.

What Luther was actually doing, and one of the main reasons for the great influence of his teachings, was challenging the entire penitential system of the church, and with it also the way in which Christians had understood the process of salvation for at least twelve centuries. Like Augustine, and partly out of his own experience, he had a keen sense of the enormous consequences of sin, its insidiousness, and the human inability to be rid of it. Like Augustine, he was led by his own experience to declare that sinners have no freedom to do good, that their will is so subjected to the power of Satan, that it is as if the will were a horse ridden by Satan. Like Augustine, he insisted on the priority of God's action in salvation. Salvation is not something we attain on our own, but something that God grants. Like Augustine, he was led by these premises to the doctrine of predestination—which, however, he did not develop with the same inexorable logic as Augustine, for he was rather dubious of the powers of the mind to penetrate the mysteries of God.

Unlike Augustine, however, Luther did not believe that salvation was attained by the merits one earns by doing good works with the aid of grace. Unlike Augustine, he was convinced that grace is not a power or a fluid that God grants sinners—infused grace—but is rather God's attitude of love toward the sinner. Unlike Augustine, he did not believe that grace and the resultant good works made a sinner just or righteous before God. For Luther, salvation is by grace; but not a grace that transforms the sinner so that the sinner is intrinsically acceptable to God. Grace remains always on the part of God. Grace does not make sinners acceptable, but simply accepts them. Justification is not a process by which God makes sinners objectively righteous or holy, but a declaration on God's part that the sinner, even though remaining a sinner, is accepted by God as justified. In Luther's own words, a Christian is at the same time a sinner and justified—*simul justus et peccator.*

Salvation and Sanctification

Given his experience of anguished years trying to earn salvation, or to justify himself, Luther was leery of any teaching or practice that might even remotely open the door for justification by works to reappear. He was convinced that the very nature of sin is such that sinners will try to justify themselves, and therefore he feared that religious practices could easily slip back into attempts at self-justification. For this reason, although he believed that Christians should try to please God, he said very little about the sanctification of believers.

It was the next generation of Protestant theologians, and particularly John Calvin, who worked more assiduously on the subject of sanctification. While agreeing that sinners are not justified by their own righteousness, but by the righteousness of Christ, Calvin asserted that this justification by grace is followed, also thanks to God's grace, by a process of sanctification by which the sinner is brought closer to the will of God:

> We confess that while through the intercession of Christ's righteousness God reconciles us to himself, and by free remission of sins account us righteous, his beneficence is at the same time joined with such a mercy that through his Holy Spirit he dwells in us and by his power the lusts of our flesh are each day more and more mortified; we are indeed sanctified, that is, consecrated to the Lord in true purity of life, with our hearts formed to obedience to the law. [2]

For Calvin, this has to do with the very purpose of human life and of the Christian faith, which is not merely to enter the gates of heaven, but to glorify God and to become what God has willed from the very act of creation. In his *Reply to Sadolet*—a Catholic cardinal—Calvin sets this forth bluntly, implying that a religion whose main concern is one's salvation is lacking an important dimension:

> It certainly is the duty of a Christian man to ascend higher than merely to seek and secure the salvation of his own soul. I therefore believe that there is no man imbued with true piety, who will not regard as in poor taste that long and detailed exhortation to a zeal for heavenly life, which occupies a man entirely concerned with himself, and does not, even by one expression, arouse him to sanctify the name of the Lord. [3]

As a result, the Reformed tradition—that stemming from Calvin and the Swiss reformation—has traditionally laid much more stress on sanctification than has the Lutheran tradition. For Calvin, the purpose of religion is not merely to attain heaven, but even more to please God—to become what God intends. Sanctification is part of the purpose of God for creation, and specifically for human beings, and therefore a full Christian faith must lay stress on it. Luther's stress on justification, even while the sinner remains such, and his fear of a relapse into justification by works resulted in his avoidance of too much emphasis on sanctification. The sinner, even though justified, remains a sinner. Thus, Luther's use of the Law of God was mostly negative—as a means to show our sinfulness and our inability to do God's will. Its positive role has to do with society at large, as guidance for the ordering of the civil community. In contrast, Calvin and the entire Reformed tradition saw a more positive value in the Law, which, after showing us our sinfulness, continues calling us to greater obedience and conformity with the will of God—in other words, to sanctification. The Law certainly shows us our sinfulness; it is also given as guidance for society, but its role as guidance for the believer must not be forgotten.

Given this difference in emphasis between the Lutheran and the Reformed traditions, it is not surprising that, while the latter has often been tempted by legalism, the great temptation of the Lutheran tradition has been antinomianism—the theory that the Law no longer has any value as guidance or commandment for believers, who therefore may do as they please.

The legalistic overtones of part of the Reformed tradition became prevalent in British Puritanism, in which one finds beliefs and statements that come dangerously close to salvation by works and even to Pelagianism—on which, see chapter 5. For instance, one of the most popular religious writers of the eighteenth century, William Law, wrote:

> We cannot offer to God the service of angels; we cannot obey Him as man in a state of perfection could; but fallen men can do their best, and this is the perfection that is required of us; it is only the perfection of our best endeavors, a careful labor to be as perfect as we can.
>
> But if we stop short of this, for ought we to know we stop short of the mercy of God and leave ourselves nothing to plead from the terms of the gospel. For God has made no promises of mercy to the slothful and negligent. His mercy is only offered to our frail and imperfect but best endeavors to practice all manner of righteousness. [4]

Complete Sanctification

During his early years, John Wesley felt profoundly the effect of William Law, whom he considered one of the best religious writers of his time. Convinced that God has "made no promises to the slothful and negligent," Wesley made every effort to lead a holy life. This was the inspiration behind the Holy Club at Oxford, and this was also the inspiration behind his missionary attempts in Georgia. Eventually, however, he came to the conclusion that such extreme legalism, with its Pelagian overtones, was not conducive to true faith, which consists in trusting Christ for one's salvation and one's entire life. On May 14, 1738, just a few days before his famous experience at Aldersgate, Wesley wrote to Law a respectful yet very critical letter:

> It is in obedience to what I think the call of God that I take upon me to speak to you of whom I have often desired to learn the first elements of the gospel of Christ....
> For two years more specially I have been preaching after the model of your two practical treatises. And all that heard have allowed that the Law is great, wonderful, and holy. But no sooner did they attempt to follow it than they found it was too high for man, and that by doing the works of this law should no flesh living be justified.
> To remedy this I exhorted them, and stirred up myself, to pray earnestly for the grace of God, and to use all the other means of obtaining that grace which the all-wise God has appointed. But still both they and I were only more convinced that this was a law whereby a man could not live, the law of our members continually warring against it, and bringing us into deeper captivity to the law of sin.
> Under this heavy yoke I might have groaned till death had not an holy man to whom God lately directed me, upon my complaining thereof, answered at once: "Believe, and thou shalt be saved.... This faith, indeed, as well as the salvation it brings, is the free gift of God."...
> Now, sir, suffer me to ask, How you will answer to our common Lord, that you never gave me this advice? [5]

Even though disagreeing with orthodox Calvinism on such matters as predestination and irresistible grace, Wesley was very much part of the Reformed tradition in most other respects. Hence his early penchant toward legalism, and the attraction of views such as that of Law. Significantly, the "holy man" to whom he refers in his letter to Law as the one who brought him back to salvation by grace was himself a Moravian—a member of a Pietist community very much influenced by Lutheran theology. Thus, while remaining a Calvinist in matters having to do with the use and value of the Law, Wesley returned to the emphasis of Luther—and also of Calvin, if not always of later Calvinists—on justification by grace. Needless to say, his letter to Law was not well received, and Law never forgave him for having written it. Still, in an action that was typical of his openness to differing views, Wesley included Law's book in his *Christian Library*, in which he included what he considered to be the best books on matters of faith available in English. He made it quite clear, however, that this book was valuable as a guide for believers who already know the grace of Jesus Christ, and not as a set of instructions to come to know such grace.

While rejecting the legalism that characterized much of the Calvinist tradition of his time, Wesley did agree with Calvin that the purpose of religion and human life is not mere admission into heaven. Justification must be followed and confirmed by sanctification—which became one of the hallmarks of the Wesleyan tradition. This becomes clear as one reads Wesley's sermons—a number of which he collected as the standard introduction to his theology, to be followed by Methodist societies and preachers. In the sermon *The Almost Christian*, he describes a person who would be an ideal church member. This person attends church regularly, tithes, visits the sick, has a personal devotional life, and so on. Yet, if such an ideal church member does not know the grace of Christ and his love, that person is no more than an "almost Christian." The justifying grace of God is the very foundation of Christianity, and without it one is not a Christian, no matter how many good deeds or acts of devotion one performs. The bulk of his sermons, addressed at believers, underscore the need for obedience to God in ways that may even sound legalistic, were it not for Wesley's constant emphasis on the grace of God. Justification must be followed by and manifested in sanctification. Furthermore, sanctification is not something one does on one's own after one is justified. Sanctification, like justification itself, is a work of the Holy Spirit, and not of the believer.

In all of this, Wesley generally agreed with Calvin. Where he disagreed was on how far one should expect this process of sanctification to go. Calvin had made it quite clear that, even though sanctification is a work of the Spirit in the believer, this is never carried to its fulness in this life, for sin always remains with us:

> But even while by the leading of the Holy Spirit we walk in the ways of the Lord, ... traces of our imperfection remain to give us occasion for humility... Let a holy servant of God, I say, choose from the whole course of his life what of an especially noteworthy character he thinks he has done.... Undoubtedly he will somewhere perceive that it savors of the rottenness of the flesh, since our eagerness for well-doing is never what it ought to be.[6]

In contrast, Wesley preached the "Christian perfection" of "entire sanctification"—and these have become hallmarks of the Wesleyan tradition. Wesley felt that preaching on sanctification and calling people to it require that such a goal be attainable in the present life. On this point, however, some clarification is necessary. By "perfection" Wesley did not mean freedom from error, from temptation, or even from wrongful deeds. One is "wholly sanctified" when one acts out of great commandments of love—or, to use Wesley's favorite phrase, when there is in one "the mind that was in Jesus Christ." Even when so acting, one is never certain that one's action is the best, for it is quite possible to err. Christians never come to a point at which they know all things, and this lack of knowledge lends a certain provisionality to even the most loving acts. Then, entire sanctification does not free from temptation, which is always present during this earthly life. Christians, no matter how "perfect," are still tempted. The obvious corollary of this is that "entire sanctification" is never final, for one can always succumb to temptation, or the temptation would not be real—hence the possibility of "falling from grace," or in more common language, "backsliding," which has distinguished the Wesleyan tradition from its Calvinist counterpart with the latter's doctrine of the perseverance of the saints. Then, even though many later Wesleyans have departed from Wesley on this point, he never expected entire sanctification to be a common experience among believers. He never claimed it for himself; and when asked to give examples, there are three that he repeatedly mentions: Monsieur de Renty, Gregorio López, and John Fletcher. Of these, only the third he knew personally—and he named Fletcher as an example of Christian perfection only after his friend's death. Even in such cases, and even though believers must be invited to seek it, entire sanctification is not the result of human effort, but of the work of the Holy Spirit. This is why in Methodist circles it became customary to speak of it as a "second blessing" beyond the experience of justification. Finally, and most important, Wesley's understanding of "perfection" is not static—as if having reached it that were the end. In words that may sound strange to modern ears, he declares that "there is no perfection ... that does not admit of a continual increase."[7]

At any rate, Wesley's emphasis on entire sanctification stands behind much of the holiness movement, which arose as people of Wesleyan background felt that traditional Methodism had ceased preaching entire sanctification—and perhaps, as some claimed, any sanctification at all. The holiness movement, begun late in the nineteenth century, is thus an attempt to return to Wesley's teachings on holiness of life, with a goal of entire sanctification. While much of this is what Wesley taught, some in the holiness movement came to claim that the experience of the "second blessing" of entire sanctification was much more common than Wesley had claimed. Later, as charismatic gifts—particularly speaking in tongues—began to appear within some branches of the holiness movement, the "second blessing" was equated with "baptism by the Spirit," and in some cases came to take the place of the long process of continual sanctification that Wesley had envisioned. Thus the Pentecostal movement emerged from within the holiness tradition.

Contemporary Relevance

There is, however, another aspect of Wesley's view of sanctification that is often neglected in discussions on the matter. For Wesley individual sanctification is part of a process whereby God is bringing humankind—and indeed all of creation—to its intended purpose and order. Sanctification is never a private matter. Wesley expounded on this subject in several of his sermons, in which he explains why Christianity must be seen as a "social religion." In the preface to one of his hymnals he put it quite bluntly, declaring that "holy solitaries is a phrase no more consistent with the gospel than holy adulterers."[8]

Although in most of these passages Wesley refers to the community of believers as the society within which Christianity is always placed, this does not mean that holiness is to be limited to acts of devotion within that community. Holiness also has implications for Christians' participation in the ordering and governance of society. It was his understanding of holiness that impelled Wesley to launch blistering attacks against slavery—as well as against the rebellious American colonies, whose leaders called for freedom while they denied it to their slaves. The same understanding of holiness led him to study social and economic conditions in England itself and to offer a rather perceptive analysis of the causes of hunger among the poor.

As one reads Wesley, all of this was not simply an attempt to "apply" Christian values to the surrounding society. It actually stemmed from a holistic view of salvation as the fulfillment of God's purposes, not only for individual believers, but also for society at large and even for the whole of creation—to the point that on occasion he can imagine cats in heaven!

This understanding of salvation as having social and cosmic dimensions may be seen as a corrective to the development that took place centuries earlier, and summarized at the beginning of this chapter. In that process, it will be remembered, the Christian understanding of salvation was slowly transformed by the views prevailing in the Hellenistic world, in which salvation was seen as salvation *from* creation, rather than *into* the new creation of God, which is the fulfillment and completion of the old.

When so understood, Wesley's doctrine of sanctification, and his cosmic understanding of its implications, may be seen as a forerunner of one of the dominant themes of theology toward the end of the twentieth century and early in the twenty-first century. This is the theme of salvation as a holistic work of God bringing not only individuals, but all of society and all of creation to their intended end. As part of this movement, biblical exegesis has reaffirmed "salvation," not only as what God does for the souls of believers, but also as what God does for their bodies, and what God does in freeing Israel from the yoke of Egypt. This is also the reason why many of today's theologians reject the traditional distinction between "salvation history" and "world history"—as if the history of the world were not leading to its salvation or its fulfillment. Finally, this understanding of salvation stands behind the insistence of various liberation theologies on liberation as an aspect of salvation.

For Further Reading

Newbigin, Lesslie. *Sin and Salvation*. Philadelphia: Westminster Press, 1956.

Tamez, Elsa. *The Amnesty of Grace: Justification by Faith from a Latin American Perspective*. Nashville: Abingdon Press, 1993.

Taylor, Barbara Brown. *Speaking of Sin: The Lost Language of Salvation*. Cambridge, Mass.: Cowley Publications, 2000.

Toon, Peter. *Justification and Sanctification*. Westchester, Ill.: Crossway Books, 1983.

Verkuyl, J. *The Message of Liberation in Our Age*. Grand Rapids, Mich.: Eerdmans, 1970.

Notes

1. *Preface to the Latin Works,* Lewis W. Spitz, trans., *Luther's Works* (Philadelphia: Muhlenberg, 1960), 34:336-37.

2. *Institutes*, 3.14.9 (Philadelphia: Westminster, 1960), 776.

3. *Reply to Sadolet* (*Calvin: Theological Treatises*; Philadelphia: Westminster, 1954), 229.

4. *A Serious Call to a Devout and Holy Life* (New York: Paulist Press, 1978), 67.

5. Frank Baker, ed., *The Works of John Wesley*, vol. 25 (Oxford: Clarendon Press, 1980), 540-41.

6. *Institutes* 3.14.9 (Philadelphia: Westminister, 1960), 776.

7. *Plain Account of Christian Perfection*, 12 (Jackson edition, 11:374). The same words appear in his *Sermon* 40.1.9.

8. Preface to the hymnal of 1739 (Jackson edition, 14:321).

10.

TRADITION

*For I received from the Lord what I also handed on
to you, that the Lord Jesus ...*
1 Corinthians 11:23

One often hears that one of the main points of disagreement between Catholics and Protestants at the time of the Reformation was the authority of Scripture. This is not strictly true. In general, Protestants and Catholics agreed on the authority of Scripture. Where they disagreed was on the authority of tradition, particularly for the interpretation of Scripture. Indeed, as a result of the Reformation and other developments in modernity, one of the main themes of theology during that time was the value and authority of tradition. Therefore, in this chapter, rather than focus on the authority of Scripture, I shall explore the role of tradition in the church, as well as its relation to Scripture.

The Importance of Tradition

The Latin *traditio*—tradition—means both something that is passed on and the act itself of passing it on. In this sense, it is like the English "transmission," which may mean the act of sending something as well as whatever is sent. Thus, when one speaks of "tradition" in a theological context, this may mean either the act of passing teachings and practices from one generation to the next, or those teachings and practices themselves.

There is no doubt that tradition plays a very important role in Christian faith. This is so because the essence of Christianity is not found primarily in a series of doctrines or principles that one could discover on one's own, much as any observant person may discover that clouds bring rain. At the very heart of Christianity stands a series of events—particularly the life, death, and resurrection of Jesus—that cannot be known unless one is told of them by someone else, much as one can only know of the Declaration of Independence if one is told about it. If tradition is the act of passing on a teaching, a practice, or the news about some event to others who would not otherwise know of them, Christianity is essentially a matter of tradition. We have all been told of Jesus, either directly by others, or indirectly by the writers of the New Testament—most probably, by both. If such is the meaning of tradition, then Scripture is one of the main agents that Christianity has had through the ages to bring others in contact with the tradition, with the historical fact of Jesus of Nazareth.

Furthermore, if the very heart of Christianity is the life and teachings of Jesus, then, in opposition to much of our modern mentality, older is better. If, on the one hand, Christianity were a matter that one could discover by research and experimentation, like biology or astronomy, then the latest should be regarded as the best. If, on the other hand, Christianity centers on certain events in the past, then what is close to those events—that which is oldest—is better than anything new.

Along similar lines, it is also important to remember that much of Scripture itself was preceded by an oral tradition before it was written. The stories about Jesus and his teachings were passed from disciple to disciple long before they were written—and much of what was then written, the writers knew through such oral tradition. Paul himself, when telling the Corinthians about communion, tells them that he is passing on a tradition, something he has received: "I received from the Lord what I also [delivered] to you" (1 Cor 11:23). In that passage, the words for both receiving and delivering are derived from the Greek equivalent of "tradition."

In the discussion in chapter 7 about the doctrine of the church, we saw a hint of the significance that tradition had for early Christians, particularly as they sought to refute the many doctrines of those who claimed to have secret knowledge about Jesus. As we saw, Christian leaders developed the principle of apostolic succession precisely as a means to claim that they and their church were the true guardians and teachers of the tradition stemming from Jesus. Apostolic succession was not a mechanical passing of a power from one generation to another; it was rather the guarantee that present-day teachings were in continuity with the teachings of the apostles—in other words, that they were within the tradition of the apostles. This in turn gave greater authority to the bishops, who through their mutual agreement were the main guardians of the tradition. For this reason, most of the early writers against Gnosticism and other heresies insisted on tradition and their being part of it. Irenaeus repeatedly says that what he is teaching he learned from Polycarp in Smyrna, who in turn was a disciple of John.

When Irenaeus wrote, the canon of the New Testament was still relatively fluid, so that an appeal to Scripture—particularly the New Testament—was not as convincing as it became later. Furthermore, when it came to the Hebrew Scriptures, Christians were proposing their own interpretations, which in many cases differed radically from Jewish interpretations. In such circumstances, it was not possible simply to appeal to the authority of Scriptures. Such an appeal had to be accompanied with the claim that whatever interpretation one was offering was in accordance with the tradition of Jesus and the apostles.

Tertullian, who had a knack for using phrases and arguments that would become crucial in later centuries, wrote a treatise, *Prescription Against Heretics*, in which he argued that the church was the owner of Scripture and that therefore no one else had the right to use these texts that were the possession of the church: "It ought to be clearly seen to whom belongs the possession of the Scriptures, that none may be admitted to the use thereof who has no title at all to the privilege."[1] On this basis, any whom the church does not consider a true Christian has no right to use the Scriptures: "not being Christians, they have acquired no right to the Christian Scriptures."[2] What Tertullian is doing here is claiming that the true interpretation of Scripture lies only with those who are part of the true tradition of the church and that the church has the right to determine who is part of that tradition and who is not. The immediate consequence of such a view is that when there is a disagreement of such magnitude as to cause some Christians to abandon the church or to be expelled from it, those who have been declared no longer part of the church cannot argue for their position on the basis of Scripture, which their opponents will now see as their own possession, which only they have the right to interpret. If both sides follow this view, then the debate is no longer about what Scripture says, but rather about which of the two sides is the true church—which side truly represents, upholds, and owns the tradition.

Tertullian's position seems final, leaving no room for debate. However, Tertullian himself proved that things are not that simple. When he came to the conviction that the church at large had become too lax in its morals and had lost much of its eschatological expectation, he abandoned it, joining the Montanists—whom the church at large considered a heretical sect. In so doing, Tertullian became a clear example of the weak link in his argument: suppose that the church no longer upholds the tradition, or that it comes to accept a false tradition, does such a church still own the exclusive right to interpret Scripture? Does it own any right at all to Scripture? Thus, the debate that was shifted from the meaning of Scripture to the question of which church has the right to interpret it now moved to the question of which church is the true representative of the tradition. Tertullian's disagreement with the church at large, leading him to become a Montanist, was not about the authority of Scripture, nor even about which church could claim an uninterrupted link of apostolic succession. It was about tradition—about which of the two rival bodies continued the tradition of the apostles, therefore owning Scripture, and therefore having the right to interpret it and even to control its interpretation. As we shall see, similar issues were at the heart of theological debates during the time of the Reformation.

Tradition and Innovation

Even in Tertullian's time, not all agreed that old was best, and that one should limit one's thoughts to what had always been taught by the church. While the main concern of Irenaeus and Tertullian was to preserve Christian doctrine against heretics, others, while also rejecting those whom the church declared to be heretics, sought to delve more deeply into Christian truth. For a long time, Greek culture had admired those whose love of wisdom—*philo/sophia*—impelled them to inquire into the nature of truth. Now there were Christians who felt that their love of God and God's truth ought to lead them along similar paths of inquiry. If one loves God truly and deeply, one will love God with the entire mind and will devote to the knowledge and service of God all the gifts with which God has endowed the intellect. This was essentially the position of a number of Christian thinkers and teachers, mostly in the city of Alexandria, known then as the intellectual center of the Mediterranean basin. Clement of Alexandria, Origen, and several others believed that the mind is a gift of God for the service of God, and that therefore to think or even to speculate about God is no sin, but is on the contrary an act of deep devotion. This did not mean that they were willing to abandon the tradition of the church. In his writings, Origen repeatedly distinguishes between what is part of the "rule of faith"—which he wholeheartedly believes and supports—and his own speculations. He has no desire to allow his intellectual inquiries to lead him to reject Christian orthodoxy—that is, to contradict the tradition of the church. But he also has no desire to limit himself to such orthodoxy or to such tradition.

The Alexandrines did this by applying to the Christian faith many of the methods and presuppositions of the Platonic philosophical tradition—which to them was the only philosophy worthy of the name. We have already seen some of the consequences this had, for instance, in the way the church came to think about God. Still, one must recognize and admire the love of truth of this "tradition beyond the tradition"—the tradition of thinkers and scholars willing to ask new questions and to seek new answers, not necessarily for the sake of innovation, but for the sake of truth.

Needless to say, Tertullian would have none of that. He was convinced that the reason heresies abounded in his time was that philosophy had been allowed to enter into the arena of theology. Hence his lapidary words, also from the treatise quoted above: "What indeed has Athens to do with Jerusalem? What concord is there between the Academy and the Church? What between heretics and Christians?"[3]

Throughout the history of Christianity, these two tendencies have appeared repeatedly. To complicate matters, sometimes the innovation has become part of the accepted tradition. A case in point is the work of Augustine, clearly the most influential theologian in the history of Western Christianity. We have already met him repeatedly—when discussing the doctrine of God, when dealing with sin and its consequences, with predestination, with the sacraments, and the like.

He dominated Western Christian tradition throughout the Middle Ages—and to some extent he still does. Yet in his time he was often seen as a radical innovator, and this on several fronts.

By employing Neoplatonism to help him out of his Manichean phase, Augustine came to speak of both God and the soul as incorporeal realities. Most of his contemporaries had no objection to such an affirmation in the case of God; but they were not quite ready to say the same about the soul. To many of us, the notion that the soul is incorporeal may be something we take for granted. Yet, particularly in the Western part of the empire, where Stoic philosophy vied with Neoplatonism, there were many who objected to this. For them, only God was incorporeal, and to be a creature is to be corporeal. This was also connected, as we saw earlier, with their view of original sin and its transmission. From their perspective, Augustine was introducing innovations that threatened the received tradition of the church. They were right to a certain extent, not because Augustine was contradicting the received doctrine of the church, but because he was delving into questions that had not been treated before with as much detail and systematic thought. The debate continued for decades, but eventually what Augustine taught on these matters became the accepted tradition of the church.

Something similar happened with Augustine's views on grace and predestination. There is little doubt that much that Augustine said in this regard was an innovation. Before his time, Christians—including Paul—had spoken of predestination and of human inability to do what God requires. However, it was Augustine who systematized all of this, asking questions that had not been asked before, and therefore giving answers that were not part of the accepted tradition. In this case, as we saw in chapter 5, what the church generally did was to declare itself in favor of Augustine's teachings while at the same time interpreting them in a very mitigated form. This created an inner contradiction within the received tradition, which declared Augustine to have been right and yet interpreted him in a way Augustine himself would have rejected. Thus, those who interpret Augustine in a more moderate fashion have repeatedly rejected every attempt to restore the full teachings of Augustine. Examples of this pattern are the cases of Gottschalk, in the ninth century, of Luther and Calvin, in the sixteenth, and of the Jansenists, in the seventeenth.

This serves to point out that much of the history of Christian doctrine has been a struggle over tradition—that is, over the question of who is the true representative of tradition, and whose views uphold or deny the tradition. One could even say that most of the debates among theologians and churches has been over the issue posed long before by Tertullian: who is the true owner of tradition.

The Vincentian Canon or Rule

In the year 434, as part of the controversy surrounding Augustine and his theology, a monk in southern France, Vincent of Lérins, published a brief writing that would become influential in later discussions regarding tradition and orthodoxy. His *Commonitory* may be said to be the first treatise on the development of doctrine. There, Vincent states what appears to be a very conservative position on the matter, arguing for the rule that

> all possible care must be taken, that we hold that faith which has been believed everywhere, always, by all [*quod ubique, quod semper, quod ab omnibus*].... This rule we shall observe if we follow universality, antiquity, consent. We shall follow universality if we confess that one faith to be true, which the whole catholic church throughout the world confesses; antiquity, if we in no wise depart from those interpretations which it is manifest were notoriously held by our holy ancestors and fathers; consent, in like manner, if in antiquity itself we adhere to the consentient definitions and determinations of all, or at least almost all priests and doctors.[4]

With these words, Vincent is trying to respond to a question that Tertullian had already faced. He was convinced that the final authority in all matters of doctrine is Scripture. Yet he saw that Scripture was interpreted differently by proponents of different doctrines or positions. He thus offered tradition—the universal tradition that has been held by all, everywhere, and always—as a guide to the interpretation of Scripture. In so doing, he was opposing both Augustine and the Donatists. It is mostly against the Donatists that he stressed universality [*quod ubique*], for Donatism was essentially a North African church. To refute this movement, Vincent felt that it sufficed to show that it lacked the universality that is characteristic of true tradition. Against Augustine's innovations, he stressed antiquity *[quod semper]*. Augustine may be widely read and influential all over the church; but still his doctrine is an innovation and therefore must be rejected.

This aspect of Vincent's writing is often cited to show his conservatism. When it came to Augustine's innovations, or to the claims of the Donatists, he certainly was conservative. Yet, Vincent is the first Christian writer to consider the possibility—and even the desirability—that doctrines may evolve. He admits that there must be "progress" in the church and that such progress is to take place, not only in size, organization, and the like, but also in doctrine. Comparing the church to a living organism, he says:

> The growth of religion in the soul must be analogous to the growth of the body, which, though in a process of years it is developed and attains its full size, yet remains still the same.... In like manner, it behooves Christian doctrine to follow the same laws of progress, so as to be consolidated by years, enlarged by time, refined by age, and yet, withal, to continue uncorrupt and unadulterate, complete and perfect....[5]

Thus, the task of the church when it comes to doctrines is threefold:

> If there is anything which antiquity has left shapeless and rudimentary, to fashion and polish it, if anything already reduced to shape and developed, to consolidate and strengthen it, if any already ratified and defined to keep and guard it.[6]

The Growing Authority of Tradition

During the rest of the Middle Ages, tradition came to be regarded with increased reverence. As education declined, there was little sense that thought and ideas—including doctrines—had developed. People living in the ninth century were convinced that all their religious practices and beliefs were exactly the same as those of the apostles and that the tradition had remained unchanged over the centuries. The relatively few writings remaining from antiquity came to have an authority they never claimed. A century after Augustine's death, he was quoted with a respect almost equal to Scripture.

Another important development regarding tradition took place during the Middle Ages. This was the claim that there was an oral tradition that had not been written down by the apostles and that on the basis of that tradition the church could proclaim doctrines that had always been part of tradition, but had not been generally acknowledged as such. Bonaventure (1221–1274), for instance, declares that "the apostles passed on [as a tradition] many things that are not written."[7] For him, and for most Franciscan theologians with him, this included matters such as the Immaculate Conception of Mary, which was not proclaimed a dogma of the Roman Catholic Church until 1854 (almost six hundred years after Bonaventure's death).

Perhaps the most significant medieval development regarding the use of tradition was the scholastic method, which was based on a strong sense of the authority of tradition and antiquity. In that method, a question is posed, followed by various quotations from "authorities"—Scripture, ancient Christian writers, philosophers— that would seem to support a positive or a negative response. After providing his own answer to the question, the scholastic teacher had too respond to the authorities that had been adduced for the other side, not usually by rejecting them, but rather by showing how they too would agree with the answer given. Quite obviously, this method is built on the presupposition that the "authorities" quoted are indeed authoritative and that one cannot answer a question in a way that would contradict them. Thus, within medieval scholasticism the authority of tradition was imbedded in the method of theology, which was often understood as a systematization and clarification of tradition.

It is often said that at that point theologians placed tradition on a par with Scripture. Although this may be true of some, and was certainly the case in much of the devotion of the time, it is not strictly true of the best medieval theologians. Saint Thomas Aquinas agrees that arguing on the basis of authorities is most fitting in theology, whose first principles are based on revelation and therefore can only be known by the testimony of those who received them—that is, through tradition. But then he makes it clear that of these authorities only Scripture is to be taken as absolutely certain. He lists three sorts of authorities usually adduced in theology: the teaching of the philosophers, Scripture, and the "doctors of the church"—by which he means ancient Christian writers. But these do not have the same authority: "One must note that sacred doctrine uses these authorities [the philosophers] as extraneous yet probable arguments; those of Scripture, as proper and definitive; and those of other doctors of the church, as proper, but only probable."[8]

In short, the Middle Ages had a very high concept of the authority of tradition; but this was seldom put on a par with the authority of Scripture. During a time in which there was very little notion that things were not as they had always been, and therefore there was little sense of history, people could generally accept the practices and doctrines of their time as essentially the same as those in the New Testament.

The Challenge of New Discoveries

The end of the Middle Ages was accompanied—and, to an extent, caused—by the discovery that many authorities had erred and that in any case there had been a historical process resulting in a present that is very different from the past. For centuries, theologians had seen a vestige of the Trinity in the world consisting of three land masses: Europe, Asia, and Africa. Now, it turned out that there were huge continents that the ancients had not even suspected. How could one still sustain the authority of a tradition that was based on such an erroneous view of earth?

Just as Columbus was "discovering" America, other momentous discoveries were being made by scholars in Europe. The Donation of Constantine, the document on which the Papacy based many of its claims, was discovered to be spurious. Through a long process of copying and recopying—in other words, by a "traditioning" process—countless errors had found their way into ancient writings. Now, with the invention of the printing press, these errors became glaring, to the point that scholars found it necessary, through a long and tedious process, to seek to recover what the ancients had actually said. After the fall of Constantinople in 1453, Greek scholars flooded Western Europe, bringing with them manuscripts, traditions, and ideas that differed significantly from those of their Western counterparts.

The result of all of this was a desire to return to the sources of antiquity. Under the motto *ad fontes*—to the sources—scholars sought to rediscover what Augustine, Jerome, and others had actually written. Under the same motto, Erasmus and others set out to produce new editions of the Greek New Testament—editions devoid, to the degree possible, of all the accretions and variants accumulated over centuries of manuscript tradition. In Italy, there were those who looked to classical Greece and Rome—and to a time even before the advent of Christianity—for models to imitate. (Significantly, the cathedral of St. Peter in Rome, for many today a symbol of tradition, was built by popes who felt that the Middle Ages had departed from the true canons of the beauty of antiquity, and who sought to go to a time before the medieval tradition for such canons.)

Luther and Tradition

This was the atmosphere prevailing in much of Europe at the time of the Reformation. Luther himself was scarcely aware of it. He knew of the work of biblical scholars seeking to reconstruct the original words of Scripture, but he did not see this as requiring a major overhaul of Christian tradition. He certainly had little interest in the art and the glories of the Italian Renaissance. Yet, since the return to the sources that had been obscured by tradition was a dominant theme in his time, this was the atmosphere he breathed, and eventually the movement he started would lead to a conscious effort to return to the sources of Christianity—particularly to Scripture.

Luther did not set out to contradict or even to change the tradition of the church. On the contrary, he had great respect for that tradition. He did not see his initial protest against the sale of indulgences as a rejection of tradition, but as a defense of tradition against recent innovators. He was slowly and reluctantly driven to reject much of the medieval tradition as it became increasingly clear that some of it contradicted his own understanding of Scripture. Even in the midst of that struggle he declared that "hearing or believing anything against the common witness, faith, and teaching that the entire and holy Christian church has sustained from the beginning until the present—for over fifteen hundred years and throughout the world—is perilous and terrible."⁹ Even though he had serious conflicts with the popes of his time, he insisted that "the papacy has God's word and the office of the apostles, and we have received the Holy Scriptures, baptism, the sacrament, and the office of preaching from them." [10]

This last quotation points to another important aspect of Luther's teachings regarding Scripture and tradition. For him, Scripture was part of tradition. It certainly was the oldest extant witness to tradition; but it, too, was part of tradition. Thus, when his Catholic opponents argued that it was the church and its tradition that had determined the canon of Scripture, and that therefore tradition is above Scripture, Luther responded that the final authority is neither Scripture nor tradition. The final authority is the gospel. It is the gospel that gave birth to the church, and it is the gospel that produced Scripture. This explains why he was able to speak negatively of books such as the Epistle of James, in which he found little but "straw." Yet, he was sufficiently respectful of both tradition and Scripture that he would never have struck James from the canon.

In brief, Luther was always as positive toward tradition as he could be. He refused to discard any traditional teaching or practice until he was convinced that it was contrary to the gospel. He kept as many of the prayers, hymns, and other liturgical elements as he could. Those he could not, he modified by eliminating whatever lines or other elements he found offensive to the gospel. He staunchly resisted the many claims by more radical reformers to eliminate or tear down anything that could not be found in Scripture—such as the images of saints, crucifixes, vestments, and so on.

Other Views

There were many who felt that Luther had not gone far enough in his restoration of scriptural Christianity. Once convinced that tradition could err, and indeed on many points had led the church astray, these more radical reformers insisted that anything that is not biblical must go. Even among Luther's colleagues in Wittenberg, some held these views. When Luther was hidden from imperial authorities in Wartburg, Karlstadt and others wrought such havoc in the churches that Luther had to leave his hiding place and return to Wittenberg to reestablish order. In Zürich, Ulrich Zwingli

(1484–1531) held similar ideas, forbidding the use of instrumental music in worship. Eventually, this more radical wing of the Reformation crystalized into Anabaptism, a diverse movement of people who sought to restore purely biblical Christianity, and therefore rejected infant baptism, as well as many of the accommodations between church and civil society that had evolved through the centuries. Some offshoots of the movement claimed to have received direct revelations from God, and then set out to build the kingdom of God on earth by leading revolutionary movements that were drenched in blood. Others—notably, the Mennonites—insisted on pacifism as a fundamental element in the teaching of Jesus and as a result suffered repeated persecutions and exiles.

This contrast between Luther and the more radical wing of the Reformation may be expressed in a nutshell. Luther saw a positive value in tradition and believed that only that in tradition which clearly contradicted the gospel should be abandoned. In contrast, the radical Reformers saw tradition as an obstacle in the way to true obedience to Scripture, and therefore they insisted that anything in tradition that could not be shown to be part of biblical Christianity should be rejected.

Calvin agreed in principle with Luther, showing great respect for the early tradition of the church and repeatedly quoting ancient authors such as Augustine and Gregory the Great. Like Luther, he felt that during the Middle Ages much of the ancient tradition of Christianity had been warped and that tradition therefore needed to be corrected. He did differ from Luther in declaring that many of the ceremonies of his time, with the accretions that had been added to them through the ages, obscured the gospel they were supposed to announce. In consequence, he simplified the practices of worship to a degree that Luther had not done. Here again, it was not so much a matter of the authority of Scripture as it was of the authority and value of tradition—what traditions ought to be kept, and what are the standards for deciding on the matter.

The English Reformation, precipitated by the marital woes of Henry VIII, at first followed the lead of Luther—and of royal policy—keeping as many of the traditional practices as were not in direct contradiction with Scripture or with the teaching of the Reformation itself. During the reign of Mary Tudor (1553–1558), many of the English reformers fled to the Continent, where they found refuge mostly among Calvinists in Switzerland. Upon returning after the death of Mary, these Calvinists sought a more thorough reformation, while Queen Elizabeth preferred to follow the policies of her father Henry VIII, so as to unsettle the faithful as little as possible. The result was the Anglican "via media," in which people of widely divergent convictions could come together, as long as they subscribed to the Thirty-nine Articles, promulgated in 1562, and in worship followed the directives of the Book of Common Prayer. Toward the end of Elizabeth's reign, the more radical Calvinists were showing dissatisfaction with such an arrangement and claimed that it was necessary to purify the church of all "popery"—for which reason they were called "Puritans." Eventually the Puritans rebelled, the Parliament they controlled beheaded the king, and they set in motion their plan of radical reformation. However, after the restoration of the monarchy, the Church of England returned to its "via media," which has characterized it ever since.

Roman Catholicism and Tradition

Meanwhile, already in the late sixteenth century, the Roman Catholic Church had established its position regarding the relationship between tradition and Scripture. Although at a time the advocates of reformation had hoped that their differences with the rest of the church would be resolved by an ecumenical council, when the council did meet, at Trent (1545–1563), it was clear that its purpose was not to discuss who was right on each of the points under discussion, but rather to reiterate the Roman Catholic position against every point advanced by the Protestants. Regarding the issue of tradition and its authority, the council affirmed that there is an oral, not written, tradition and that this has an authority on a par with Scripture:

> Since this truth and this morality are contained in the written books and in non-written traditions that have been received from the very lips of Christ by the apostles ... the Council, following the example of the orthodox Fathers, acknowledges all the books of the Old and the New Testament ... as well as the traditions regarding both faith and morals, as coming from the very mouth of Christ or dictated by the Holy Ghost and preserved in the Catholic

Church by an uninterrupted succession, receiving and venerating them with the same respect and the same devotion.[11]

In conclusion, although at times it would seem that the main issue in the entire process of the Reformation was the authority of Scripture, there is a sense in which Catholics as well as Protestants agreed on the authority of Scripture. The issue was rather the authority of tradition—its value, its permanence, and its role in the interpretation of Scripture.

The Challenge of Modernity

The modern age brought with it issues and perspectives that were very different from any that the church had faced before. Until that time it was generally agreed that whatever is older is usually better than an innovation, but the spirit of modernity moved in the opposite direction. Truth was not in the past, but in the future—in some golden age that humankind would eventually achieve by means of innovation, invention, and progress. As a result of scientific research applied in technological advances, the world of nature seemed to be opening up with infinite possibilities. Old systems of government—monarchy in particular—must be left behind as relics of the past. The wave of the future was democracy, education, free enterprise, and advancement through free inquiry.

In general, Protestant and Catholic theologians reacted to these new conditions in diametrically opposite ways. Protestant theologians sought to show that modernity was compatible with Christianity (see chapter 3) and even that Protestantism was the form of Christianity most suitable for the modern age. This meant a general abandonment of tradition—or at least relegating it to the rank of "past superstitions." Christianity had little to do with all those doctrines and practices that had developed over the ages. In fact, Christianity was a fairly simple thing. Typical of the age was historian Adolph von Harnack, who summarized the essence of Christianity as: "Firstly, the kingdom of God and its coming. Secondly, God the Father and the infinite value of the human soul. Thirdly, the higher righteousness and the commandment of love."[12]

In such modern depictions of Christianity, the authority of Scripture counted for little. This was even more so, since the critical and historical study of Scripture, which flourished within Protestantism precisely at this time, undercut many of the old presuppositions about the origin and composition of the Bible. Thus, while Protestant theologians claimed that they valued Scripture above tradition, in reality they valued modernity above both. Clearly, this was not the attitude of the rank and file within Protestantism. Even so, the notion that Protestantism was to be preferred because it was modern did penetrate deeply among the body of believers.

In contrast, Roman Catholicism tended to see modernity as the bane of Christianity. As a result of the ideals of modernity, that church had lost its position of practically exclusive dominance over much of western Europe. The French Revolution, with its ideals of freedom, equality, and fraternity, had resulted in great loss to the church in that nation. Many of the new states declared themselves to be secular and free from any guidance on the part of the church. They also claimed the education of their children as their responsibility and were committed to doing this apart from the dictates of the church. Freedom of thought and of speech resulted in the publication of many books that the church considered blasphemous or immoral. In 1871, most of the papal possessions in Italy were annexed by the Italian government. Not surprisingly, Roman Catholicism tended to see in all of this a serious threat to Christian tradition, and therefore it set itself to defend tradition over against the innovations of modernity. In 1854, Pope Pius IX reasserted papal authority by proclaiming the dogma of the Immaculate Conception of Mary—the first time in history a pope had proclaimed a dogma on his own. Ironically, this innovation was made in the name and in the defense of tradition. In 1864, Pope Pius issued *Syllabus of Errors,* which condemned several of the basic tenets of modern democracy and the modern secular state. In 1870, the First Vatican Council declared the pope to be infallible. Even then, the dominant anti-modern attitude of the official stance of the Church did not go unchallenged. The Roman Catholic "modernist" movement—quite different from Protestant modernism—suggested that, no matter whether the present doctrines and practices of the church reflect those of the first century, one ought to look not at the ancient church, but at the church of the present and what it has become thanks to the Holy Spirit. In 1908, its leading figure, Alfred Loisy, was excommunicated.

Thus, while Protestantism erred on the side of embracing modernity too glibly, Catholicism erred in the other direction, rejecting much that was modern almost as a matter of course. In consequence, the gap between the two main branches of Western Christianity was wider in the nineteenth century than it had been even in the sixteenth, at the high point of the Reformation. Since this gap could be summarized as opposing attitudes towards tradition, the authority of tradition became one of the main dividing lines between the two—even though most Protestants still insisted that the gap was on the authority of Scripture.

Contemporary Relevance

During the twentieth century a very different situation emerged. Within Roman Catholicism, John XXIII's emphasis on *aggiornamento*—updating—as the main item in the agenda of the Second Vatican Council (1962–1965) brought a new attitude of openness toward a number of elements in modernity—as well as toward Protestantism. Among Protestants, thanks in part to Neo-orthodoxy, there was a renewed emphasis on the authority of Scripture and on its value both for the life of the church and for the theological enterprise. Catholics shared in this renewed study of Scripture. On the matter of tradition, Catholic historical studies showed that it was not as monolithic as had been thought. On their part, Protestants came to a new appreciation of tradition.

Then, late in the twentieth century, people began talking of the end of modernity and speaking of "postmodernity." In postmodernity, they said, the canons of modernity no longer hold. The great "metanarrative," or foundational myth of modernity that the world was moving toward the universal acceptance of a purely rational and objective system of truths, no longer holds. All knowledge is marked by the perspectives and the interests of those who know. When looking at the past, there is no longer a single tradition, but a variety of traditions that interweave in ever-changing ways. Scripture itself—as any other reality—is always read and interpreted from the perspective of the reader, so that there is no longer a universally valid and absolutely demonstrable reading of Scripture.

Within the life of the church, the enormous demographic changes of the twentieth century made these issues much more urgent. By the beginning of the twenty-first century, it was clear that the centers of Christian vitality and growth were no longer in the North Atlantic, nor even in traditionally Christian areas. Furthermore, instead of one, there were many centers, each set in a different culture, speaking different languages, cherishing different traditions.

Given such circumstances, Christian theologians in the early years of the twenty-first century are engaged in the task of elucidating how the gospel can be one in so many different incarnations. It is no longer a matter of the authority of tradition, but rather a matter of a variety of traditions, and the need to recognize and cherish their differences while somehow clinging to the notion of one gospel and one tradition. The issue of tradition is not dead; it is just much more complicated and more urgent!

For Further Reading

Allchin, A. M. *The Living Presence of the Past: The Dynamic of Christian Tradition*. New York: Seabury, 1981.

Congar, Yves, O.P. *The Meaning of Tradition*. New York: Hawthorn Books, 1964.

Hanson, R. P. C. *Tradition in the Early Church*. London: SCM Press, 1962.

Jenkins, Daniel. *Tradition, Freedom, and the Spirit*. Philadelphia: Westminster Press, 1951.

Pelikan, Jaroslav J. *The Vindication of Tradition*. New Haven: Yale University Press, 1984.

Notes

1. *Prescription Against Heretics*, 15 (*Ante-Nicene Fathers*, 3:251).
2. Ibid., 37 (Ibid., 3:261).
3. Ibid., 7 (Ibid., 3:246).
4. *Commonitory*, 2 (*Nicene and Post-Nicene Fathers*, Second series, 11:132).
5. Ibid., 23 (Ibid., 11:148).
6. Ibid., 23 (Ibid., 11:149).
7. *Commentary on the Sentences*, 3.1.2.6.

8. *Summa Theologica*, Part I, question 1, art. 1.

9. *To Albert, Margrave of Brandenburg* (1532).

10. *Sermon on John 16:1-2* (*Luther's Works;* Saint Louis: Concordia, 1961, 24:304).

11. Heinrich Denzinger, *Enchiridion Symbolorum*, 31st edition (Barcelona: Herder, 1957), 783.

12. Adolph von Harnack, *What Is Christianity?* (New York: Harper and Brothers, 1957), 41.

11.

THE SPIRIT OF HOPE

And I saw the holy city, the new Jerusalem, coming down out of heaven from God, prepared as a bride adorned for her husband.
Revelation 21:2

There are two important points of Christian doctrine that have scarcely been mentioned in the previous chapters. These are the doctrine of the Holy Spirit—pneumatology—and the doctrine of last things—eschatology. One reason these two items have not occupied us to this point is that there is no particular moment in the past when they became the central issue at hand, when they were given their definitive shape. More important, however, these two items have been left for this last chapter because they are the points of doctrine likely to dominate much of the theological discussion during our lifetime. This has much to do with the emerging shape of Christianity in today's world.

The New Geography of Christianity

The most significant change that has taken place within Christianity in the last hundred years is that it has ceased being the religion of the West—or, in the case of Protestantism, of the North Atlantic. In the West itself, a series of events and developments have resulted in the increased marginalization of Christianity. In many traditionally Christian countries, church membership and church attendance have declined rapidly. In spite of a number of rearguard actions and attempts to restore "Christian values," mostly on the part of the "Christian right," and even in spite of some temporary victories in such actions, it is clear that in general the old Christendom is moving toward a "post-Christian" society. Both in the United States and in Europe, one frequently hears Christians bemoaning the declining membership in their churches and sometimes even doubting that there is a future for the Christian faith.

While this is taking place in the traditionally Christian West, almost exactly the opposite is happening in the rest of the world. In Asia there are now denominations that are larger than their mother churches in the United States or in Europe. In several countries in Africa, Christian growth is nothing short of explosive. Among Protestants in Latin America, the growth of Pentecostalism is to the point at which it is beginning to challenge the traditional hegemony of Roman Catholicism.

The stage for all of this was set years ago, mostly in the nineteenth century, which was the century of the great missionary expansion of Christianity—particularly of Protestant Christianity, for Roman Catholicism had also expanded enormously in the sixteenth century. The churches that the missionaries of the nineteenth century planted have served as the springboard for the unprecedented growth of the late twentieth and early twenty-first centuries.

However, the growth that has taken place is very different from what most of those missionaries foresaw. The most progressive among them hoped for a day when nationals would take over the churches the missionaries were founding, when these churches would support and govern themselves, and when they would take up the missionary torch. These goals were sometimes called the "three selfs": self-government, self-support, and self-propagation. They have been attained in many of the "younger churches" in what has traditionally been called the "Third World." But that is not all that has happened. Christians in those younger churches have also begun to seek their own ways of being the church and are developing perspectives and theologies that take their own context into account. There is a fourth "self" that very few envisioned: self-interpretation, by which many Christians in traditionally non-Christian cultures reinterpret the faith and reshape worship in ways that are more amenable to their own cultural traditions. In many cases, this has led to the birth of autochthonous or independent churches, which have little or no connection to the churches that sent the first missionaries. Thus, the enormous growth of Christianity in Africa is due not only to conversions to Anglicanism, Methodism, or Roman Catholicism, but most particularly to the great attraction of independent, indigenous churches—many of which Anglicans, Methodists, or Roman Catholics would hardly recognize as the result of their labors. In Latin America, while Methodists, Presbyterians, and others are growing, Protestant growth is due mostly to Pentecostalism—and in particular to Pentecostal denominations that have arisen on Latin American soil.

The Holy Spirit

These new conditions lead us to consider the doctrine of the Holy Spirit. Many in these "younger" churches are convinced that the manner in which Christianity has adapted to their own national or local environment is the work of the Holy Spirit. If Christianity speaks to a culture or a class in a concrete and innovative way, this is not because its leaders have been particularly insightful or creative; it is because the Holy Spirit leads them through the changes that are necessary in that particular setting. As has been the case throughout the history of the church, in these newer expressions of Christianity there is a close relationship between worship and theology. An emphasis on the freedom to worship in ways that are quite different from the way earlier missionaries taught, and in some cases a parallel emphasis on the freedom of the individual to express emotions that seemed to be suppressed in more traditional worship, find theological expression on a similar emphasis on the freedom of the Spirit to move the church and its members in new directions.

Significantly, many of these developments are taking place in societies that have a high regard for tradition, and quite often the "new" forms of Christian worship bear the mark of the traditional practices within those societies. Thus, it would not be entirely accurate to say that these newer, autochthonous expressions of Christianity are against tradition. Although many have inherited the notions taught by Protestant missionaries who spoke of the superiority of Scripture above tradition, and might even speak disparagingly of the tradition of the church, what is in fact happening is that their openness to the Spirit is allowing them to claim the action of God in their own cultural and traditional ways. Thus, for instance, there is much in some forms of Pentecostal worship in the Caribbean that is reminiscent of Afro-Caribbean religious practices—just as there is much in the "traditional" worship of the West that derives from Mithraism, from ancient fertility cults, and from the lore of the druids. In brief, as Christianity becomes incarnate in a variety of cultures, a process takes place in many ways similar to what we saw when early Christians sought ways to appropriate the best of Hellenistic culture and philosophy. Perhaps the main difference is that, while Hellenistic civilization had the notion of the Logos, what permeates many of these other cultures is the notion of spiritual presence. Hence another reason for the prevalence of theology about the Holy Spirit as a means of bridging the gap between Christianity and the traditional culture, just as the second-century church developed a theology of the Logos for a similar purpose. Just as in the early centuries of Christianity there was within the church a very serious struggle to determine the true nature of the faith, similar struggles and disagreements now appear throughout the world. If there are dangers in this—which is certainly the case—these are no more serious than the dangers involved in the earlier Hellenization of Christianity. The vast majority of Christians today find themselves in situations in which they have to reconsider most of the issues discussed in the rest of this book. This is not a purely intellectual task; it is a task that involves all the aspects of a given culture—intellectual, emotional, aesthetic, and so on—and a task one does not dare undertake without divine guidance.

The net result is a growing interest in the Holy Spirit, at least for three reasons. First, the Spirit plays an important role as the power connecting believers with the main events of the gospel and making those events come alive in a different culture. Second, it is also the Spirit who inspires and guides Christians in various cultures to appropriate the gospel within the context of their own traditions and to be able to claim that these are not simply innovations they have introduced into the life of the church, but the result of God acting within the community of believers. Finally, in a worldwide church that seems to be increasingly diverse by its very incarnation in such a variety of cultures, the Spirit is the bond of love that makes unity possible.

Given such circumstances, it is not surprising that the doctrine of the Holy Spirit has become one of the main subjects of discussion among theologians and church leaders throughout the world. It has often been said that pneumatology—the doctrine of the Spirit—has been relegated to what amounts to an afterthought in Christian theology. This is true. In the previous eleven chapters in this book, we have come across the doctrine of the Spirit only in what are almost passing references. The first was in chapter 4, in which I said that during the discussions regarding the divinity of the Second Person of the Trinity, some were willing to affirm the divinity of the Son, but not of the Holy Spirit. Then, again in the same chapter, we came across the controversy regarding the *Filioque*, which dealt with the procession of the Spirit, but in truth focused on the Trinity and on the alteration to the Nicene Creed. Much later, in discussing the sacraments, there was mention of the role of the Spirit in them—particularly in the context of Calvin's understanding of the presence of Christ in communion. If anything, these three examples serve to prove the point: pneumatology has often been examples neglected to a secondary role. It has always been in the background of Christian theology, which has constantly taken cognizance of it; but very seldom has it become the focus of attention.

There have been reasons for this. The Spirit of God is by definition uncontrollable, blowing freely in whatever direction the Spirit wills. In the early church, leadership and structure were usually determined by the signs that a person gave of having received from the Spirit the particular gifts necessary for a task—if that task was teaching, the gift of teaching, and if the task was presiding, the gift of presiding. Historians usually refer to this sort of leadership as "charismatic," not in the sense that they were necessarily like today's charismatics, but in the sense that it was the gifts that determined the office, function, and authority of a person. There are early Christian documents that speak of wandering Christian prophets or preachers going from place to place with no other validation than their gifts.

However, such "charismatic" leadership also poses some problems. The same documents that speak of wandering prophets also point to some of the problems inherent in this sort of leadership. How does one know who is really gifted by the Spirit and who is a

213

self-appointed leader or—even worse—someone simply profiting from the credulity of people? The *Didache*, a document from the late first or early second century, tries to set standards for measuring who is a true prophet and who is a false prophet. One such standard is that someone who asks to be fed or who stays several days enjoying the hospitality of believers is not a true prophet!

As the second and third centuries progressed, and particularly in view of the need to resist erroneous teaching, these difficulties became more and more serious. Clearly, it was no longer wise to receive any wandering prophet as authoritative. The question became urgent: Who is a qualified exponent of Christianity, and who is teaching false doctrine? The result of all this was a move away from such "charismatic" leadership, and towards a more institutionalized system of government and of validation of leadership. The emphasis on apostolic succession, discussed earlier, was one of the means to make certain that whoever claimed to be a Christian leader was indeed authorized by the rest of the church. Similarly, the practice of having neighboring bishops examine the theology of a newly elected bishop had the same purpose. Bishops and other leaders were elected by their congregations, who should have a fairly clear idea of their gifts; but they had to be validated by their peers. Thus it was hoped to achieve a balance between the "charismatic" and the institutional.

However, the fourth century tipped the balance in the other direction. Once the empire became Christian, bishops and other leaders tended to derive their authority from their office rather than from their particular gifts for that office. Clearly, a more institutionalized church was more fitting for the new situation, and also more manageable by the civil authorities. Thus a long process began, through which the authority of bishops and other church leaders came to depend exclusively on ordination—to the point that eventually ordination became a sacrament. Such leadership had little interest in restoring the earlier balance by allowing for a different sort of leadership based on gifts rather than function—even though there were always people who were particularly respected for their wisdom and holiness. Since an emphasis on the freedom of the Spirit could easily undercut the power and authority of the existing institutionalized leadership, the net result was that discussions of the Spirit were normally limited to matters such as how the Spirit acts in the sacraments, or in the inspiration of Scripture. The neglect of the doctrine of the Spirit was not therefore a mere oversight. It was more the result of fear of what an emphasis on such a doctrine might do.

This is no longer the case. The doctrine of the Spirit is being discussed in many different quarters and in very different theological settings. Yet it is important to note that such discussion is not due simply to a logical need to present a fuller picture of the Trinity, nor is it just a corrective to what was an omission in the past. It is a burning issue for our time. Quite often new movements claim that if they are challenging the established order and leadership—and certainly their style of worship—of the church, this is because they are moved by the Spirit to do so. The established authorities retaliate by denying and ridiculing the claims of those who challenge them. Where there should be dialogue and sharing of experience and insights, there is resentment and mutual recrimination.

It is for these reasons that the doctrine of the Spirit is likely to be one of the main themes of theology during the twenty-first century. It will certainly be debated with at least as much zeal as Pelagianism was debated during the fifth century, or the authority of tradition during the sixteenth. In today's debates, acrimony will be inevitable. Yet, as we move into the twenty-first century, we would do well to remember that the debates of the past were eventually settled and that this was brought about by the power of the one who, as Augustine would say, is the bond of love between the Father and the Son, and is therefore also the bond of unity among Christians. Indeed, as one looks back at the history told throughout this book, one is actually looking at the work of the Spirit guiding Christians, quite often in spite of ourselves, toward "all the truth" (John 16:13).

Thus, the paradox, the tragedy, and the hope of our struggles and debates over the Holy Spirit is that we are quite often arguing about the Spirit who is our bond of unity and that in the end we will come to truth and unity, not necessarily because of the power of our arguments or the strength of our convictions, but through the work of the very Spirit about whom we argue!

Is it possible to foretell the outcome of our debates on these issues? Probably not. Yet, if doctrine is a series of foul lines or fences whose purpose is to keep us from falling where others have fallen, it may be well to point out at least some of the fences that should guide our discussion on today's issues. First of all, there is the unity of God.

The Spirit is not a "second" or a "third" God. The Spirit does not undo or contradict or correct the work of God that is traditionally associated with the other Persons of the Trinity. Second, because there is only one God, there is also one purpose. This was expressed earlier in terms of the continuity between creation and redemption. In the case of the Spirit, it will be expressed in terms of the continuity between creation, redemption, and sanctification. It will be expressed in terms of the inspiring action of the Spirit, not only upon the original writers of Scripture, but also upon the reading community of the faithful. It will be expressed in self-emptying love, for the Spirit is the Spirit of Christ, and Christ offered himself to be crucified out of love. Third, since this one God is love, the work of the Spirit will always be a work of love. Hatred, bigotry, and injustice are never the work of the Spirit.

Finally, but most important, the Spirit is a Spirit of hope. The Spirit is "the pledge of our inheritance" (Eph 1:14). In the midst of our current disagreements, it is far too easy for us to forget that the future is not in our hands. It is in the hands of God. For that we can be thankful, for we know that of which we are capable, and we better trust that of which God is capable!

Christian Hope

This leads us to the other neglected doctrine on which the twenty-first century is focusing, eschatology. From its very inception, eschatology—the branch of theology dealing with the "last things"—has been a central element of Christianity. Jesus himself announced the good news of the kingdom of God, and much of his preaching was eschatological. The main issue of disagreement between those Jews who became Christians and those who did not was whether or not Jesus was the fulfillment of the hope of Israel—in other words, whether his life, death, and resurrection were eschatological events. In most early Christian writings the hope and the expectation are expressed that God will establish a new order, a reign of abundance, peace, love, and justice.

In those early Christian writings, this expectation is not primarily about going to another place called heaven. It is rather about a new order, a "new heaven and a new earth," which God will establish.

Significantly, the two main metaphors expressing that expectation are political in nature—a kingdom and a city. Again, as we have seen, salvation was not *from* creation, but *into* a new creation; it was not primarily a matter of leaving this "valley of tears" and passing on to a purely spiritual life. Salvation would be fulfilled in a new city, in a new kingdom, in a final resurrection *of the body*.

Although Christians did not set out to subvert or to overthrow the state, there was a subversive element in such eschatological hope. To announce that one is awaiting another kingdom does not sit well with the present kings. Rome considered itself the great civilizer of the Mediterranean basin and prided itself for the peace it had brought to the area. It had established its own system of laws that it considered eminently just—even though it was based on rights, privileges, and discriminations that today would be considered unjust. The emperor claimed to have his authority from the gods, and it was expected that upon his death he would become a god. Now, out of a corner of that vast empire, came a group of fanatical dreamers claiming not only that there is only one God, but also that this God will bring about a new order, a new kingdom, a new state—for that is the meaning of the term *polis*, usually translated as "city." Even though Christians were surprised that the empire persecuted them when all they did was pray for the emperor, the authorities had ample reason to consider them dangerous subversives.

Things changed when the empire embraced Christianity. Some Christians saw in Constantine the new David establishing the kingdom of God. Many now objected to the book of Revelation, with its negative statements about Rome. The eschatological expectation of a new kingdom of God supplanting all human kingdoms was soon transmuted into the hope of the soul's going to heaven. Rather than focusing on the future of the entire created order—a new heaven and a new earth—Christian hope now focused on the future of individual souls. Since this was very similar to what most of the Hellenistic world understood by "salvation," and since it had already begun to make inroads into the Christian view of salvation (see chapter 9), the change was almost imperceptible. Throughout the Middle Ages, while the coming reign of God was still mentioned on occasion, all of Christian life and devotion focused on the continued life of the soul in another realm beyond the physical world. In this respect, the Reformation changed little, for the main disagreement between

Luther and the Roman Catholic tradition had to do more with how salvation is attained rather than with what it is. It was some of the more radical Anabaptists who recovered the New Testament vision of a coming reign of God. But then, as they tried to bring that reign by their own means, establishing theocracies that quickly lapsed into fanaticism and chaos, their rediscovery of the centrality of the kingdom was discredited.

This has changed in recent years. Some of that change has to do with the new demographic configuration of Christianity described at the beginning of this chapter. Today most Christians live in the poorer nations of the world. They have very little reason to hope for much from the present order. Many have learned through painful experience that simply overthrowing a government does not really change their conditions of poverty and deprivation. Yet, while others lose hope, many of these Christians have reaffirmed their hope in the final outcome of creation. Having to live in constant awareness of physical suffering, seeing their loved ones suffer, feeling the pangs of hunger and the pain of humiliation, living as "strangers and exiles on the earth," they seek a "homeland" (Heb 11:13-14), a new reign of abundance and peace and justice.

In different ways, other excluded groups, even in the more affluent parts of the world, find themselves clinging to hope against hope. Racial and ethnic minorities, women, and others who for whatever reason experience exclusion and oppression frequently turn to eschatological hope in the midst of their apparently hopeless situation.

For all these reasons, eschatology, not so much as the doctrine of the last things, but rather as the doctrine of hope, is very much in the center of theological reflection today.

In this case, as in the case of pneumatology, it is impossible to predict where the present reflections and discussions will lead. Perhaps all one can do is mention some of the "fences" that will likely serve as guidelines for the emerging eschatology. First of all, the emerging eschatology will affirm once again the continuity between creation and redemption, and their fulfillment. The new heaven and new earth are the creation of the same God who made the first heaven and the first earth. Eschatology must not be a negation of creation, but rather its affirmation—the affirmation of a creation freed from its bondage to sin and decay. Second, eschatology is about hope and is not a "program" for future events. It is not like *TV Guide,* in which is a listing of coming programs. It is not a matter of finding out what "trumpet" or what "bowl of wrath" we are in. The great affirmation of eschatology is not who will be "left behind," but the final victory of the One who made all things and saw that they were good. Third, eschatology is not about how to bring about the reign of God. On this point, both liberalism and many conservatives err: liberals by thinking that they will usher in God's reign by means of social progress, and conservatives by believing that God is waiting for us to meet certain requirements—completing the task of preaching to the nations, restoring the state of Israel to its ancient borders, and so on—before bringing in the kingdom. Fourth, eschatological hope is not a sense that a good outcome is likely. Eschatological hope is the confidence that the future is in the hands of God, and that therefore it is just as certain as the present. Fifth, and most important, eschatology is about the sort of hope that shapes present life. It is not a passive hope, as when we sit around and wait for something to happen. It is an active hope, as when we prepare for a future we know is coming.

The Spirit of Hope

These two, the Holy Spirit and hope, are closely connected. Calvin held that in communion the Holy Spirit takes the church into the presence of Christ at the final banquet (see chapter 8). To this, we must add that the Holy Spirit is the source and the guarantor of eschatological hope and that, even though the new conditions in which Christians find ourselves may at times be disheartening and even frightening, thanks to the presence of the Spirit we may face the future—we may look at future theological debates and even acrimony—with the certainty of those who know that our future is in the hands of the God of love.

For Further Reading

Heron, Alasdair I. C. *The Holy Spirit: The Holy Spirit in the Bible, the History of Christian Thought, and Recent Theology.* Philadelphia: Westminster Press, 1983.

Jenkins, Philip. *The Next Christendom: The Coming of Global Christianity.* New York: Oxford University Press, 2002.

Moltmann, Jürgen. *Theology of Hope: On the Ground and the Implications of a Christian Eschatology.* New York: Harper & Row, 1967.

Wilmore, Gayraud S. *Last Things First.* Philadelphia: Westminster Press, 1982.